THE

INHERITANCE

OF

SHAME

A MEMOIR

PETER

GAJDICS

BROWN
PAPER
PRESS

Brown Paper Press
6475 E. Pacific Coast Highway, #329
Long Beach, CA 90803

FIRST EDITION
Designed by Alban Fischer

Distributed by SCB Distributors

Library of Congress Control Number: 2016959770
ISBN 978-1-941932-08-7
978-1-941932-09-4 (ebook)

Printed in the United States of America

All quotes from *A Course in Miracles* are from the First Edition, published in 1976. They are used with written permission from the copyright holder and publisher, the Foundation for Inner Peace, P.O. Box 598, Mill Valley, CA 94942-0598, www.acim.org.

10 9 8 7 6 5 4 3 2 1

Canada Council   Conseil des arts
for the Arts   du Canada

We acknowledge the support of the Canada Council for the Arts, which last year invested $153 million to bring the arts to Canadians throughout the country.

Nous remercions le Conseil des arts du Canada de son soutien. L'an dernier, le Conseil a investi 153 millions de dollars pour mettre de l'art dans la vie des Canadiennes et des Canadiens de tout le pays.

Author's Note

Much of what is in this book I started writing years ago, as early as 1997. I have used my personal journals, as well as tape recordings, therapy sessional reports, and my own medical records to help guide me in the reconstruction of events, interactions, and conversations. Even friends, some from whom I was estranged for years, helped me fill in a few missing pieces. Memory, however, is subjective. I have written what I believe to be true and accurate, but I would be remiss not to add that this book is based on my experience of these events. This is my story and no one else's. Only names have been changed.

I DEDICATE THIS BOOK TO ALL THOSE WHOSE
LIVES HAVE BEEN SACRIFICED BECAUSE OF
SOMEONE ELSE'S INTOLERANCE OR PREJUDICE.

1

BY THE THIRD TIME his car had circled the block, I knew the man was interested. He pulled over and lowered the passenger-side tinted window. I walked to the curb and leaned in—the way I'd seen other young men in the neighborhood do it for months.

"Are you busy tonight?" he said.

"That depends," I answered.

"How much do you charge?" he said.

"What do you want?"

"A blow job."

"Fifty dollars."

For a moment I wondered if my price was too high.

"Okay," he said. "Get in."

I wasn't nervous when he said he knew where we could go. I wasn't anything. We drove for more than thirty minutes. He offered me cigarettes, Benson & Hedges. I smoked. We didn't talk. After several minutes I wanted to take a better look, so I glanced over. He was no one I would've chosen to be with.

It was late, well past midnight, when we arrived. The road inside the forest was unpaved, shrouded by trees and shrubs, guarded by a Do Not Enter sign. I wondered if he'd been there before; maybe he'd brought others before me. We stopped only when the road stopped. If it hadn't been for the light inside the car I wouldn't have seen a thing, not even myself. He opened the glove compartment and took out a condom. It hadn't occurred to me to bring one. I suppose I should've since I was more at risk than he, but I unwrapped the plastic and waited as he unzipped his pleated slacks. The smell from his groin reminded me of rotting fish I'd found once on the beach as a child. Foul, not to be touched.

I slid the condom down over him and lowered my head. The taste of rubber, like a pencil eraser, was not something I enjoyed, but at least I knew there'd be no contamination. He moaned. I felt his hands on my head, one on either side like two clamps, pulling me up and pushing me down. There was rhythm to his needs that I obliged. I didn't gag: the fact made me feel good. I was good. At some point his groaning increased to a growl then a high-pitched cry, and suddenly the rubber swelled.

I sat back up. The car windows were clouded with our heat, his breath. I didn't watch him pull off the rubber, but I think he used a tissue. His car seats were real leather, after all.

"Would you like some air?"

"Sure," I heard my voice say from far away.

He started the car, cracked my window, backed out. Then we were on the road again, beneath lights, lit.

"I know an ATM machine where I can get your money."

For a moment I almost asked him what he meant, but then I remembered.

We drove for twenty minutes, then he pulled up at the curb. I recognized the bank as one which I too used.

"I'll be just a minute."

The night sky hovered. From the car I looked out over the downtown maze of skyscrapers and crisscrossing bridges and speeding cars. All had continued, without change. Life had not shattered into unmendable fragments.

He returned to the car, buckled up, pulled out his wallet that was filled with colorful credit cards, and handed me one crisp and still warm fifty-dollar bill.

I didn't thank him.

"Can I drive you home?"

"Sure."

I told him where I lived, but lied and had him drop me two blocks from my basement suite. As I exited his car I wondered if I should thank him for the ride, but, again, decided against it.

"Maybe I'll see you again," I heard him say when I was already outside.

He drove off.

For a moment I didn't move. I watched. Not just him, but also me watching him. Then I walked to a nearby corner store, bought bread, milk, filtered Camels, two bananas. I unpacked the groceries when I arrived home and smoked a cigarette before brushing my teeth and climbing into bed. If I thought of anything that night as I lay waiting for sleep it was that sex with him had been no different than with all the rest, except that this time I'd made some money.

2

I was born at the tail end of the Baby Boom generation, in Vancouver, British Columbia, on the west coast of Canada, December 13, 1964. "A Sunday child," my mother told me years later, "a special gift from God."

When I was an adult, she told me that my father cradled me to sleep in his arms until he also drifted off, while my four older siblings—Pisti, Barbara, Frank, and Kriska—were tucked fast asleep upstairs in bed. She'd sneak out of their room in the middle of the night, a single nightlight shining down on Dad with his newborn son, both asleep and at peace in his living room sofa chair. Sometimes, still bundled in his arms, I awoke and looked up at my mother. I hardly ever cried as a child, my parents always said, and I laughed a lot.

God the Father, God the Son, and God the Holy Ghost made up the One Trinity, and my father, who'd been born someplace far away called Hungary, explained it all to my siblings and me when we were children.

"The Bible is God's plan," he told us Saturday nights after we knelt in the living room and said the Rosary as a family, "and as good, honorable Catholics, it's our duty to live according to Scripture."

The house my parents bought on the west side of Vancouver in the year before my birth cost either $12,000, according to my father, or $15,000, according to my mother. They took out a twenty-five-year mortgage. My father's job at the saw factory paid him $4.85 per hour, a fact I kept to myself and knew as a child only because I peeked once at his Thursday paycheck kept hidden in my mother's jewelry box. Our fridge was always full of food, and glass bottles of milk that the milkman brought to our back door every Friday morning. Peanut butter smudged between stacks of Ritz crackers and slices of Kraft cheese were my favorite after-school snack.

My mother baked all her own cakes, something she called "tortes," from scratch, just like her mother and two grandmothers back home in "the old country," not far from where my father was born, in another strange-sounding country called Yugoslavia. I never knew a time when my mother didn't preface the fact that she was from Yugoslavia by saying she was German, which always confused me, because I couldn't understand how she could be German if she'd been born in a country called Yugoslavia. I had been born in a country called Canada and was called Canadian. For the most part, however, I didn't think too much about Yugoslavia, or Hungary, or even, for that matter, Canada.

Attending the 11 o'clock mass each Sunday morning was ritual, a high point to a week well lived. Saturday nights after Rosary, Pisti, Frank, and I polished our best black Hush Puppies and lined them up next to the oatmeal-colored sectional in the den for our father's inspection. There was a "right" way to polish our shoes, and there was a "wrong" way to polish our shoes, and our father showed us the difference. Then came Sunday, the day of the Lord, scrubbed faces and combed hair, pressed gray dress pants, crisp white shirts, and clip-on bow ties for the boys, pleated skirts worn well below their knees, blouses, and tiny purses for my sisters, walking as a family three blocks to our steepled church, Our Lady of Perpetual Help, or OLPH, as we called it, adjoined to our elementary school. All the kids often joked, away from the grown-ups, that OLPH really stood for "Old Lady's Pool Hall," but it was where the nuns in old-fashioned habits, like Sally Field in *The Flying Nun*, one of my favorite shows, taught us our lessons. It was where we grew up.

Girls were the ones I played with by the monkey bars or swing sets in the schoolyard during recess every day, and boys were the enemy, or at least they were not like me, even though I was also a boy. I liked hopscotch and jacks, singers like Captain & Tennille, Donny and Marie, and the Carpenters. Boys liked punching faces and playing football, hitting hardballs with baseball bats, Black Sabbath, Judas Priest, and AC/DC.

Boys liked guns. Once, I told a crowd of boys that I liked guns too, even though I didn't, and then Ritchie Rogers, one of the worst of the pack, told me I was his new best friend. We laughed after school and we walked home side by side, arms around each other's shoulders like best buds. While I liked having a new best friend who was a boy, the sudden change of events confused me. Guns were definitely not something that I liked, and if Ritchie liked me because I liked guns, then I knew he didn't really like me at all but, rather, a me who wasn't really me. A week later I told him I didn't like guns after all, then Ritchie said we were no longer friends.

What I liked more than anything was cutting out paper dolls and drawing pictures with my Crayola crayons, weaving macramé, painting stained-glass windows, cutting out all the movie listings in the weekend newspaper and pasting them inside my large, hardcover scrapbook, collecting bouquets of colorful autumn leaves, and building snowmen in our backyard during winter. Even though Christmas was the Lord's birthday, I liked Christmas because of *Frosty the Snowman* and *A Charlie Brown Christmas*, Bing Crosby and Rosemary Clooney singing "Count Your Blessings (Instead of Sheep)" in *White Christmas*. Gingerbread men and fruitcake with marzipan icing that my mother baked. I especially liked the Douglas fir that the Christmas angel left in a bank of snow by the side of the house every year for us to find on a wintery morning.

I kissed my parents goodnight in the living room before bed every night when I was a young boy, but my father's body was wooden and unresponsive, like my hugs were not a language he understood. Upstairs, in the sloped-ceiling attic room I shared with Pisti, my mother sat on the edge of my bed, singing "Que Sera, Sera," as I drifted in and out, like on a swing, back and forth, opening and closing my eyes between this world and that one.

"*Peterle, mein lieber Peterle,*" she'd sometimes say following her song, even though I couldn't understand her German, "*was hast Du mit mir gemacht, dass ich keine Ruhe finde.*" ("Peter, my dear little Peter, what have you done to me that I can find no peace.")

I loved my mother, and even when I should've closed my eyes and given in to sleep, I couldn't help but stare up at her and smile, smell the sweetness of her Chanel N°5, which I knew she used discreetly. Sometimes, as she bent back down to kiss me goodnight, I saw her breasts through her pink flannel nightie that draped wide open like the curtain in a breeze. I always tried not to look, but if I glanced and saw them dangling high above me, a bolt of terror struck through my body like a whiplash that left me breathless in her wake.

When I was six years old, my mother was the president of the Catholic Women's League. We were all so proud of Mommy, and she was good at her job. She planned tea parties and Church bazaars and rummage sales to raise money for the parish. The white elephant table was always my favorite because I found Christmas decorations for our tree and used 45 records, like "Yesterday" and "Do Wah Diddy Diddy."

I was standing in a crowd in my school basement, feet from where my mother was working behind a table during one of the bazaars, when a fat, balding man asked me to show him to the little boys' room. I did as I was asked, and I took him down the hall, away from the crowd, and pointed to the door.

"Can you take me inside, please?" he said.

I didn't understand why I needed to go inside, but I'd been brought up to be kind and obedient, so I walked ahead of him into the brightly lit room with five cubicles, a lineup of stained enamel urinals and sinks and black, chain-mesh grating on the windows high up near the cobwebbed ceiling.

He walked to the last cubicle, and he turned around.

"Can you come with me inside, please?"

Now my heart was pounding, like when I ran home for lunch except my body wasn't moving. He waited. My legs were knee-deep in mud, but I walked over. He went inside and motioned for me to follow. Saying no to adults was not ever a consideration.

In my memory the incident never ends, and I remember the months that followed.

I remembered it when my mother tucked me in at bedtime, sang me her song, and said, "I love you," but all I heard was the fat man in the toilet stall still telling me he loved me too.

"*I love you*," he'd said, his arms like bands around my back, pulling me into his fat belly, opening his pants. Then my mother was gone from my bedroom and the lights were off, except for the hallway nightlight, which cast shadows across my walls, shadows I tried not to notice because they moved, creatures, fat monsters, shape-shifters morphing all around me, closing in on me, like the fat man pushing his penis into my mouth, up and down.

Falling to sleep had always been like a borderless crossing where I was never quite sure in which country I resided. But after the incident at school, when my eyes snapped open from sleep, all I saw now was my mother's naked body with three breasts floating next to me beside my bed.

Or else I crept down the stairs and through the house, terrified of returning to my mother's hovering flesh still up, outside my dream, inside my room. If Pisti or my father ever found me huddled in a corner, I'd start to cry and say that I had died upstairs in bed.

"You're not dead," they'd say. "You're just asleep." And then they'd lead me back up to the nightmare in my room.

Other times I'd run screaming from my bed and through the house, arms flailing, voice ripping both my parents from bed—"I'M DYING I'M DYING I'M DYING!"—until my father held me down while my mother spooned hot beef consommé down my throat, which I'm sure was meant to calm my body, but always, in my mind, I knew that somewhere in the air there was a hole through which I could escape, return from wherever I'd arrived, if only I could find it. Later, all three of us spent, my mother returned my body to my bed, my coffin, where I felt myself dying in the arms she'd wrap around me like a warm blanket.

By grade six, I began skipping out of school midday, raising my hand in Sister Agatha's catechism class and, instead of going to the bathroom, walking the three blocks home, sneaking in through the basement, past my mother, who seemed to always be in the kitchen, aproned and baking, up the second creaking flight of stairs, around the corner, and down a bookshelved hallway to my room, and crawling into bed. Buried beneath comforters during the day there were never any nightmares, only dreams in which my arms turned into wings and I flew far away.

‖‖‖‖‖‖‖

My mother always helped me make each of my annual Halloween trick-or-treat costumes: a giant stick of "Juicy Fruit" gum, constructed out of colored cardboard that we bought at our local five-and-dime, which slipped over my head like a bodysuit with holes for arms and head; the Tin Man from *The Wizard of Oz*, made from old soup cans and a funnel for a hat from my father's toolshed; a magician, with black cape, top hat, and wand.

Every Christmas she took Pisti and me on the bus to the big downtown department store in a red brick building with the animated Santa Claus, reindeer, and elves in its storefront windows. In the food court on the main floor, she bought bags of Pascall White Heather Chocolates so we could string them for our Christmas tree back home. Sometimes we ate slices of pie in the diner on the mezzanine, looking down on all the twinkling lights and decorations. Before bed, I told my mother that I loved her more than the distance from our house to that downtown department store because nothing in the world was bigger or farther away than the distance from our house to that store.

Twice a year we also bussed to a European delicatessen that smelled of candied coffee and crème pastries. The aisles were overflowing with all sorts of boxed nuts and dried fruit, jars of jams and tin cans of special cookies and exotic teas, grains, and beans. Behind the glassed-in countertop full of freshly baked tortes, the woman, with jet-black hair and a thick accent like my father's, ground bags of poppy seeds fresh for my mother. Back home, my mother mixed the black bitter seeds with milk, sugar, and lemon rind on the stove, kneaded out dough on the floured tabletop, then rolled a dozen strudels stuffed with the hot, creamy filling, while my father tried his best to teach me the correct pronunciation for poppy seeds in Hungarian.

"*Mák*," he'd say.

"Muck."

"Not muck. *Mák*. It's a long á, *mááááák*. Try again."

"Muuuuck."

However the word was pronounced, one of our favorites was

definitely *mákos tészta*, or poppy seed noodles—freshly cooked German egg noodles tossed in butter and *mák*, sugar, and lemon rind. While my brothers and sisters were out on the front street playing softball or hide-and-go-seek with the other neighborhood kids every weekend, I was in the kitchen with my mother, cooking and baking, helping to cut up the chunks of stewing beef for Hungarian goulash, stuffing the cabbage rolls, and sprinkling paprika on the chicken goulash, or *paprikás csirke,* as my father always corrected me.

Desserts like *palacsintas,* or Hungarian crepes, with sweetened cottage cheese, raisins, and lemon rind were reserved for Sundays, but during the week, we sometimes devoured prune pockets— gnocchi dough stuffed with sweetened prunes, boiled like pasta and then fried in butter and breadcrumbs. *Zserbó* squares—yeast dough between layers of apricot jam, ground walnuts and sugar, then strawberry jam, ground walnuts and sugar, and topped with chocolate ganache—was a dessert my mother explained had originated all the way from a *konditorei* in Budapest, the capital city of Hungary, called Café Gerbeaud. I asked my mother to translate *madártej,* and she said it was "birds milk," but I didn't see any birds, only cooked egg whites floating in vanilla custard. A *Dobos torte*, which looked like its translation of "drum cake," was the most special dessert of them all and always brought streaks of panic across the faces of any schoolmates at our birthday parties as father cut through its caramelized, candied topping with an electric knife.

And then there was *aranygaluska.*

"There is no translation for *aranygaluska,*" my father had explained several times before. "But *arany* means 'golden,' so I suppose you could call it 'golden dinner cake,'" which is precisely what we did. I had the most important job, or so my mother said, sprinkling ground walnuts, sugar, and raisins between layers of yeast dough cut into discs. Then my mother baked it till the whole house smelled like caramelized yeast.

"We always ate *aranygaluska* after a clear soup back home," my mother said one Sunday afternoon as she prepared the finishing touches: the custard sauce that we'd pour over the warm *aranygaluska* before eating. She had told me "the story" before.

"First we ate our clear soup . . . maybe a chicken soup. Then we ate our *aranygaluska*, like a dessert but really as a main course."

"When I grow up I'm going to go to Hungary," I said, "just like my daddy."

"No you won't," my mother said.

"Why not?"

"Hungary is behind the Iron Curtain."

I knew that curtains, like the green ones in our living room, were made from fabric, so I could not understand how an entire country could be behind a curtain made from iron.

Helping my mother bake anything from the "the old country" always meant listening to her talk about her childhood, which would inevitably lead us to "the camps," where she had learned, before her escape, about the scarcity of food. My siblings and I always knew somehow not to leave a scrap of food on our dinner plates. We didn't need to think of all those starving children in Ethiopia. Our mother told us about our starving relatives in the camps, deaths from dysentery, her own malnutrition, lice in the barracks. Anything we did end up leaving on our dinner plates—a lump of mashed potato, a carrot, or a Brussels sprout—our mother promptly swept onto hers and gobbled it down herself. Even chicken bones, clean of meat, our mother sucked dry. *All good, loving mothers had once escaped these camps*, I thought as a child, *just like my mommy*.

Once, in the middle of her baking, "Those Were the Days" started playing on our portable Sony AM/FM transistor radio.

"Oh I love this song," she said. "We listened to this in Russian back home."

Suddenly she clasped my hands, and we started waltzing through the kitchen, laughing and singing along with Mary Hopkin.

> *Those were the days my friend*
> *We thought they'd never end*
> *We'd sing and dance forever and a day*
> *We'd live the life we choose*
> *We'd fight and never lose*
> *For we were young and sure to have our way.*

||||||||||

The night my sister, Kriska, ran away from home, I was watching *The Brady Bunch* in the den. I was eight; she was sixteen. The last thing I saw as she walked through the room clutching a handful of laundry, turned the corner, and disappeared down the basement stairs were her eyes.

Goodbye, I could have sworn they'd said.

3

MY PARENTS NEVER FOUGHT, but they often debated, especially around anything to do with the political history of the Austro-Hungarian Empire; European war pacts and peace treaties; the occupation and oppression of various territories and minorities; and neighboring countries whose borders changed, and the resulting change of citizenships to national citizens. No simple question, like "Where were your parents born?" was ever answered simply. My mother's father, born Austrian in a town that, at the time of his birth, 1899, was Austria-Hungary, later "became," as a result of shifting borders, a citizen of Romania, whose region changed again soon after to the newly formed but short-lived Kingdom of Serbs, Croats and Slovenes. "Everyone sat in everyone else's backyard," my mother used to say when I was still young, and then she'd leave it at that, as if that explained it all.

Whenever I'd ask my mother for more details on her upbringing, which I did progressively as I got older, she said that she came from a long history of eighteenth-century German pioneers who had settled in a region of the Balkans called "the Banat." Together, they were considered *Volksdeutsche*, or German nationals living outside the borders of Germany. But she had also been a Yugoslav citizen because she was born in Modosch, a village that at the time of her birth in 1924 had still been part of the Kingdom of Serbs, Croats and Slovenes, later to become, in 1929, Yugoslavia.

"Wouldn't that make you Yugoslavian?" I'd ask.

"I am German, through and through," she'd repeat.

"I don't understand. How can you be German if you were born in Yugoslavia?"

Ethnicity—a person's cultural heritage—was not the same as citizenship, which changed often in Europe as a result of a change to borders or country names, both my parents tried to explain, as if their explanations helped clarify anything, except my unending confusion. "You can look at a map of Europe," my mother said once, "and still have no idea of the culture of each of its country's inhabitants."

High above the chatter and the smells of goulash cooking in the kitchen, the damp and drafty attic of my family home became my only haven. I made a nest from moth-ridden clothes, and there I'd lie for hours, typing on my father's old 1950s Remington, whose keys looked like a skeletal ribcage.

Fully formed inside that typewriter's cavity lay buried all the secrets of the world, I imagined, waiting to be discovered.

Of the countless black-and-white photographs I found stashed in their dusty old travel trunks, the few of my father were of him and his Hungarian buddies after their arrival in Canada—the gang of them driving across the country in a brown Studebaker, dressed in gray flannel suits like the Rat Pack, smoking Marlboros, and wearing fedoras and turbans. Most photographs of my mother had been taken near Liverpool, a few years after her escape from the camp. Sometimes I read old letters that my father had written to my mother after they were married in northern British Columbia, while he was working in various construction jobs around the province. His English was still broken, but he called her "dearest" and "darling," said that he loved her, like I'd heard him say a thousand times in the house.

"I love you, dearest," he'd say, and then they'd hug and kiss on the lips, sweetly, and I knew that the world was safe and at peace, even though all the nuns at school repeated that someone called Brezhnev could put his finger on a button and blow us all up on any given day.

Reading through my father's letters in the attic, often I wondered what his life had been like as a child, before fleeing Hungary. One night, as I was reading a letter, he appeared from behind a stack of boxes, flashlight in hand, calling me to dinner. When he saw the trunks thrown open and the pictures strewn across the wooden floorboards, he asked me what I was doing.

"You should never look at another person's property, Peter," he said to me from the doorway. "We each have our lives, and you must respect the privacy of another person's history. Now come to dinner, and forget about our past."

I knew, instantly, that what I'd done was bad, but was it my reading the letters or attempting to unlock the mystery of who they really were? The political history of Europe, which both of my parents discussed without hesitation, interested me far less than their personal experiences of war, which neither would even mention. I could never ask them anything about their "emotional lives" in Europe, that much I knew. Silence was a language best understood by children, and already I was a master of intuition.

ıııııııııı

My own silence resolved around sex. Boys were still the enemy, but their bodies now gave me all sorts of butterflies, made me light-headed, and aroused fantasies of touching them, their skin, and kissing their lips.

I wanted their bodies, or at least that's how I thought it to myself. In my child's mind, "wanting their bodies" meant replacing my own body with one of theirs, because their bodies were good and strong, whereas mine was bad and weak. Boys did not like other boys; only girls liked boys. If I'd been born a girl, or had a girl's body, then it would've made sense for me to like boys. Except I didn't want to be a girl or have a girl's body. I wanted a boy's body, to remain a boy. Confusion lapped onto confusion, and nothing made sense, least of all boys, or bodies.

Before my mother went to work as a librarian, she stayed home to take care of her children, but she did take night classes at a nearby university. She wrote stories with made-up names, but they really were all about her home country, the camps. Her teacher told her she should try to get them published, but she never did.

"One day I will write my memoirs about Europe," she'd tell me over and over again. "One day . . ."

"Three Candles to Light" was one of her stories she wrote for school. She asked me if I wanted to read it when I was thirteen.

"It's about my first Christmas in the concentration camp," she said.

I said of course, yes, I wanted to read it, but I didn't understand much of any of it, or even, still, what concentration camps were.

Then the television miniseries *Holocaust* aired in 1978, and *Sophie's Choice* a few years later. Instead of waiting for her to talk about the camps, now I asked questions.

"Those films are about National Socialist concentration camps, the Nazis," she'd try to explain. "I was in a communist concentration camp, in Yugoslavia."

I still couldn't understand how she could've been German if she'd been born in Yugoslavia, nor could I differentiate between National Socialist, or Nazi, concentration camps, which were only starting to receive some media attention, and communist concentration camps, least of all in somewhere called the Banat, a province of Yugoslavia, under the rule of some dictator called Marshal Tito.

What I did understand, implicitly, was that anything I could ever say, do, or feel about my own life would never rival my mother's grief and anger over the injustice of how "her people" had been incarcerated, rounded up like cattle and moved into concentration camps, tortured, and murdered, left to die. Shame silenced any possibility for redemption, and my own shame silenced me absolutely.

||||||||||

Boys turned into men, and when I was fourteen, I had sex with another man.

I had skipped out of school, was steps off the bus downtown, when I saw him, a perfect stranger, on the street. He was blond, with a handlebar moustache, and I remember that he licked his lips and motioned for me to follow him, which I did, like a sleepwalker, through the underground shopping mall, into a department store parkade, and down into the bottom of a concrete stairwell. Neither of us said a word the whole time we walked. Words weren't necessary.

The stink of piss and cum dizzied my mind as the stranger pushed me up against the graffitied wall and kissed me, hard, on the lips, held my hands above my head, and devoured me, as I did him, each of us like sexual cannibals, starved for what the other had to give. When I opened my eyes, two other men were five steps up, like on a balcony, rubbing crotches through bulging 501s, kissing, entering each other's flesh while spitting, sweating, watching.

When he knelt down before me, for an instant the image of Sunday Mass flashed across my mind, then joined the memory of the fat man in my elementary school toilet that seemed suddenly like it had never left me and had now only surfaced. But then a pressure peaked in my groin as the man's hands slid up inside my shirt, and out came from inside of me all thought, and memory, and fear.

"Thanks, boy," he said, wiping his mouth, zipping up.

There was a gap in my thinking where I followed his lead and thanked him as well. I looked up the stairs, but the other men had disappeared. When he pushed open the heavy aluminum door, the sight of an alleyway lined with drunks and junkies rushed inside of me with a gust of fresh fear.

With every panicked step toward the bus around a corner, I repeated to myself that what I'd done could not be done again, would not be done again.

||||||||||

That same year, in my grade nine sex-education class at my all-boys Catholic high school, I learned all about the "lifestyle of the homo-sexual," which sounded frighteningly similar to the life that I was already living. Like a revised Book of Revelation, the final chapter of our textbook explained it all, beginning with the homosexual's choice to act on an immoral and intrinsically disordered behavior and ending with their self-imposed misery, diseased body, and assured annihilation. There was no happy ending for the homosexual.

If I thought of anything during the endless hours of English, French, Mathematics, Catechism, History, and Social Studies, I thought only of how I could divide myself in two, like a wishbone, stray as far away from my desires as possible. Instead of homework each night, I lip-synched songs from my black Denon portable turn-table: Elton John's "Someone Saved My Life Tonight" . . . Three Dog Night's "The Show Must Go On." The Rolling Stones scared me because Kriska had listened to the Stones before she ran away from home. Maybe if I listened to the Stones then I, too, would end up like her: an outcast, unloved, a runaway. So I listened to Queen instead, alone in my bedroom after dinner, acting out the lyrics to "Bohemian Rhapsody."

> *Is this the real life? Is this just fantasy?*
> *Caught in a landslide, no escape from reality . . .*

Despite my prayers the night before, the blinding light of day forced me up and out of the house each morning and back to school where facts and figures from all my classes flowed over me. Nothing stuck; nothing was absorbed. If the Catholic Brothers, each of them cassocked and clutching long wooden rulers, didn't mock me, make fun of my endless failed exams, my sixteen percents, then, when they read my grades aloud for all to scorn, they'd pronounce the first syllable of my last name like the severest of punishments.

"Let's see how poorly Mr. '*Gay*-dicks' did on his French exam today, shall we?" Or else the other boys crowded 'round me during recess like crows around a carcass, chanting "*Gay-dicks . . . Gay-dicks . . . Gay-dicks*," as if my name were the worst thing I could be.

None of that stopped Tommy, my best and only friend at school, and me from expressing all our private yearnings in secret gestures and coded language. Amongst teachers and schoolmates, we talked openly about being "Final Chapters," or else we hung our hands over the edges of desks and tables to say, without uttering one word across crowded rooms, that we were "hands at the edge of a table": limp wristed. Neither of us was the least bit interested in each other "that way," which made everything so much simpler. The fact of our Final Chapter-ness was like a mathematical equation, and as long as no one, particularly our parents, ever found out about it, everything would be fine.

And then there was a dark force that took hold of my senses, which I kept concealed even from Tommy.

I skipped out of school.

I bussed downtown.

I walked through crowded shopping malls for hours, back and

forth from one public washroom to another like a zombie, down into the guts of that parkade. If I had sex and then held a man and told him *I love you*, my words always reminded me of the fat man who'd said he loved me too, and I knew I'd never have to see any of these other men again so it didn't matter what I said. Some of them scrawled their names and numbers on a piece of paper, and as I walked away, I'd see their faces, hopeful that I'd call them one day soon.

I would smile—always the polite Catholic boy—and tell them that I would, then throw their number away as soon as they were out of sight. Sex with men had nothing to do with who I was in my real life, I told myself. Sex with men was something that I did, but it was not who I was. And always, when I got on the bus to return home, sex with men was part of another world that I left downtown where it belonged.

I learned to hitchhike when I saw a boy my age stick out his thumb and a car pull over. Days later I followed suit, and sure enough, a car pulled over for me. The man inside asked me how far I was going. "All the way," I told him. Halfway home he rubbed his hand over my leg. Within the month, I was hitchhiking home every day, picked up by a different man two or three times my age. Sometimes I bussed downtown, where I was more likely to get picked, just so I could hitchhike home. Often I asked them why they liked to "do it with guys." Mostly, we never talked at all.

Maintaining the contradiction that my life had become grew increasingly difficult. Fear of discovery was always imminent. After one dinner at home, I told my parents that I thought I was a "Final Chapter." They just stared at me, as if I'd spoken a foreign language. And, in a sense, I had. But having said that much, codified as it were, released the pressure to tell them all, to tear the mask completely off the actor, then live to regret it.

Some weekends I slept over at Tommy's house, a sprawling estate high atop the British Properties in West Vancouver. As an only child, Tommy could do as he pleased, and his parents hardly noticed. We lay out by his pool, listened to ABBA, held séances with black candles after his parents had gone to bed, and read excerpts aloud from The Shining until, freaked, we'd have to talk about I Love Lucy, giggling, just to calm down.

||||||||||

After school one afternoon, when I was sixteen, I dashed into my bedroom, reached beneath my top mattress for one of the *Honchos* and *Blueboys* that I'd been stealing from a downtown magazine store for years. Instead of the pornos, I found only a Bible, and inside its cover, addressed to me, a note: *Read this instead.*

I panicked, fearing my worst nightmare had come true: my parents had discovered my secret. I grabbed my coat and ran down the stairs to the basement door, but before I could leave my brother, Pisti, called out to me from behind.

"Did you find the Bible?"

I thought of all his *Playboys* stacked four feet high in our bedroom, all of which he occasionally bragged about to our parents, and my fear shifted to anger, then betrayal.

"Stay out of my life!" I screamed, and slammed the door behind me.

Several weeks later Pisti again confronted me. He had been following me for months, he said: he knew that I'd been having sex with men downtown. He threatened to tell our parents unless I confessed everything to Father Raphael, our parish priest. Receive absolution. Repent. Change my ways.

I fell to my knees and begged him to reconsider.

Then his story changed.

"I never followed you, but I had a hunch," he said. "Now that I know the truth, you need to confess everything to Father Raphael, or else."

A week later I confessed my sin to Father Raphael.

He "forgave" me.

"It's just a phase of life," he said in the confessional. The slotted screen obscured my face, but still I feared he'd know me from my voice. "It's completely natural for boys your age."

For two weeks I was elated, believing that God would save me from my sins.

But my desires only deepened.

Every night I prayed for God to take me in my sleep, and every morning I awoke to feel my body, alive and heavy with despair. Why was I sentenced to a life of sin? Why did God hate me so? How was it even possible that I was "becoming" as my name, pronounced "Gay-dicks," implied, while my two older brothers, by every indication, weren't? If my name had been like flesh, I would've burnt it from my bones, and said to everyone, to all my Tormentors, *Look, see, I am not the name you call me.*

But I was. I was everything they named me, and more. My name was like marrow, built into my bones. There was nowhere I could go to escape my insides.

Nearly every weekend, by the early 1980s, Tommy and I danced for hours at the Gandydancer, a lone, unmarked gay dance club in an otherwise derelict part of town filled with abandoned warehouses built on rail platforms with cantilevered canopies. We'd drive around town in his father's steel blue Park Avenue model automobile, singing along to tapes of our favorite songs—Midge Ure's "If I Was" or Wham!'s "Careless Whisper"—stopping at Doll & Penny's café in the city's West End gay district near English Bay beach for a 2 a.m. drag show while munching on baskets of fries with mayonnaise.

All the dancing and drag in the world, however, couldn't stop the clouds of despair from darkening my mind. Through the fog of my depression, I could hear my parents and my siblings ask me what was wrong. But at nineteen years old, lying face up on my bed, nearly catatonic, there were secrets from my past and fears about my future that I could not share with anyone.

4

I HAD SEEN THE movie *Fame*, with Irene Cara, in theaters every weekend for four months in 1980. It was all about young kids in the High School of Performing Arts in New York City who had big problems with ambition, competition, betrayal, and even homosexuality. So when the American Academy of Dramatic Arts, a college for acting training from which Robert Redford, among others, had graduated, held auditions in Vancouver in 1983, I jumped at the chance and made an appointment.

Sammy's monologue from William Inge's play *Dark at the Top of the Stairs,* the same as Montgomery's in the opening of *Fame,* was my audition piece.

"I always worry that maybe people aren't going to like me . . ."

Two months later I was accepted as a first-year student, and, to my parents' unremitting disapproval, took a Greyhound bus in January 1984 to Pasadena, California. Best of all, my new home would be more than 1,200 miles away from all the sex that I had wanted to escape, but had found no way to avoid.

Acting, as a means of hiding from what I didn't want to see, had come naturally to me in my private life, but the formal creative discipline of acting as a means of facing deeper truths within oneself in order to transmute them outward to an audience was another matter entirely. Still, my creative juices overflowed: tap dance, jazz, and ballet; singing songs from musicals like *A Chorus Line*, *Fiddler on the Roof,* and *Company*; method acting and rehearsing scenes from plays by Lillian Hellman and Clifford Odets.

Friendships were forged, a sense of camaraderie established. Within months, I even had a girlfriend—another student at the

Academy. Cecilia, an Armenian from Los Angeles, had rented the apartment next door to me in our two-floor walk-up with a pea-nut-shaped outdoor pool, three miles from campus. When we started sleeping together, nightly, in my apartment, I worried that she might somehow discover all the gay porno magazines that I kept stashed beneath my top mattress. When she broached the subject, after months of heavy kissing and even the occasional dabbling into oral sex, that we should "go all the way," I told her that I didn't think she was "ready."

Like any skilled actor, I could play the part of boyfriend to girl-friend, but the role I was playing was not me. When I arrived home one night with a hickey, she thought for sure I'd been with another woman and begged me to tell her the truth. I could not tell her that it was true I'd had sex, but it'd been with a man, in a video arcade. Porno theaters and late-night trysts in cars with men twice or three times my age: the secret life I'd left behind had followed me to Hollywood, land of make-believe and shattered dreams.

After one year at the Academy, I returned to my home in Vancouver and moved back into my parents' house. Second-year's studies were by invitation only, and so I waited for their letter. The Academy's director, Bryn Morgan, wrote and said that he thought I needed to live in the world for a while, instead of a theater.

"Life is what you need to experience," he wrote, "not a character." I was not invited back.

I was devastated.

||||||||||

One night after dinner, as I was washing the dishes, my mother handed me a document.

"It's about some of my experiences in the camps," she said. "Hopefully this will help clarify things." Then she closed the door and left me alone. I sat down and started to read, beginning with the opening phrase, "For your eyes only."

Sometime before the end of the war, in late October 1944, all ethnic Germans living in the former Yugoslavia were branded as fascists and stripped of their civic rights, declared enemies of the people, and interned in concentration camps. At the train station, as she was about to be deported along with hundreds of others to a forced labor camp in Siberia, my mother, twenty years old, slipped beneath the tracks of the cattle car and escaped back to her hometown of Modosch. Captured by the OZNA, the Serbian secret police, days later, she was jailed in one of the most notorious death camps in Petrovgrad, known for having nightly "killing parties." Runnels had been dug in the earth, and every night a dozen prisoners would be led outside and horsewhipped till their blood flowed through the channels below, like veins in the earth, to a large pit at one end of the camp. From inside the barracks, huddled together with all the women, my mother listened as the prisoners' flesh was ripped from their bones. One month later, she stopped menstruating. Two years later, she attempted to escape, but was caught near the Romanian border and returned to the death camp.

The next morning, she was ordered to report to the commandant's office, where she sat waiting most of the day. Late at night a car drove up and the commandant, whom she had come to know as her tormentor, got out and led her into one of the offices.

The moment they entered, he slapped her across her face.

"Why did you try and escape from my prison?" he asked, towering above her.

"I am not going to starve to death in your—" she began, before he struck the other side of her face, sending her crashing to her knees.

He waited until she'd picked herself back up, then asked again, "Why did you try and escape from my prison?"

"I am not going to starve to death in your camp."

She awoke later, alone, slumped on the floor, bruised and too weak to move.

My mother spent her twenty-second birthday in solitary confinement, where she wrote poetry, or prayers, as she preferred to think of them. Each morning she laid out the theme in her mind: on All Soul's Day, a prayer to her recently deceased mother, asking for her guidance; on her own birthday, a prayer for the deliverance of her soul to God, should she die in the camp. All day, every day, she'd work on her prayer in her mind, replacing one word for another, until she knew it was ready to be scratched, with her only hairpin, into the chalked walls of her cell. Some were no more than ten words; others were longer than ten lines. She wrote in German, and in Serbian; she wrote for the ones who would come after her. One prayer for each day she was imprisoned. This, she wrote, is what kept her sane.

After a month in solitary, my mother was transported to the labor camp in Kikinda, and six weeks later to the concentration camp in Molidorf. As a form of torture and to prevent further attempted escapes, her tormentor jailed her in a bunker filled with waist-high water. There was one window inside the cell, and so she pulled herself up out of the water and onto its large, brick windowsill, where she remained, perched, knees bent, dripping wet, chilled. When her tormentor found her there, hours later, he demanded that she get down off the sill and stand in the water. She refused. He waded through the water and pointed his rifle at her head.

"Get down or else I'll shoot."

"Then shoot me," she replied, grasping the window's iron bars.

He left.

The next morning she was transported once again by train back to her hometown, whose former town store had since been appropriated by the OZNA and made into their new headquarters. All entrances to the building were now boarded up, with the police quartered in beds that filled the large kitchen and the servant's room next to a pantry, where she was jailed. Rats and mice had eaten away at the loosened floorboards, and every night she heard them below, squeaking and scurrying in all directions.

Sometimes, in the darkness, she recalled her home life before they'd all been dispossessed. Violin lessons on Wednesdays. Waking to the fragrance of lilacs growing outside her bedroom window. Espalier grapes trailing up the sides of their home, some so large and juicy her mother had called them "goat tits" because each was more like a meal. Fresh eggs from their backyard chickens. Oozing cherries from her Oma's garden. Her father's vineyards, the smell of his pipe, a mixture of hickory and cocoa. Men gathering in their home from all around the village to talk and drink a glass of homemade brandy. Sausages and spec hanging upstairs in the attic and her mother's *speise* lined with jars of peach and plum jam, apricot for special occasions. Palacsintas with sweet cottage cheese filling on Sundays and honey bread for lunch.

In her memory there was much of everything and everything was warm and sunny. She could hear her parents' laughter, lulling her to sleep. They loved her. Hunger was not something she had ever known. Ending her life was not something she had ever contemplated. God was still with her.

Midway through her story she stated, tangentially but categorically, that she had not been raped. It was a statement that seemed almost to come out of nowhere, to answer an unasked question. But then she shifted topics again and went on to describe a visit, four weeks later, with her hometown priest, who was being jailed in another part of the same camp. The moment he saw her he broke down in tears. He spoke to her of destiny, of freedom, of a world beyond her confinement. Only if she firmly believed, he told her, would it all come to pass, would she be able to escape.

"Forget if you can," he cautioned, clasping her hands in his. "But above all else, *above all else,* you must learn to forgive. Hate destroys the hater, never the hated. Grievances buried will one day surface. And with renewed vengeance."

Before the prison guards returned her to the pantry, where she was jailed for five more months, the priest told her he would pray for her freedom.

She believed he had.

|||||||||||

With no clear direction in my life, at twenty years old, I enrolled at Vancouver Community College. Acting had not turned out well, so I registered in creative writing.

When I told my parents I wanted to move out on my own, my father exploded.

"What will you do for money? If you think we're going to support you . . ."

I found a basement suite on the east side of town whose owners discounted the rent to $300 per month because I was a student. An actor's agency in town signed me on and sent me out for auditions. My school newspaper published some of my poetry. Inspired by the character of Maggie the Cat in Tennessee Williams's play *Cat on a Hot Tin Roof*, I wrote my first one-act play, an absurdist black comedy called *Killing Maggie Cat*. Then I read an ad at a local theater that said a television station was interested in filming short plays, so I sent them mine. Weeks later, the producer called and said she liked my play, and then she connected me with two local student actors.

By day, I was a starving actor and creative writing student, working part-time as a waiter, directing my play for television, and attending cattle calls for commercials and bit parts in TV and film. But by night, every night, like the bulimic facing a plate of food, I bicycled to a downtown parking lot by the ocean where I knew men cruised—"the fruit loop," as it was commonly known—and I didn't go home until I was full.

Four years earlier, I had called the crisis center helpline in a fit of desperation about my attraction for men, panicked at the thought that my only solution in life would be to kill myself. Then I volunteered to work there myself, and within minutes of meeting Pearl, another volunteer, discovered our shared passion for the confessional poets, like Sylvia Plath and Anne Sexton, probably because we had both been keeping secrets.

"I cut myself," she told me that first night over tea. She was dressed in a black bohemian skirt with too many colorful bracelets on her wrists to count.

"Why would you do that?"

"It releases the pressure inside."

"What sort of pressure?"

"There's a disconnect between the way I feel and how I act, like a road inside that spreads in two and never meets. Cutting myself is the only way I've found that brings them back together, reconnects the two, if only for a moment."

From that moment on, Pearl and I became inseparable: reading poetry and plays aloud till all hours of the morning; lying tangled like weeds on our beds, listening to This Mortal Coil's *Filigree & Shadow*, dressed in drag at midnight screenings of *The Rocky Horror Picture Show* and Pink Floyd's *The Wall*; sitting up all night on my frayed, plaid sofa to watch a sunrise, then falling asleep in each other's arms moments before it did.

Once, following dinner at a downtown restaurant called Penny Lane that played nonstop Beatles, both of us moderately inebriated and taken with each other's charm, I pulled her into the shadows of a condemned office tower where we kissed for hours, passionately, without reservation. When she asked me to take her home and make love to her, I froze. As with Cecilia, there was a sense of validation and intoxication from my relationship with Pearl that had remained elusive with men, whom I'd continued meeting secretly, in bushes and in bars, in "tearooms," and in bathhouses. Two worlds anchored in me but never met.

Then I told her.

In the middle of one night in my basement apartment and a pack and a half of Camels later, I told her that I was a man who liked other men, that I was a "homosexual."

"I thought as much," she said, without so much as flinching.

"You mean you knew?"

"I had my suspicions. Most straight men I know don't read Christopher Durang and Joe Orton. It's okay, Peter. Really, it is."

But it was not okay, at least not to me. Every movie I had ever seen had portrayed gay men as self-destructive and unhappy—*The Boys in the Band, Some of My Best Friends Are . . . , Cruising*. Even the TV movies *The Day After*, about nuclear Armageddon, and *An Early Frost*, about a new gay disease called AIDS, seemed to me to be about essentially the same event. Being gay meant staring down the barrel of a loaded gun. At least that's what the media said. The Catholic Brothers had been blunter: If homosexuals were lucky enough to make it out alive, their souls would burn in Hell for all eternity.

I knew no other way of connecting my own divergent roads— who or what I knew myself to be with how I presented myself to the world—than to tell my parents my secret.

I wrote them The Letter.

I left it on their bed when they were out of the house.

Later that night, they arrived at my apartment with a bag of groceries and a leather-bound copy of *The New American Bible*. In and out, no discussion.

Several days later, my mother phoned and said she wanted me to come to the house "for a talk." Once there, she led me upstairs to my old bedroom, where we sat, facing each other, backs up against opposite sides of the room.

"Your father sobs," she starting by saying. "Do you know he can't even sleep nights because of what you've done to us?"

"What I've done to *you*?"

"Oh, you are cruel, aren't you? Cruel and self-righteous, caring for no one but yourself."

"What did you want to talk about, Mother? Why I'm a homosexual?"

"Don't say that."

"I am not going to argue who I am."

"You're not—*that*."

"You don't want to talk to me, you want to change me."

"I've read articles in the library, about homosexuals, the types of things they do. They say that once you've tried homosexuality, it's very difficult to do anything else."

"Right. I don't think so."

"You are so naive," she said.

"And don't call me naive. I am not naive. I may be a lot of things but I am not naive."

"Your father's not naive. He doesn't like to read about these sorts of things, he doesn't like to be reminded, but he is not naive."

"So he reads the Bible instead."

"Yes, he reads the Bible, it's what he believes. It's what we both believe. God created—"

"Can we please leave God out of this?"

"No. You talk about what you believe; this is what we believe. God created man and woman so that they might procreate. Have children. To be united with someone forever is what God intended."

"Why? Why is it so wrong for me to love another man?"

"No, that's—"

"A sin. I know."

"Peter, you are asking your father and me to choose between everything we believe, our faith, and—"

"Me. Your son."

My mother looked away, breathed and clasped her hands.

"Mother, I just want to be happy."

"So, you're going to sell yourself, body and soul."

"Excuse me?"

"There's more to life than being happy."

"Now I'm not supposed to be happy?"

"You've been seduced into becoming a homosexual. Seduced by some old pervert. That's not happiness, that's perversion."

My mother and I had never discussed the event in my elementary school toilet. So overwhelming was my fear that I would end up like the man who had abused me that in an instant I was buried beneath the shame of her words.

"Homosexuals live lives of promiscuity and debauchery. All they care about is their next sex partner. Anonymous, dysfunctional sex: that's all they care about. Fornication, sex between two unmarried people, it's a sin."

Her final words blinded me with indignation. I lashed out, knowing full well that my eldest sister, Kriska, had been born not seven months after our parents' marriage, a fact my siblings and I had always known somehow never to mention.

"Were you a virgin before you got married?"

"I was raped in the concentration camp."

My mother looked stunned, as if this, her confession, were as much a shock to her as it was to me.

Then she doubled over, still sitting but clutching at her stomach, sobbing. I rushed to hold her in my arms.

"Please don't tell your father," she begged, cradled in my arms. "I've never told your father, you won't tell him, will you?" Her eyes, like those of an orphan, gazed up at me. I'd never seen her cry, but tears were coursing down her flushed cheeks.

"Please don't tell him . . . please . . ."

"Of course not," was all I could say, as I held her in my arms. "Of course not . . ."

Days later, the entire confrontation still left me in shock. A salient pact had been forged between us, and yet—had I not come to talk to her, at her request, about my own "confession"? Conflicted by the news of her rape, my promise that I never mention it again to anyone, least of all my father, and the ongoing need to talk about my own sexuality—and my own sexual abuse—a divide between my parents and me only widened in the weeks and months that followed. Soon, it became clear to me that to mention anything about my sexuality would be a reminder of her rape. I didn't want to cause my mother more pain, and so I learned what not to say, do, or feel, in order that she not be reminded of her past. In essence, our pact had bound me to a deafening silence. And beneath my silence, festering rage.

ıııııııııı

My need for sex, meanwhile, consumed me like an itch I felt compelled to scratch. I stopped returning calls to my agent. Never showed up for planned auditions. Pearl left me a series of desperate messages on my answering machine, pleading for me to call and tell her where I was or what was going on. I escaped into a world driven by anonymous sexual encounters with men.

Poppers, amyl nitrate, became a staple at the local gay bathhouse. The drug seemed to release me from myself, from where I was and what I was doing, if only for the moment. Once, while kissing a man inside a cubicle, my feelings of shame beating down against the pleasure of the experience, I grabbed the bottle and inhaled the liquid deep into my lungs.

"Hey, watch that stuff," the man warned, as I pulled him into me, our bodies, tongues, cocks, limbs, tangling, merging into one. The heart palpitations, a violent drunkenness that stole me from myself, came instantly and lasted seconds, seconds I would have risked my life to repeat, no doubt, before the sickness erupted through my gut. When the vomit burned the back of my throat I pushed his body, unwanted flesh, away from me and rolled onto the floor. I was a man whose food seemed poisonous to his hunger.

Two weeks later, I bused downtown and stood with the prostitutes.

By the third time his car had circled the block, I knew the man was interested. He pulled over and lowered the passenger-side tinted window. I walked to the curb and leaned in—the way I'd seen other young men in the neighborhood do it for months.

"Are you busy tonight?" he said.

||||||||||

My decision to leave, to remove myself physically from my immediate environment as soon as possible, appeared inside of me with panicked urgency the morning after the night with the man who paid money.

I called the University of Victoria on Vancouver Island, a two-hour ferry from my hometown of Vancouver, and asked for all the paperwork for undergraduate studies.

I told my parents I was moving to Victoria to start my bachelor's degree in creative writing; then, to assuage their visible concern, added, "maybe journalism."

Pearl knew nothing about the incident with the man. I told her my plan, and the day I left, on September 1, 1989, she helped me pack my books and clothes in her Toyota, and we drove to the ferry. In Victoria, I rented a room on the top floor of an unmarried couple's home.

Before my first day of classes, I made an appointment to see a new near-retired general practitioner, referred by my general practitioner back home. When I saw him the next week, I told him that I needed to see a psychiatrist.

"Can you please itemize for me what you're looking for?" he asked. Staunchly British, like much of the older generation in the province's capital city, the doctor asked questions like he was completing a national survey.

"Some sort of therapy where I can do more than talk, although . . . I guess I also need to talk. I need . . ." I pushed my fist into the pit of my stomach, near my belly button, like I was trying to reach my own umbilical cord. "Something . . . deeper. I know I need to cry. But I don't want to take medication."

"There is one doctor, a Spanish man, who's just moved to the city from back east. Quebec, I think. He's also the only psychiatrist practicing psychotherapy that's accepting new patients. I'll see what I can do . . ."

5

I WAS SITTING ON the only metal chair in a yet-to-be finished waiting room when I smelled his pungent cologne, like the scent of an animal that had laid claim to its territory. Moments later, his office door swung open with a gust of wind.

"Are you Peter?" he said in a pronounced Spanish accent. "I'm Dr. Alfonzo."

The smell was his.

I stood up and smiled, shook his hand, and followed him back through two adjoining doors that opened up inside a large, empty room, a windowless chamber, still being constructed.

"My furniture's being delivered next week. Until then, we can sit here," he said, pointing to two rickety stools.

We sat, and he started writing notes before I'd said a word. Olive skinned and around fifty years old, he was dressed in black, head to toe, with short, graying hair, wild, bushy eyebrows that hung over his long, dark lashes, and a closely cropped goatee. No doubt he'd once been handsome. Now he looked more menacing and slightly disheveled.

I glanced up, above his head, to a large framed quote from something called *A Course in Miracles*, hanging on the wall.

> *This is a course in miracles.*
> *It is a required course.*
> *Only the time you take it is voluntary . . .*

"How do you pronounce your last name?" he asked.

"'Guy-ditch,'" I said. "As in a 'guy-in-a-ditch.'" I cracked a smile.

He was not amused. "When I was a kid we actually pronounced it 'Gay-dicks.'"

He looked up from his yellow, legal-sized notepad. "Why would you do that?"

"My father Anglicized his name after the war. I guess he wanted to make it easier on North Americans."

"Which war?"

"World War II. He didn't really know what he was doing, changing the pronunciation to 'gay.' He's Hungarian; he couldn't speak English. Growing up was a cruel joke."

"Why?"

He waited for me to explain what I thought had been obvious. "Well, growing up with the name 'Gay-dicks,' and turning out gay."

"You're gay?" He raised an eyebrow, scanned me up and down.

"Yes . . ."

"You told your parents?"

"Last year."

"What did they say?"

"That they'd never accept it, that it was immoral, and I should never talk about it again."

He looked back to his notes and scribbled away. "Tell me about your parents."

Before thinking, I blurted out the first thing that came to mind whenever I was asked about my mother. "My mother escaped from a concentration camp."

"You're Jewish?"

"Catholic. At least I grew up Catholic."

"Why was your mother in a concentration camp?"

"All the Germans where she lived in Yugoslavia were placed in concentration camps after the war. Communist camps."

I tried to focus on our conversation, and his eyes, not to glance down at the tickling of what I knew was crawling on my forearm. There was no way of knowing exactly when the transfer had occurred, when I'd been contaminated, but the signs had started three nights after the night in the local gay bathhouse, two weeks earlier. I was in my bedroom, working on an assignment for one of my creative writing classes, when I realized I'd been scratching my crotch for twenty minutes. I went to the bathroom that I shared with another student down the hall, pulled the string to the light bulb dangling from the ceiling, latched the wooden door, lowered my pants and underwear. What at first looked like nothing more than a freckle, a grain of sand, began to move, crawl with legs that stretched from its oval body across the fuzz of my black pubic hairs. I smudged it between my thumb and forefinger. Then I saw another, near the hair follicles. And another. All across my skin, my arms, legs, torso, I saw them, crawling. I was infested with body crabs.

"Mr. Gajdics?"

"Sorry, what was the question?"

"And your father?"

"I don't really know that much about my father. He's never liked to talk about his past. Even now he won't mention it. Sometimes he hit us when we asked him questions."

"So . . . why do you want to see a psychiatrist?"

"Why? I guess . . . I want to feel more control in my life."

"You feel out of control?"

"I feel like I've lost everything that matters to me: my parents, their love. I was trying to be honest, telling who I am. And now . . ."

"Yes?"

"How do I come to terms with who I am when who I am causes so much pain and suffering to everyone I love?" I started crying.

"We won't have any of that." He motioned with a flick of his pen for me to cease all tears and to get on track. "No crying. Not now. Not yet." His thick accent shook me from my pain. He looked back to his notes as I closed the door to my tears, something I'd become an expert at since childhood.

"How's your sleep?"

"My sleep?"

"Do you sleep through the night?"

"Not usually."

"Are you depressed?"

I blushed. The truth was I had lived in the country of depression for so long it felt like my home. "I suppose."

"Do you have a boyfriend?"

"No."

"Do you want one?"

"I don't trust men."

He glanced up again, but this time his eyes seemed to be photographing my every inch for future recollection: my swarthy complexion, my long black hair tied back in a ponytail, my closely cropped beard and mustache.

"And women?"

"I've always had women friends, a girlfriend, even, but . . . sexually, that's never really worked."

"You can't maintain an erection?"

"No. I mean, that's not it, it's just . . . I always end up thinking about men when I'm with women. But when I'm with men, I . . ."

"Yes?"

"I feel like a crippled heterosexual."

The words hung between us like an onerous confession. He turned back to his notepad and scribbled some notes. I tried to fix my eyes on the upside-down writing, but all I could decipher were arrows and tables and what looked like some kind of shorthand.

"There was also an incident," I added, almost as an afterthought. "When I was six."

"Incident?"

"Sexual abuse."

"You were abused?" His interest peaked. "Who abused you—a family member?"

"A stranger. During a church bazaar in my elementary-school bathroom."

"Where were your parents?"

"Somewhere in the crowd, I don't know."

"How did it end?"

"I don't remember it ending."

"Did you tell anyone?"

"No."

"You never discussed it with anyone?"

"Not really."

"What do you mean, 'not really'?"

"When I was thirteen, my mother sat me down in the kitchen after school one day and she told me that there were dirty old men who kidnapped little boys and made them do really bad things that turned them into perverts for life. Then she just stared at me."

"What did she mean by that?"

"I don't know. I was too afraid to ask. 'Beware who you've become,' I guess."

"Meaning?"

"Like I said, I didn't ask her, and she never explained. I was too scared."

"I'm thinking of setting up a group solely for gay men," he said. "I think you'd be a perfect fit. But we need to take care of what's really bothering you. It would be a mistake to focus on your homosexuality. Your sexuality will take care of itself."

He was silent for a moment, still studying my face, then continued.

"Read *The Primal Scream* by Arthur Janov, and also these papers," he said, handing me a copy of "The Etiology of Neurosis and the Role of Reparenting in the Healing of the Inner Child," which he'd had published somewhere in Europe.

Then he pulled out what appeared to be a prescription pad, scribbled for a few minutes on it, and handed it to me.

Rivotril and Surmontil.

"Fill this prescription and follow the directions on how to take the medication. If you decide this isn't for you, that's okay. But you're going to have to stabilize your sleep patterns before embarking on any type of therapy. You can't do therapy without restorative sleep."

|||||||||

I left Alfonzo's office and walked straight to a nearby pharmacy. I decided not to fill his two prescriptions until I'd had a chance to read up on each of the drugs, but I wanted to buy more of the skin cream that already hadn't worked twice before.

"Sometimes you need more than one application," the pharmacist explained in a hushed tone at the back counter. "Because of the larva, the eggs." I left the store with two more bottles, prepared to repeat the procedure as many times as necessary.

I would have rushed home and smeared my body, but I had to bus up to a second-year poetry workshop at the university. Surrounded by nine other students and my professor, an emaciated older man who seemed to take pleasure out of tearing apart not only the word choices but the entire self-worth of each of his twenty-something-year-old students, not once did I not think about what I could not escape.

After class I quickly researched the two prescriptions in the school library. Rivotril, or clonazepam, I read in a pharmaceutical directory, belonged to the class of medications called benzodiazepines, generally used as a sedative or to decrease seizures or anxiety. If used over a period of time, the drug was known to become addictive. Surmontil, or trimipramine, on the other hand, was one of many types of tricyclic antidepressants. "Tricyclics," as they were commonly known, were most often prescribed in cases of clinical depression.

My choice was not a difficult one to make: I didn't want to get addicted to anything, and I had never thought of myself as "clinically depressed," so I decided to skip both medications. Alfonzo would understand, I told myself. After all, he was a doctor, and doctors, I'd always believed, were compassionate and respectful of their patients.

After the fourth page of his scientific paper, which read to me like gibberish, I still had no idea what to expect from his therapy. But he did reference Alice Miller's *Prisoners of Childhood*, a book I'd read repeatedly for years, and still had a highlighted, dog-eared copy in my backpack.

Instead of busing home, I walked to a nearby stretch of beach flanked, at one end, by jagged cliffs. I wanted my body to be shocked, so in the winter breeze I unzipped my jacket. Seconds later, I heard a voice call out to me from behind.

"You work at the university."

When I turned around, another student from my university, a man of about my age who ate almost every day at the student union cafeteria where I worked part-time as a cook and cashier, picked up his speed to walk alongside me.

"Yes," I answered. "You're a student at the university, right?"

His face was clear and open, with walnut eyes that looked intently into mine. "Do you live around here?"

"No, I, no. I live close to the university, actually. I was just out, walking . . ."

"Mind if I walk with you?"

"Sure . . ."

"What are you studying?"

"Creative writing."

"An artist. So, are you a sensitive young man?"

He smiled. I glanced at him, as we continued along the shore. He was smartly dressed in a black turtleneck and pleated brown cords, and his hands, I noticed, remained tucked inside the pockets to his beige, unbuttoned trench coat.

"And you? I mean, what are you studying?"

"Engineering."

"So, that means you're not sensitive?"

"I am, actually."

Beneath the flood of a street lamp, we stopped. In the corridor of wind, his scent blew up against me. I couldn't escape his eyes, his body, what they did to me. I froze.

"I think there's a coffee shop around here," he said, glancing back. "Would you like to grab a coffee or . . . something?"

A familiar loss of breath, desire mixed with panic, took hold.

"Maybe . . . another time," I managed to say. "But thanks . . . "

I didn't look back, but felt his eyes on me, behind, as I disappeared into the night.

6

I MET WITH ALFONZO a second time a week after our initial consultation.

"I wouldn't worry too much about my paper," he said. "The world of academia can be quite stuffy. All the terminology is necessary for publication, but it can be an Achilles' heel to the public."

I glanced down to a copy of the paper, the sections I'd highlighted throughout. "So, this word you use . . . 'abreaction.'"

"Feeling."

"Feeling?"

"Well, feeling at the level of change."

Deep, transformational change, Alfonzo explained, occurred only when a person's inner child was accessed, their "primal pain" experienced, and any lessons learned were integrated. Then they could finally "grow back up" to their "chronological age."

"And all of it," Alfonzo said proudly, "can occur during a single primal session."

He stared at me for a moment, searching my eyes for some reaction.

"No other therapeutic process can claim to do what I've perfected in this therapy. The way the patient dips back down into the world of their childhood, their primal world. It's like peeling an onion, session after session, layer upon layer, until you reach the core. But first you have to find a way of peeling the onion. It's Alice down the rabbit hole. You'll see. You'll experience it for yourself. Then you'll know exactly what I mean."

"So, what's at the core of the onion?"

He smiled. "Nothing. Everything."

"And this other word you use . . . 'introject'?"

"Your internalized parents."

"That's it?"

"That's it. Like I said, I wouldn't worry about the paper. You'll learn how to do the therapy yourself. I'll teach you, then you'll feel it for yourself."

We were nearing the end of the session when I realized I'd never seen any diplomas or certificates anywhere in his office, not on the walls or on his desk.

"Can I ask you about your background?" I asked. "Where did you go to school?"

"Are you implying that I don't know what I'm talking about?"

"I was just wondering where you studied."

"You were just wondering where I studied," he repeated, singing my own words back to me. He ignored my question but continued writing notes. "How are you finding the medications?" he asked.

"I decided not to fill the prescriptions."

He stopped writing, placed his pen on the desk, and stood up.

"Are you questioning my authority?" He turned and paced toward the window, three steps ahead, then back and stopping only because he'd reached the foot of my chair. "You think you know more than me? Is that it? Listen here, sonny boy, I was a doctor before you were born."

His eyes narrowed, his finger was pointed in my face. I was speechless.

After a moment he lowered his hand, returned to his seat, finished his notes, then said something about making another appointment for the following week. But I was holding my breath and only thought about getting out the door before the tears came again. This time I wasn't sure I'd be able, or even want, to turn them off.

The next day I returned to the general practitioner who'd referred me.

"What sort of issues are you struggling with?" he said. "I don't think you told me this before." He glanced at my chart.

"Issues?"

He sat back on his swivel stool in the pristine examination room and waited.

"Well . . . I moved to Victoria to go to school, but . . . that was really an excuse to escape my family. We've been fighting for months. I can't sleep. Sometimes I have these . . . episodes."

"What kind of episodes?"

"Like I'm looking through a tunnel. I can't breathe. It feels like I'm going to die."

"You wouldn't rather see a clinical psychologist?"

"I can't afford a psychologist. I know psychiatry is covered under my provincial health plan, though, right?"

"Dr. Alfonzo is the only psychiatrist in this city who's accepting new patients. If you want another referral, you may end up waiting another two years."

"Two years? I can't wait two years . . ."

I didn't leave.

"Was there something else?"

"Well, yes . . . actually."

He waited.

"I had . . . I mean, I've had . . . crabs . . . body lice. I've tried twice to get rid of them, but I think they're coming back. I feel like I'm being eaten alive."

Through his thick bifocals, the doctor's eyes swelled. "If the cream doesn't work, you need to try it again. Wait one week and reapply as the directions instruct. Meanwhile, you may want to limit your sexual partners."

My only wish, as I lay in bed that night with twice the recommended remedy searing my flesh, was that I could get at the roots, kill the eggs. No matter how I tried, it seemed there was always something left inside of me I couldn't quite clean.

|||||||||||

Alfonzo called me at home the next day.

"I was just wondering how you're doing. Have you decided about my therapy?"

"Not really," I said, knowing I could always hang up and never go back if he attacked me on the phone. "I still have some concerns."

"What would they be?"

"Well, the medications, for one. I don't really want to take medication."

"Okay," he said, calmly, "that's your choice." All his patients started off on at least one of the tricyclics, he explained—to ensure their sleep patterns stabilized before treatment began. "But if you're not comfortable with medication, then we won't use any medication. Anything else?"

"Your scientific paper is still confusing to me. I'm trying to wrap my head around your form of treatment. What exactly happens during a therapy session?"

"Have you read *The Primal Scream* yet?"

"I started . . ."

What I'd read, in fact, had intrigued me. In the 1960s, American psychologist and psychiatric worker Arthur Janov claimed to have "discovered" primal therapy as a "cure" for all psychological neurosis. His actual treatment seemed to involve a two-phase process. In the first phase, patients experienced intense bouts of crying and screaming, known as "primal regressions" or "primals," through controlled acts of breathing while lying on their backs. The second involved vivid, psychological insights into a particular historical event of trauma. Janov's fame grew when the Beatle John Lennon took his treatment and incorporated screaming into one of his songs.

"I don't like to call my therapy 'Primal Therapy,'" Alfonzo continued on the phone, "especially since Janov trademarked the phrase back in the sixties. He used to sue people who violated the copyright. But the idea behind our therapy's the same: regressions. Of course, Janov never provided reparenting, like I will."

"What do you mean by 'reparenting'?"

Alfonzo's plan, as he continued to explain, was to hire a woman in the next six months—"to act as a surrogate parent" following all my primal sessions in the office. "Nurturing the child is what's most important," he said. "You won't find anyone else offering this type of experiential therapy, Peter. Not anywhere in the city, perhaps not anywhere in the world. You won't find the nurturing, that's for sure. But my patient list is filling up fast, so . . . if you're interested, you better make up your mind soon."

Alfonzo's words rang through me throughout Christmas season—during the two-hour ferry back to Vancouver and the ensuing festivities with my family that had brought me joy as a child, but which now left me cold, resentful, and detached. I thought of nothing but my need to talk to someone, anyone, about my parents who'd said they loved their son but rejected his homosexuality. How they could separate the two, me from my sexuality, I did not know, and only knew I could no longer do that in myself. Maybe Alfonzo would decide not to use a surrogate parent; maybe he'd decide that this sort of nurturing was not the best idea, not for me, because even the thought of it made me anxious.

In the background on several television sets, I saw newscasts about the Berlin Wall, the fall of communism, the end of the Cold War. Walls were coming down as others, between my parents and I, went up. When my parents asked that I attend Christmas Mass with them at Our Lady of Perpetual Help, I wanted to say, *Why would I go to church after everything the church has told me about who I am? Why would I do that to myself?*

But I went.

My parents and I sat in the same third pew from the front as my whole family had when my siblings and I were children: me next to my mother, my father next to her. I looked around but recognized no one from my past. All the families with their ten, twelve, thirteen children were replaced with families of three, maybe four. As the congregation started singing, and I didn't, I thought about the last time I sang at church. I was eleven.

My mother and I had been sitting side by side, as usual, holding hands, the rest of my family lined up next to us. The priest began his sermon. He praised our Lord God, Creator of life and the Universe, and his only begotten Son, Jesus Christ, Savior of mankind. But then he started talking about purgatory, damnation, the fires of Hell, that we were sinners, every last one of us, and that judgment day was growing ever nearer. When he mentioned "all the homosexuals, the lot of them condemned to Satan," my palms began to sweat, my throat constricted. His eyes, which seemed to be burrowing into me, my soul, burned with all the hatred I imagined lay waiting for me at judgment. I tried to uncurl my fingers from around my mother's, but she squeezed them tighter, pulled me into her.

The sermon ended. The congregation stood to sing. But when I opened my mouth to join in, nothing came out: no sound, no music.

My mother noticed my silence, a paleness that had washed over me, and bent down and whispered. "What's wrong with you? Why aren't you singing?"

I couldn't sing. Music was no longer in me to sing.

There was never any choice but to line up behind my parents, along with all the other parishioners, for Holy Communion. Step by step, I approached the altar, could not even hear the hymn above the pounding of my heart.

Yea, though I walk through the valley of the shadow of death . . .

As I stepped forward I neared a cliff; to turn back would have drawn undue attention to myself, contravened all duty to my parents, my faith, the Church; to step forward and receive Christ's Body in my mouth would be to drop unrepentantly into my own damned soul, after which there would be no forgiveness, forever.

I shall fear no evil . . .

I received the Body of Christ. But as I returned to our pew, a faint resignation of hope shuddered through me, like a cold, quiet sweat.

. . . for thou art with me; thy rod and thy staff they comfort me.

The start of damnation.

Sitting now in the same third pew during Christmas Mass, I still didn't sing. During all the hymns I stood beside my parents, closed-mouthed. My mother glanced over at me, but said nothing. I also had not lined up for Communion in years, but my parents had long since stopped asking me why not. They received the Body of Christ as I waited for Mass to end.

After the Christmas season, on the last day of the year at the end of the decade, I said goodbye to my parents and returned once again by ferry to my new life as a university student. For the first time in weeks, my skin was calm, uninfested, but a hole inside my heart had become like a crater in my soul. Standing in a cold winter fog on the outside deck, I knew that sex was what I'd used to kill my pain, and sex was what was causing me pain, and that if I did not talk to someone, fast, sex would kill me.

|||||||||

Three weeks later, I followed Alfonzo through the inner chamber, "the workroom," as he called it, and into his adjoining private office. Slits of light streamed through the shutters. There were leafy plants and overcrowded bookshelves. He sat on a black leather recliner in front of his L-shaped desk and motioned for me to sit in the chair across from him.

"I'm placing you in a group of heterosexual men and women," he said.

Tears flooded my eyes. "But . . . I thought . . . you said something about a group with other . . . men."

"That's not going to happen." To supplement my groups, he explained, I would have to begin individual sessions with him. Except he didn't want me to talk. "Not yet. First you need to learn how to do the therapy. Then you can talk. Your thoughts are still far too disorganized."

He stood and told me to follow him back into the workroom. Since my previous visit, all the walls had been constructed, with the framed quote from *A Course in Miracles* hanging above a blacked-out window at one end of the room. He dimmed the lights and plopped himself into a squat chair, similar to a waiting-room chair but with its aluminum legs sawed off, positioned in the middle of one side of the room, back up against the wall, so that he was at eye level to a large sheeted mattress in the middle of the floor.

"Lie down," he said.

I lay down, now mere inches from him.

"First, close your eyes and breathe in deeply through your nose, then exhale with a grunt through your mouth. In through your nose, out with a grunt. Keep doing that. And start moving your arms and legs, like you're walking down the street. Don't stop."

I did as I was told: closed my eyes, breathed as he'd instructed, moved my arms and legs on the mattress.

"Next I want you to think about a person or event from your past.

Something that's troubling to you. Keep vocalizing your breaths while thinking about that event, and continue moving your arms and legs like you're walking."

I felt a weight with every breath, a crushing pressure on my chest, like a body, forcing its way inside. Random memories emerged, each as if they'd never ended, only waiting to be felt.

My arms and legs kept moving; but in my mind, I saw myself, six years old, inside the toilet stall. I felt myself forced back against the cold metal door behind me, my little boy's body squished up against the fat man's stomach, like a drum, held solidly between us. On the mattress I breathed in, then out, in, out; and then I heard Alfonzo, like a voice in my head, reminding me not to talk, but to "focus on the past."

And I did: I couldn't stop, couldn't help but see the man, the three-quarter crown on top of his head with dandruff, like snow, dusting his shoulders and the front of his body; the dirty blue lint, like stuffing from his insides, falling out of his navel; his nose, bloated and purplish, that looked like it would crack wide open and spill out yellowish pus.

All I wanted was to move, if not away from him then outside myself. But then he was reaching down between his pale, hairy legs, and his eyes, they flickered, like he was dreaming. When he groaned I smelled his breath, dirty, cigarettes, and I heard the sound of a zipper being pulled down as his fingers reached around inside my pants.

"I love you," he whispered, pulling me in toward his cracked lips. "I love you."

"Keep moving!" Alfonzo screamed. "Faster!" I did: my legs and arms clipped faster, faster, as my heart pounded in my ears. "Faster!"

Then I was running, running on the mattress, kicking on the mattress as the pressure rose from within. When my back arched up, up off the mattress, I heard the scream, like a windstorm through the channels of my body, echo out of me and off the walls as I lay there, frozen, drenched and dizzy, spinning, extremities tingling, ears ringing, lightheaded, as if I'd dove off a cliff and was falling through air.

Only after the dizziness stopped, minutes later, did I open my eyes. I saw snow.

"Sit up," Alfonzo said. "Slowly."

I did.

"Now . . . I want you to go to the batting station—Peter, can you hear me?"

"Yes . . ."

"I want you to go to the batting station, at the end of the mattress. Then I want you to kneel in front of the punching bag and face the wall."

Beneath the window at the head of the mattress was a boxer's punching bag lying on the floor. There was an aluminum baseball bat next to it, and on the wall directly in front a large "X," marked like a bull's-eye with red electrician's tape.

I did as I was told and crawled over to the "batting station."

"We lie on the mattress to connect with deep pain. If we feel anger, even the slightest bit of anger, we move directly to the batting station. Pick up the baseball bat."

I picked up the bat lying next to the punching bag.

"Keep looking at the red 'X' on the wall, and start hitting the bag."

I didn't move.

"Did you hear me?"

The whole exercise seemed foolish. I didn't feel angry. If anything, I was still weak and weighted with sadness from the exercise on the mattress.

"I'm not angry," I said.

"I said hit the bag."

"I don't want to."

"Peter, this is not a question. I said hit the fucking bag."

I tapped the bag, halfheartedly, with the baseball bat.

Alfonzo stood up and walked over to me, took the bat from my hands, and knelt down next to me. "Do you see what I'm doing? Watch me. Grip the bat, and hit the bag. Simple."

He handed the bat back to me, and I started to hit the punching bag, weakly at first, but quickly picking up speed.

"That's it," he called out over my bats. "Don't forget to breathe.

And remember: no talking. Think about your mother or your father. See them sitting before you when you stare at the 'X.' And keep vocalizing your breaths: in through your nose, out with a grunt through your mouth. Don't stop till I tell you to stop."

Soon I was whacking the bag with all my strength, grunting all the while.

||||||||||

With each subsequent session lying on the mattress, eyes closed, limbs moving, I'd visualize myself at seven, already withdrawn but with a fury in my eyes that both frightened and surprised me in the present. When the rage came like a heat wave through my body, I didn't even stand but scurried on all fours to grip the bat, cold and hard, and channel whatever I'd never been allowed to feel into repeated swings high into the air with every muscle in my back, shoulders and arms constricted, then down with a stabbing thump against the bag, like a body, lying passively before me.

For the next several weeks, we excavated my body. Every time I backed away from a memory, a feeling, rage, Alfonzo was there, nudging me on into myself, deeper into the fury, like a room I'd long since abandoned out of fear. Those feelings still took up residence in me whether I acknowledged them or not. Nothing was taboo, no memory off limits. All was encouraged, welcomed, given room to breathe, to spread its arms as if waking after a long night's sleep and ready itself to stand up and be.

Be angry. Become it, because that was the point, this was the time, there were no excuses.

Alfonzo, it seemed, could see inside my room, the room of my fury: he knew what was in me and how to coax it out of me. After weeks of me kneeling, grunting, batting, he called out to me from across the workroom.

"What have you always wanted to say to your mother and your father?" he said as I imagined the bat like all the knives I'd ever wanted to slice into them, into everyone who'd teased me, mocked me, called me names, or worse: who'd denied me my feelings, aborted them, each and every one, as if they'd been unwanted children—my sadness, my terror, even my joy.

"Say it now!" he screamed. "Say all of it! Only this time, win! You have to win! Scream twice as loud as their denial! Don't back down!"

Breaths and grunts morphed into words as I screamed at my mother, at both my parents, asked them why they'd never talked to me about the fat man in the toilet stall, why I'd been silenced, as if bound and gagged, throughout my childhood, why they'd never come to rescue me, to help me. Didn't they love me?

Then one day, while "walking" on the mattress in the middle of a session, an image popped into my mind, as clearly as if I'd opened up a curtain and allowed in the light. The fat man and I were still inside the stall, but thirty feet away, outside the bathroom door, standing like a guard, I saw my mother. As if I were above it all, omnisciently looking down upon a scene from my life, I was witnessing what could not have been, what I could not comprehend.

And then the image cut forward, like from a movie, and I was back with my mother in the church bazaar, holding her hand amidst a sea of people. The fat man approached us. I had stopped moving on the mattress and my palms were sweating, my heart, thumping. I didn't want to look, to see, but when I did I saw his stained and jagged teeth, fangs. Then he handed her money, "For your son's hospitality," patting my head, before he turned and walked away.

"Go to the bat," Alfonzo called out.

But I could not move. I could not stand, roll over, or crawl anywhere. I could not believe what I was seeing, imagining, and I did not want to fight.

"Stop," I heard him say. "Peter, open your eyes. Do it. Now."

My eyes opened. Everything looked blurry, surreal.

"Sit up."

I didn't want to move, but I did as I was told.

"I want you to listen to me. Peter, are you with me?"

"Yes," I said, because I knew that's what I was supposed to say.

"When you connect to a painful memory it's vital that you go to the batting station. Do you hear me?"

"Yes . . ."

"You can't just lie there and stop moving. If you do, you'll go into despair. This is how it works. This is how everyone does it, how it's always been done, and if you don't follow the rules, you're out. Out. Do you understand me?"

"Yes."

"Do you?"

"Yes," I said, lying.

7

GROUP THERAPY STARTED IN late January 1990, several weeks after my individual sessions. I could only imagine the other patients had all been referred to Alfonzo through their general practitioners, as I'd been through mine. Alfonzo sat on his squat chair in the middle of one side of the room, with ten of us in a circle, backs up against the outer walls, around the mattress. Yvette, his secretary, a French Canadian, took notes on a pad at one end of the group.

"I could summarize my therapy with three C's," Alfonzo said, holding up his three middle fingers for added effect. "Confession. Confrontation. Communion. First you confess your story—tell someone your life, expose your shame. Then you confront those who wronged you in some way, which is why we have the batting station over there. And finally—and this is the most important part—you commune with the divine through the act of reparenting. Without this final step, receiving the love you were denied as a child, no true healing occurs. *A Course in Miracles* says it all: 'Only love is real, all else, illusion.' A loveless mind is a mind in error. And a mind in error can only be corrected with the help of my therapy and the aid of reparenting."

Understanding Alfonzo through his Spanish accent was sometimes difficult, but everything he said about only love being real, all else illusion, made sense to me, much more than the Catholic doctrines of my youth, which had taught me sin and forgiveness. I listened to him, we all listened to him, as he continued on about his theories around reparenting, which, he explained, had evolved over the course of his own therapy, beginning in the late 1960s with none other than the father of primal therapy, Arthur Janov, at his Primal Institute in Los Angeles.

"It's amazing to me now, the fact that Janov never thought to bring us Mommy. All of us, a sea of primal patients, all lying on our own mattresses in a room as big as a gymnasium, crying out for Mommy's love, and Janov never thought to give us the obvious: Mommy's love. Reparenting with the mother, and to a lesser degree, the father—it's the glue that holds that baby's mind together. It's the missing link in all of psychotherapy, and I discovered it. Such is the level of denial of the male mind. But of course you can't get to Mommy and Daddy before going through yourself."

He stopped talking long enough to look at us one at a time, each as if we were merely obstacle courses he was about to begin.

"So, who goes first? Who wants to confess their shame?"

All our eyes turned to the floor.

"No volunteers?"

An image of Brother Roberts, cassocked and white collared, popped into my mind—the way he roamed the aisles of my grade nine sex-education class, all of our faces, mine especially, buried in our books as we prayed he wouldn't call on us to read aloud.

"Okay then. We start at one end and go in a circle."

Just like class, I was sitting somewhere in the middle, time enough to mentally prepare or pray for the hour to end before it was my turn to speak.

First up was a woman who we all could see was anorexic, even before she opened her mouth. Her voice, when she started explaining her reasons for not eating, was frailer than bone china.

"Speak up," Alfonzo repeated throughout her meek, disjointed soliloquy, her skeletal arms wrapped tighter around her body each time she heard his voice.

Next up was a mid-thirties Rastafarian who wore faded Bob Marley T-shirts. He shared his story about his wife he'd not had sex with for over three years. "I don't know what her problem is," he explained, tugging at his dreadlocks.

"Maybe there's nothing wrong with her," Alfonzo reproached. "Maybe there's something wrong with *you*."

"My sixteen-year-old daughter's the problem," another patient, a late-thirties, single mother, shared with the group. "She stays out late, comes home drunk, skips school. And now I've met her dropout boyfriend, who I'm sure is a member of some pot-smoking gang."

"So why are you here?" Alfonzo asked.

"Well, I wanted her to come, but she refused."

"So why are *you* here?" Alfonzo repeated.

"I don't know. My daughter's the problem."

"Okay. Get on the mattress."

"What?"

"Lie on the mattress, and let's see what's inside you."

And so she did, reticently, moving her arms and legs as if she were underwater, the sound of her voice bubbling up but blocked somewhere between her chest and throat. After twenty minutes on the mattress her body broke open, like Pandora's box.

"You think I wanted you?" she screamed, her body thrashing on the mattress, eyes locked shut, limbs like clubs against the insulating mattress beneath her. "You think I wanted to have some ungrateful brat I never loved I never wanted I never asked to have and now I have to support and feed and worry about all the time? Just die, goddammit, just die and leave me to my life so I can *live* my life!"

The woman's eyes flashed open, and she tumbled off the mattress and toward the door while looking back as if the mattress itself had possessed her into what she'd said, into what she'd felt, into what had come from her.

She left before the end of the hour. We never saw her again.

The anorexic also didn't return the following week. When Alfonzo told us she would not be returning, he added that her eating disorder, her refusal to feed her body, was directly related to her fear of love.

"Love is to the self what food is to the body," he told us. "Without it, you die. You understand what I'm talking about, don't you, Peter?"

Everyone turned and looked at me. Alfonzo smiled. I blushed but said nothing, embarrassed as if being singled out in class.

The Rastafarian lasted one week longer before he, too, vanished. Presumably, when Alfonzo called his home to check up on him, his wife said that he'd dropped off the face of the earth and that no one, not even she, could find him.

"One day he'll show up," Alfonzo told us in the group the following week. "And when he does, he'll still have the same problems that he left with when he disappeared."

Week after week, the other original patients disappeared from the group like characters killed off in an Agatha Christie novel, until all but myself of the original group had been replaced with new patients from an ever-growing list of patients referred to Alfonzo for treatment.

When it was my turn to share, to confess my shame, I told the ever-changing cast of characters about a time, after the time in my elementary school toilet, that I had sex with another man.

"I had skipped out of school," I started, still sitting in the circle.

"How old were you?" Alfonzo asked, perched on his squat chair directly across from me on the other side of the room.

"Thirteen."

"This is very important," Alfonzo said to everyone. "Before beginning a memory, you have to always say how old you are and where you are. Go ahead . . ."

"I was downtown, alone. I was in grade eight. It was '1950s day' at school so I was dressed as my favorite TV character, the Fonz. White T-shirt and blue denims. This man passed me on the street. His face was covered in pockmarks, like craters. He smiled. I glanced back. He walked back to me and asked what I was up to. I told him I was just walking around. He told me to meet him at his apartment later that afternoon."

"He *told* you?"

"I mean he asked me."

"Okay. He 'asked' you. Go on."

"I guess he gave me his address and then he walked away. All I could think about all day was maybe getting from him what I couldn't find in anyone else."

"And what was that?"

"A connection. Attention, maybe? Anyway, I waited outside his apartment for over an hour. It was late in the day, three thirty. I knew my parents would be expecting me home from school, but I couldn't leave. I couldn't go home without . . . it. Whatever 'it' was. At five o'clock he arrived. I saw him from one end of the street, strolling toward me. I was so mad for waiting all that time and then all he said was hello or something, no apology, but he told me that he was glad I was there and I should go upstairs with him."

"Upstairs?"

"To his apartment. I followed him in. He told me to get undressed . . . to lie on his bed. He scared me. He was ugly. I didn't know what I was doing, but I couldn't leave."

"Why couldn't you leave?"

"I . . . just . . . couldn't. I took off my pants. He told me to take them off. I felt ashamed of my body. My skin was still hairless. I was thirteen. Then he took off his pants, and I saw his penis. It was huge, like a club. He told me to lie on my stomach. I wanted to leave. I didn't know what I was doing. I remember thinking about my mother. I could see her at home, making dinner. And my dad . . . arriving home from work, so tired. I could see them asking where I was. I should have been home hours ago. Where was their baby boy?"

I started shivering. I glanced quickly at everyone in my group, then over at Alfonzo. I had never talked about any of these details with anyone before, and while I was scared to keep going, remaining silent, at that moment, seemed worse than the fear of anyone's judgment.

"I could feel his pubic hairs against my behind. They were sharp, like bristles. Then he . . . stabbed himself inside me. The pain was . . . raw . . . and unbearable. Jagged glass through bone. My body . . . jumped off the bed. I can still see me, running down his corridor, hysterical. Like my body had . . . burst or come undone, somehow. He got mad. I don't remember much, but I remember his anger. And then . . . I don't know. After that I don't remember. I guess I must've calmed down. I mean at some point, I must've stopped crying. Got dressed . . . put on my underwear, my pants, shirt . . . my coat. I'm here today so I must've left his apartment and walked to the bus. Rode home . . . entered the house and faced my parents. Made up some excuse about why I was three hours late. I can't remember but . . . it must've happened. My mind . . . fell out of time . . . or something."

"There's nothing gay about being gay, is there, Peter?" Alfonzo said as I finished my story, chilled, but tearless. "In all my years as a practicing psychiatrist, I have never met one happy homosexual."

In my silence, another group member, Natie, a deeply commanding, handsome, older woman, spoke up. "Maybe the reason why you've never met a happy homosexual is because you're a psychiatrist," she said, "trained to treat unhappy people, gay or straight. Besides, Peter's story had nothing to do with being gay—he was raped!"

"Are you challenging my lifetime of experience?" he said.

Natie was a therapist herself, as I'd learned from her own introduction, so her opinion seemed to matter to Alfonzo above the quibbling of the other patients.

"You had better shut up," he told her. "Or else."

||||||||||

Later that night, after my writing workshop at school, I arrived home to a phone message. Before I could hit "play," the phone rang. It was my old childhood friend, Tommy.

"Peter, what's going on?" he said on the phone.

"What do you mean?"

"This therapy, Peter, I'm worried about you. I don't hear from you anymore. I feel like this doctor is a body snatcher. What's happening to you? Have you talked to your mother?"

"No."

"Don't you think you should?"

"No."

"Well maybe she's worried about you."

"That's not my problem."

"Maybe you should think of her feelings."

"Why? Has she ever thought of mine?"

Just the thought of needing to take care of my mother's feelings, again, made me think of the baseball bat in the office, and in an instant, I was swinging it through my mind, faces smashed like piñatas in the air.

"Does this have anything to do with all those men?"

"*Which* men?" I asked, knowing full well what he was asking.

"That you've had sex with. I don't know why you can't just date one man, like me. Peter, whatever's going on, I'm sure your parents care about you and you need—"

I hung up the phone, picked up the first thing, a water glass, I saw, and threw it across the room. It bounced off the floor and landed next to my bed in a thud.

What I needed was the baseball bat.

The blinking light on the phone machine caught my eye. I pressed "play."

"Peter, it's Dr. Alfonzo. How are you? That was quite a session today, wasn't it? Peter, please don't give up hope. My thoughts and love are with you. You're not alone."

Love? Not alone? In all the time since telling my parents, "I am a homosexual," two years earlier, they had never said such supportive words to me, on or off the phone. I rewound the message and listened to it again, and again.

‖‖‖‖‖‖‖

"What I want to know," Alfonzo said, starting my next individual session, the following week, "is how a thirteen-year-old boy ends up downtown alone, getting fucked up the ass by a man three times his age."

I lowered my eyes. "You don't have to say it like that."

"Isn't that what it was?"

"I skipped out of school. I told you."

"Why? What was going on at home?"

I looked at him, but said nothing. Knew only that I couldn't be at home. Or at school. Both had been worse than wandering the streets, alone, downtown.

"Lie down," he said.

In the month that I'd been working with Alfonzo, my regressions on the mattress had been like diving back into a wreck, the furthest reaches of my past where events and circumstances, feeling images caught on film, played through me, the Moviola of my body. I never knew just what to expect, which memories I would have to swim through and survive, until I lay down, closed my eyes, breathed deeply, and moved.

When I did, there was my thirteenth birthday, the Dobos torte my mother had spent all afternoon baking just for me, and the feeling of depression settling into my young body like an influenza that I couldn't fight. I wanted to go to bed, to turn life off, as if unconsciousness could hide me from myself. It never did. In sleep, my dreams enunciated everything I couldn't bear the weight of while awake.

In one dream I was inside my parents' bathroom when I realized my thumb had been severed from my hand and that I'd have to fix it, somehow reattach it to my body. No one else could help me now. But then my mother was banging on the door, wanting to see, to help, to know what had happened, and I was hysterical, panicked, without a thumb, crazed and alone inside the bathroom. I couldn't breathe or scream for her to go away, to leave me to my shame. But what I wanted most of all was for her to come and somehow help make me into who I'd been when I was whole.

In one of my regressions, I thought of dinners, all seven of us around the blue Arborite kitchen table as my father joked with my two older brothers that they'd better not talk back to him *or else* he'd stuff them in a potato sack and tie it up so they could never get out again. Everyone would laugh, or maybe only smile. *Potato sacks aren't big enough for my brothers*, I'd think. But I understood his message perfectly well: We were not, under any circumstance, at any time, to speak back to our father. If we did, we were slapped across our face or else he told our mother to pass him the *fakanál*—the Hungarian word for "wooden spoon," pronounced "fuck-u-null"— which usually meant that someone was about to get the slapping of their lives.

Every night we listened to Walter Cronkite's voice from our black-and-white Fleetwood console in the living room, telling us of Vietnam and Watergate, the atomic bomb, of Washington politics. It seemed the world was splintered into pieces—filled with betrayal and heartache, at war with itself, imploding and coming to an end. Later, after dinner and the dishes, my brothers and I repeated our father's Hungarian word, *fakanál*, while forcing its first syllable through our lips and back and forth at each other like darts hurled through the air.

"And that's the way it is," Walter Cronkite signed out in the background of our lives, as we raced around the house, chanting "*fak*anál . . . *fak*anál . . . *fak*anál."

"Where are you now?" Alfonzo asked, and then I was remembering, seeing with eyes I'd never used before, the night that Kriska ran away from home.

"Okay, keep moving and talking," Alfonzo said as I continued to breathe, to move, to see myself lying in bed later that night, after my mother found Kriska's goodbye note on her bed.

"Your sister doesn't want to live with us anymore," she'd said, shutting my door and leaving me adrift at sea. When I cried, I begged for God to tell me why, why life took from me my sister that I loved. But no one answered, not God, not my parents. There was only silence and pain: the breaking apart of what was supposed to have always remained whole.

"Daddy's bringing Kriska home tonight," I remembered my brother, Pisti, telling me; and then I saw us, weeks later, crouched beneath the kitchen table, peering through the rain-streaked window, beyond our fenced-in yard, down the potholed laneway, at Daddy dragging Kriska by her golden hair as she kicked and punched him like an untamed animal being dragged back to its pen. When they entered the house, through the basement below, their screams were like a fire that burst us all up in flames.

"Sit at the table and eat your dinner," our mother, our protector, ordered my siblings and me before Kriska ran past us, escaped her beating in the basement to run up the stairs, through the kitchen, and around the corner to the bathroom, as our father, her captor, closed in on her; and all of it, the beating and the screaming and the fear, the threat that I could be next, that if he did it to her he could do it to me, was all like an ice storm to my body.

"Go to the bat," Alfonzo ordered.

I didn't want to, wanted instead to hide, to do what I knew and allow the quicksand called despair to take me, but I crawled to the batting station as instructed.

I had not yet learned to talk and found no words, like tools, to use against my father.

"Just keep batting," I heard Alfonzo, my leader, say. "Breathe and bat and stare at the 'X.'"

And then I was twelve, thirteen, standing in the kitchen with my father after he'd returned home from work, listening to him talk about God, His love for all His children, when all I wanted was to ask how God could love His children when he, my father, beat his own.

"Keep batting," Alfonzo called out. "And keep your eyes focused on the 'X.'"

And I did, batting up against his words as I heard him talking about Kriska, whom he'd hardly ever mentioned in the four years she'd been living with a foster family.

"She had the devil in her," he said. "You don't want to end up like her. You're a good boy. She was a troublemaker."

"Bat!" Alfonzo screamed.

"No she wasn't," I shot back to my father as a child, unable to contain myself.

"What did you say?" my father asked.

The tremor of his chin and a burn in his eyes warned of what was coming. Like a paddle he raised his hand, backed me into a corner of the kitchen.

"Bloody hell . . ."

I darted past him, heard the snap of his belt buckle, like a bull-whip, and ran, as if trying to run outside me, through the living room, the dining room, up the wooden stairs, and down the hallway to my room.

At the batting station, kneeling and still clutching to the bat, a rage pulsed through me, and all I could do was breathe, gutturally punch the air before me, and bat. Breathe, bat, and visualize all the years I'd imagined grabbing the kitchen knife and stabbing it into him, into both my parents. As a child, those thoughts were bigger than my body, were rage that blistered, then, unexpressed, deflated, leaving me numb inside an igloo of depression. Now I was breaking out, through years of ice, one bat at a time, back into the rage.

Once in my bedroom, I locked the door. Then he was pounding up the stairs; he was on the other side, banging with fists like clubs for me to open up and let him in.

"Open this door!" my father screamed in the past as Alfonzo screamed in the present for me to "Bat! Keeping batting!"

"This is my house, this is my door, as long as you live in my house you will open my door!"

As a child nothing, not one word, breath, escaped my body; everything, all fear, incomprehension, knotted in my belly. Then a stiffness I didn't want or understand swelled between my legs. Outside the door, my father gave up and returned to my mother and *The Lawrence Welk Show* downstairs. But, in my room, crazed with tension like angular objects jabbing in and out of me, I rubbed my pants to make it stop, to stop the stiffness.

"Don't stop!" I heard Alfonzo as I continued batting.

In my memory in my room something exploded, like a pipe bursting down below, and was shooting out of me, inside my pants, and then a release of all of everything that had been trapped inside me spun me down onto the floor in a flush of lightheadedness. Chilled and still dizzy, I unzipped and looked with horror at a whitish substance oozing from my penis. I had broken myself. *Oh God oh God oh God . . . forgive me, please . . .*

I finally stopped batting minutes later because of sweat pouring down my face, stinging my eyes, pooling on my back and chest, preventing me from gripping the bat one moment longer. I fell back into a sitting position, still clutching the bat, panting like a dog whose owner had forced it on a run, and no one spoke. For several minutes, neither one of us exchanged a word.

"I guess that's it," I said, dropping the bat, wiping my brow, crawling back to the mattress, where my session began.

I looked to Alfonzo for guidance. He looked at me and waited, knowing, no doubt, what I had not yet learned. Clearing away the rage had allowed the underbrush of mourning to appear. Which it did, moments later.

"Lie back down and move," he said, I think, because by then I could barely hear, could not follow instructions, thought nothing, really, was already awash in tears, mourning a constellation of losses.

He touched my chest, gently guided me back. "Move," he said, "keep moving."

I tried, but there was nothing I could do but cry, as powerless to sadness as a shore is to its waves.

And then it stopped. My body, in its infinite wisdom, knowing it had accomplished all it could for one day, stopped its tears.

Later, after I didn't die from shame, all that had remained was the experience that what came out of me that first ejaculation had released me from myself when I was still unable, like my sister before me, to escape. Whatever it was called, whatever I had done, all I wanted was to do it again, and again, for it to come out of me again, and again . . .

"Good work," Alfonzo said as I lay there, spent.

8

"So how does it feel, now that you're sharing?" Alfonzo asked me in his private office, when we were alone after one of my group sessions.

"Like I've dropped twenty pounds. Like I want to run away and hide."

"And the therapy in general? How are you finding the therapy?"

"Draining. I have to go home and sleep. I'm exhausted."

"That'll pass. In the meantime, you should take extra B vitamins."

"B vitamins?"

"For the stress. Overall, though, you find it helping?"

Was it helping? I didn't quite know what he meant, how to respond. I felt worse than when I'd started, fatigued and unable to suppress unwanted anxiety, but I figured that was normal. Poison rising to the surface before draining from the body, I told myself.

"I want to cry all the time. At work, at the student union building when I'm serving chili, or at the cash register. It's embarrassing."

"At some point you may need to take medication. For your own good. But we can talk about that another time. What about sex? Are you still having sex with men?"

His question cornered me. Despite having shared my sexual history, my shame, in groups and with Alfonzo personally, I'd still not talked much about my current life situation.

"I had sex a while ago. In a gay bathhouse."

"So, did it help?" he asked, with an edge of sarcasm.

"Help?"

"Did you get what you were looking for?"

I looked at him, unsure of how to respond.

"No," I said.

"Well then maybe you're starting to learn a thing or two? This isn't all a waste of time? You know, Peter, at some point you're going to have to make a choice between sex with men or therapy. You're like a chocolate addict who wants to go on a diet but doesn't want to give up his fix. I don't think any therapist would treat you while you're off fucking in a bush."

I was not off fucking in a bush, at least not anymore, but I received his words as if each had been hammered into me, the same tiny spot inside myself with all my other shame.

"I understand your difficulty," he continued. "Believe me. I've been on this path since before you were born. Not with men, but with my own demons. Like you, my therapy was forced upon me. It was sink or swim. I had no parents to guide me."

"You didn't have a father?"

"My father died when I was a child."

"Really?"

"He was a writer, like you. Completely outspoken. He had his own press, nothing fancy, just a little newspaper where he wrote articles against Franco and his army. One day they came to our house, took my father outside, lined him up with all the dissidents, and shot him."

"You saw this?"

"And a lot more."

"How old were you?"

"Five, maybe six."

"Where was your mother?"

"My mother couldn't help me. No one could. I was alone before I knew how to talk."

"So, your mother raised you alone?"

"Me and my brother, but . . . let's just say my mother knew how to twist the knife."

"What do you mean?"

He smiled.

"You know what I mean. Our curriculum may be different, Peter, but we're all in the same school. I left Spain to get away from her,

her and my wife. Another woman who also knew how to twist the knife. Twist and turn."

"You were married?"

"I have a son back in Spain. I hope to bring him here soon. I think he needs to get away from his mother. Before it's too late."

"How long have you been in Canada?"

"Just over twenty years. I graduated from McGill and then I worked at a psychiatric institute in Montreal. I was at the forefront of treating gay couples when you were still in diapers."

Alfonzo's disclosure, his willingness to share so much about his life, surprised me, especially considering his past reluctance to do so. But I liked that we were talking, that he was talking about himself. The inner sanctum of his thoughts and feelings was a cave into which I wanted to crawl and be comforted.

"Was this before or after you were with Janov?"

"Before. I started therapy with Daniel Casriel in New York. Have you read his book, *A Scream Away From Happiness*?"

"No."

"You should. But then I heard about Janov, and his institute in LA. After a couple of years with Janov, I got a job in a hospital in Quebec. That's when the fun and games began. I built my own sound-insulated workroom, next to my office, continued on with my primal sessions, alone. Every day, between seeing my own patients, I'd lock myself in my office and I'd lie down on the mattress, and the tears . . . well let's just say there was a sea inside, and it wasn't long before I was drowning in it. I primalled and I primalled. Without a life raft. I primalled till there was nothing left of me to primal. Till my child self was completely wiped out."

"What do you mean, 'wiped out'?"

"The tether connecting me to the mother ship had been severed. It was my dark night of the soul—an emptying of the well of my identity. My mind was shattered. You think you know grief? Anxiety and panic attacks overwhelmed my system. My sleep deteriorated. The amount of medication I was taking, just to function, would have killed a horse.

"To this day I don't know how I maintained the illusion of being a practicing psychiatrist for as many years as I did. Reparenting was something that I stumbled on by accident. There was a nurse at the hospital where I worked, a very warm and loving woman, a Mother Teresa figure.

"One day I asked her to hold me, privately, in my office. All I knew was that I needed to be held, and loved, that my child self needed to be nurtured. I never realized for a second the extent to which my child self depended on that love as a cure to all my grief. My dues have been paid with sweat and heartache. The fact is, Peter, I'm the only person alive doing this kind of therapy. No one else out there has figured out the obvious, that the child can only cry for so long before going into despair. That's where you've been for the last, well—I don't know that you've never not been in despair.

"We're all running around the same track of life, Peter. The only difference between you and me is that I'm a little further ahead of the game than you are. That's it."

||||||||||

In my writing workshop later that day, my professor returned our graded one-act plays. My play, *Off the Wall,* however, contained no grade, only the handwritten note: "Please don't write plays in the absurdist style."

I had long been a lover of existential theater, including plays by Samuel Beckett, Eugène Ionesco, and Edward Albee, and the writings of Antonin Artaud. In my own three-character play, a Young Man awoke sitting high up on the ledge of a wall, unaware of where he was or how he'd ended up on the wall. Perched next to him was an Older Woman, whose vacuous attempts to mother him, as the play progressed, left him bereft. When a Little Boy began bicycling up and down the street at the foot of the wall, and then screamed up at the Young Man, in one short monologue, about being "kidnapped" and made to do "really dirty stuff" which caused him to "grow up and see a doctor 'cause they never believe me when I tell 'em," the Young Man decided that he had to jump off the wall, no matter the consequence, which he did, moments before the play's final blackout.

Like many plays from the Theater of the Absurd, my own play

ended as it began: with the Little Boy climbing up on the wall, then falling asleep with the Older Woman still sitting next to him.

I approached my teacher, a mid-thirties gay man, during morning break. "I notice you didn't grade my play. Do you mind telling me why?"

He motioned for me to follow him around the corner, away from other students. "I didn't grade your play because . . . frankly, I don't know how to grade it. I don't understand Theater of the Absurd. I'd appreciate it if you'd not write in that style anymore."

"Oh."

||||||||||

Back home, I thought about my session with Alfonzo, the fact that my father had never talked directly to me, to any of my siblings, about his life "before" in quite the same way that Alfonzo, like a father to a son, was already talking to me about his.

My mother at least had relatives, if far away in Europe. My father, however, was like the shadow of a man without a past to call his own. Everything about him was a mystery, even the sound of his voice. As a child, I'd never thought about the fact that he had an "accent"—all I knew was that he always seemed to stress the "wrong" syllables so that his words came out sounding lopsided. He also could not pronounce "th," which, no matter how hard he tried, sounded like another "t." His English embarrassed me. *Why can't Daddy sound like other daddies?* I'd think, ashamed of my embarrassment.

The only time I'd glimpsed his history was late at night, when he played the upright Yamaha piano after dinner. Unlike my siblings and me, who all took lessons, my father could not read music. Instead his fingers seemed to channel storms still raging in his worn, weary heart.

Sometimes Pisti and I joked that Daddy should have been a priest, because the only thing he seemed the least bit interested in talking about was God.

"Don't you ever want to ask him about his own life?" I'd asked Pisti, after lights out one night. "Where he came from? His past?"

"Don't ask him. You know we're not supposed to."

"Why not?"

"Because."

"Because why?"

"Because you know what'll happen if you do."

I did know. The only questions we were allowed to ask were those that reinforced his religious beliefs. If we ever disagreed with anything he said, exerted our own minds over his or contradicted him in any way, punishment was meted out accordingly.

"What was your father like?" I'd asked him once.

When his slap came without warning, the suddenness of his fury reduced me to ashes. I ran to my room. By the time my mother arrived, seconds later, to comfort me, I was crying into my pillow.

"Doesn't he want me to know who he is? Who his parents were?"

"He's scared, that's all," she said. "He's just scared."

"One day he'll be dead, and I won't be able to remember him. I won't remember my own father because he didn't want to tell me who he was . . ."

If I begged my mother when we were alone, sometimes she offered up a morsel from my father's past, but always making me promise never to discuss any of it with him for fear of causing him more pain.

Growing up in 1930s Hungary, she'd told me once, "bastard" was not a word that anyone said aloud, but my father always knew what he was, what the other children, and even some of their parents called him behind his back.

Abandoned by his mother as an infant and sent to an orphanage in Budapest, he was shuffled from one foster family to another every two years, from one surrogate mother to another, but none belonged to him, none knew or loved him as their own. His body had not come from theirs.

Some nights, my mother said, he dreamt that one day soon he would find his way back into her arms, the arms of his birth mother. Then there would be wholeness again. Completion. Maybe then sleep might become restful, dreamless.

News of her death reached him at the age of fifteen, in 1945, while living with his latest foster parents across the border in Slovakia. It was as though my father's hope, the blood and breath that kept his spirit alive, had been eviscerated, my mother told me. Now there would be no one, not even in his dreams, to show him the way.

|||||||||

"We don't know why a person turns out gay," Alfonzo told me when we were alone in his private office after my most recent group confession. "In your case you've obviously misplaced your maternal needs. You would never have sought homosexual love if you'd received the love of your mother as a child. But then the father comes into play as well. Your father was a passive little boy with pockets of unexpressed rage, exploding onto his children. He never provided strong role modeling. I don't think you even bonded with your father. Clearly, all your sexual liaisons with men have been an extension of that need you found lacking in your father."

"So, it was my mother . . . or . . . what? I'm confused."

"You're confused because you've been searching for the love of your parents in every man you've been with sexually."

"So you're saying that no one is born gay?"

"Rarely is anyone born homosexual. Only a small percentage of people are born with a predisposition to homosexuality. But it's rare."

"Do you think I'm one of those people?"

He paused, looked me up and down.

"No. You're definitely heterosexual. You don't have any of the characteristics of a homosexual."

"Characteristics?"

"Effeminacy, passivity, desperation to get a man, a drug addict, an alcoholic: you aren't any of these things. The fact is, Peter, most gays learn their behavior. Therefore, it can be unlearned, though with great difficulty."

This had always been my greatest fear: that my attraction for men had been created, and not by God; that my sexuality had been like a descending staircase I'd been pushed down, one step at a time, into the cellar of my homosexuality. Now I was trapped inside that prison, fearful that what had been done to me as a child, I would do unto others. Alfonzo was saying that I could unlearn my homosexuality, unlock my trap door, and ascend into the light of heterosexuality. But he might as well have said that we could prevent me from becoming like the fat man in my elementary school toilet: a dirty old man, preying on innocent children. Alfonzo's words were like a lifeline, thrown out to me at sea.

"Ultimately, Peter, it's up to you. What sort of life do you want? Do you want to have a life filled with casual sex in public toilets and bathhouses, always hiding, never being accepted by friends and family, a life of secrecy and shame, compartmentalizing your relationships? Only you can answer those questions."

"Of course that's not what I want."

"Then you have to listen to me when I tell you what to do." He rocked forward in his chair. "You have to stop arguing with me. During groups, in your individual sessions: You have to do as I tell you. Do you understand me? God created Adam and Eve, Peter. He didn't create Adam and Steve."

He laughed. I forced a smile, but his joke reminded me of how the boys used to crowd around me in my elementary school playground, pecking me and calling me "faggot," or worse, simply my name, like a curse: "*Gay*-dicks."

"When you get right down to it, we're all heterosexual. Your true sexuality has been buried beneath years of self-abuse, but you're just as heterosexual as I am." His voice trailed to a whisper. "Only in my unique hands do you have any hope. You know that. You've seen what's out there. You've lived the life of a homosexual. This is it, Peter. This is your last chance. You either fix it here, once and for all, or else you go back to the life you were living. It's up to you. Only you can decide."

By late spring 1990 my primal sessions had deepened; so too had my feelings of dependency. I believed that Alfonzo understood my suffering as no one else. I began to accept—or, at least at first, to not contradict—his views about the apparent causes of my homosexuality. Both in private and in the presence of other group members, he called me his "experiment."

"I am going to revolutionize the field of psychiatry by being the first psychiatrist to find a cure for homosexuality," he told one of my groups, looking at me sitting across from him.

In a matter of weeks, I had changed from arguing with his views on homosexuality to defending him if another patient objected to the way he screamed at me. I blinded myself to his faults (the way he chastised patients whenever they stepped out of line or disobeyed his instructions) and magnified his positive traits (his unexpected warmth and charisma).

Meanwhile, the insomnia and panic attacks that had driven me to seek help in the first place worsened. To counter this, Alfonzo again prescribed a dose of Surmontil.

"It's your choice, whether or not to take the medication. But if you don't, you'll never get anywhere in your therapy. You need restorative sleep. Eventually, you won't have the energy to do this therapy without some type of medication."

There didn't seem to be much of a choice in what Alfonzo told me. Either I took the medication or discontinued therapy.

I had the prescription filled that same night.

The medication's dose was increased quite rapidly, then replaced with Sinequan, another tricyclic antidepressant, and used in conjunction with Rivotril. Elavil, yet one more tricyclic, soon followed. Alfonzo explained that we would need to "tweak" my use of various medications and that some experimentation would be inevitable. The medications led to a great deal of sleep; for the first time in years, I didn't have to worry about going to bed. No longer was I plagued by nightmares. Tossing and turning for hours, or lying in bed obsessing about what being gay would mean for the rest of my life—these all became events of the past. Sleep turned into something I no longer had to do. Sleep was done for me.

||||||||||

One night, as the city slept and I should have also, I walked the streets, past stone cathedrals, antiquarian bookstores, coffee shops and boutiques, and to his office, my new church. *Dr. Alfonzo, Psychiatrist,* I read on the roster through the chained black iron gate out front. There was a wooden bench, ten feet from the door. I sat there, maybe for an hour, taking comfort in the knowledge that I could be near the one place in my world where I felt safe, and seen, even if it was the middle of the night and I was alone.

But I was not alone. Not anymore.

"Alfonzo loves me," I said aloud to no one but myself. "I know he does. And I love him."

Several days later the two of us were in his office, after one of my individual sessions, when I told him my secret. "I wanted to ask you something," I said.

"Yes?" He looked up from his note-taking.

"I wanted to ask you, I mean . . . I wanted to tell you . . ." My voice, and spirit, faded.

"Yes?"

"Well, it's just that, I've been having these feelings lately, after my sessions. Sometimes at night. About you. And me. Like I want to tell you something." I couldn't say the words.

"Whatever it is, it's okay."

"That . . . I love you. That you're my daddy."

The moment I said the words, I wanted to rescind them. Outside the cage of my heart they frightened me, sounded obscene, too childlike for a man my age of twenty-five to be saying, admitting. I expected him to get angry, to laugh, but he didn't. Without another word he stood and opened his arms.

"Come here," he said, and then he clothed me in his arms. They were strong. His body was warm. I felt his belly jiggle as he let out a little laugh. I breathed him in and smelled his cologne.

"Do you love me?" I asked.

"Of course."

"You do?"

"Of course."

When he released me, I felt myself as half the person I'd been in his embrace, maybe less than half, because now I'd known his warmth, his love. He sat down and so I did, too. I imitated him. I wanted more, to talk some more, to tell him more, but then he was already writing notes.

"Can I tell you something?" I said.

He glanced at me.

"I was twelve. There was a boy I used to babysit."

He placed his pen on the desk, leaned back in his chair.

"One night I was standing in front of him and I pulled down my pants. I wanted him to give me oral sex."

"How old was the boy?"

"Five. Maybe six. I was in some sort of trance, like I was sleep-walking. The boy resisted. And then it's like I woke up. I saw the boy and saw myself, standing there, in front of him, what I was doing. I pulled up my pants and I backed away, terrified."

"I'm doubling your prescription today," he said, picking up his pen. "I want you to bring the extra medication back to me. Half is for me."

"Oh."

He handed me the prescription. I looked at it.

"Is this okay?" I said. "I mean, should you be doing this? You can't get prescriptions from your own doctor?"

"Peter," he said, with a sudden edge, "I have spent years on that mattress in there, paving the way for the type of therapy you're now taking for granted. Do you know how many years I've lost for the sake of your sanity? Yours, and your brothers and sisters? You owe me."

I stood, and started to leave his office, confused.

"Oh and Peter?" he said, calling me back. "Don't talk about this little arrangement with anyone. Okay?"

"Of course not," I said. "Never."

Alfonzo's secretary, Yvette, was waiting for me as I left Alfonzo's office.

"I want to talk to you before you leave," she said, drawing me into her own office. A native of Montreal, Yvette's French accent was as pronounced as Alfonzo's Spanish accent. "We're thinking of orga-nizing a house for some of our single patients, and Dr. Alfonzo and I thought that you'd be a good fit. We think that you should move in."

"What sort of house?" I asked, already a bit skeptical. "What do you mean?"

"It's nothing to be scared of. We had one back east, years ago. We called it the Sticks because it was in the middle of a forest. Somehow the name evolved into the Styx, 'S-t-y-x.' A small group of you will just rent a house somewhere and share expenses: rent, utilities, food. At least this way you can all support each other while going through your therapy. Primal can be an overwhelming experience. This can only help you, Peter."

Alfonzo entered Yvette's office behind me and said something to her in French. Like my parents, whose German and Hungarian I never understood, I had no idea what they were saying. With my parents, in fact, I remembered that they'd often use their own languages around us kids when they wanted to keep secrets.

"I don't think you can continue with your therapy if you don't live in the house," Alfonzo said to me. "It's your choice. But you either move in or we discontinue your treatment. It's entirely up to you. One of my patients from the first house is organizing the setup. He'll be calling you. His name's Clayton."

9

"Everyone calls me Clay," Alfonzo's former patient told me one hot summer's day two weeks later. We were at a beachside café, eating fish and chips wrapped in newspaper while staring out across the Strait of Juan de Fuca, and beyond, to the Olympic Mountains of Washington. "It's a pet name my first surrogate mother used to call me, in Quebec. Somehow it stuck."

"Clay . . ."

"You also probably didn't know my father's a psychiatrist."

"That must be weird. Being in therapy with a psychiatrist and all."

"Every day during my childhood he went to his office, helping psychotics and schizophrenics, manic-depressives. At the end of the day, he'd come home, pour a Scotch, then he'd chase me around the house, raging, screaming that he was going to kill me. My father was a big man, six-six. I didn't stand a chance. Finally, he'd pin me to the floor and he'd wrap his fingers around my neck, choking me. My father had thick fingers. I still remember the moment before I'd pass out, staring up at his face, the way it turned bright red—the veins in his forehead and his neck, bulging through his skin."

"How long did this go on?"

"Most of my childhood. So I decided to kill him."

"How old were you?"

"Eighteen. I mapped it all out in my mind, every detail: how, when, where. I was still weak, though. I've always been a small guy. I figured that once I killed him and got thrown in jail, for sure I wouldn't survive. That's when I met Dr. Alfonzo. The only reason I started therapy was to get stronger, you know, to build up my internal resilience so I could sustain a trial and my years in jail."

"And now?"

"Now?" he said with a slight chuckle. "Instead of killing my father I got chronic fatigue syndrome. About two years ago."

"How do you do this therapy if you have chronic fatigue syndrome?" I said, glancing at his pale, bony face, and the dark circles, like crescent moons, sleeping beneath his eyes.

"I couldn't live without this therapy. Meeting Dr. Alfonzo saved my life. I'd be dead today if it hadn't been for him. Or in jail. Where else in the world can you kill your father with a bat, every single day . . . or lie on a mattress and howl like a wolf, then go home to your own bed?"

Clay's story could have been my own. I had never plotted my father's murder, but I'd also never forgotten the way he'd chased us through the house as children, raging that as long as we lived in his house we belonged to him, our bodies belonged to him, and he could do anything he wanted to us.

In Clay I'd met a soul mate.

"How would this house function anyway? I mean our expenses, rent, food . . ."

"We'll share everything communally. Don't worry, everything will work out. We just have to support each other emotionally, that's the main thing to remember. The fact is, if you're not living in a house like this, you won't go very deep in your therapy. And everyone else—all the outpatients, who just go to the office for their sessions—they'll start looking to you for guidance 'cause they'll see how much progress you're making. And you know: the faster you progress, the sooner you finish therapy altogether."

Like the medication, there didn't seem to be much choice in what was being offered. Three times a week I was returning to my tiny rental room after revisiting the unresolved pain of my childhood. Crash-landing back inside my aloneness. Who else would understand the process of primal, if not other primal patients? I needed a family.

||||||||||

Over a period of weeks Clay and I searched the city for a house large enough to accommodate up to six patients, since Alfonzo had told us—or, at least, told Clay, who related it back to me—that he planned to send additional patients to our house for three-week retreats, or "intensives," as he called them.

Inside the first house we visited, black and yellow beach towels were tacked over all the windows, hundreds of empty glass pop bottles lined the perimeter of each room, and a series of sketched pentagrams led up the wooden stairs to a second floor that was littered with empty Styrofoam takeout containers and a sea of half-burned candles.

"It feels like little children were murdered in this house," I told Clay, as we walked from room to room.

"We could clean it up," he said.

"This house doesn't need to be cleaned, it needs to be exorcised. There's no way I'm living here . . ."

Perhaps because the first house was so dismal, we jumped at the next one, a 1970s rancher with multicolored shag carpet and wood paneling in a family-oriented area next to an elementary-school playground and a twenty-minute bicycle ride to my university. In October 1990, the two of us moved into the house with Alfonzo's only other gay patient, Brent.

The main floor of the house, off the front hallway, opened into a small living room with gas fireplace, and then two additional bedrooms, which in turn led directly into a laundry room near the back with exposed beams and half-finished walls, like the skeleton of a house beneath the facade of its exterior.

Coiled metal stairs in the front hallway rose like the steps of a submarine to the main living room on the top floor of the house, the "upper deck," as we began to call it. Running the width of the floor adjacent to the living room was one slim corridor with a bathroom at one end and three box-like bedrooms situated evenly along its path. A galley kitchen, near the opposite end of the floor, provided space for a large wooden table, six chairs, and much conversation.

No sooner had we unpacked than Brent was hanging framed male nudes throughout his master bedroom and en suite bathroom, constructed a twig canopy above his queen-sized bed, filled our living room with ten of his six feet cacti, and strung his complete collection of Carmen Miranda plastic fruit—grapes, oranges, pineapples, apples, and bananas—throughout our downstairs laundry room. Finally, as if to save the best for last, he set up a tall, husky mannequin with bouffant hair, dressed in a floral sequin gown and cowhide high heels next to the metal staircase in our front hallway.

"This is Bea," he said, introducing Clay and me to his mannequin.

"Bea?" Clay said.

"After Beatrice Arthur, you know, *Maude*? I've had her for years. We found each other in an old junk shop years ago. We go everywhere together. I thought she could greet all our guests to the house."

The next day Brent returned home with a second half-mannequin (waist and legs), which he promptly turned into a living room side table, and named "Bea's half-sister."

As Brent helped "decorate" the house, Clay took charge of converting an enclosed storage room on the ground floor into our new makeshift "screaming room" that we'd had planned to use for self-administered primal sessions. We tied old mattresses, purchased at a used furniture shop, up against its four interior walls. We lay another mattress on the floor for regressions. A punching bag and wooden baseball bat, provided by Alfonzo, were placed in one corner of the room to function as our "batting station."

It didn't take me long to learn that there were rules for everything in the Styx, and everything needed to be documented in a "house charter," which would later need to be edited and approved by Alfonzo. Our diets would be vegan. Smoking, drinking, and sex would not be tolerated. Cablevision, radio, and newspapers were prohibited. Tuesdays would become our "entertainment night," which typically meant family-oriented video rentals like *Jonathan Livingston Seagull* or *Born Free*. Movies that endorsed a parent/child relationship were especially recommended. Members were to return home to the Styx every day after work, or their sessions at the office, or in my case, school.

And social contact with anyone outside therapy was forbidden.

"Styx members are your new family," Alfonzo explained. "It's in your best interest to spend as much time together as possible."

So Brent, Clay, and I talked together, walked together, meditated together, shopped together, cooked together, and ate many of our meals together. When Brent and Clay told me that I was spending too much time in my room writing poetry and plays for school or reading books that weren't related to our therapy, I felt threatened and wanted to escape.

"You shouldn't be reading anything other than Janov's books," Clay told me. "Janov, or else Dr. Alfonzo's own scientific paper: those are the only things you should be reading."

Instead of arguing, Clay told me I should take my feelings of resistance to the workroom. "If you have an issue with any of the theories of Janov or Dr. Alfonzo, then you need to take your feeling back historically to the first time you felt this fear of being overpowered," he said, repeating what Alfonzo had said time and time again. "This is a trigger, as good as gold in therapy. You need to work it in the workroom, we all need to work our issues in the workroom, not argue them upstairs in our living room."

So that's what we did, up to four hours every night in the workroom, sometimes falling into bed only with the rising of the sun. Clay raged, with the bat, at his father; Brent begged, like a famished child, on the mattress for the love of his mother; and I screamed on both the mattress and with the bat about all the sex with men I'd had throughout my life, as if doing so I might diminish my desire for more in the future.

If primals were our gravest undertaking, dinners were our greatest reward. Every night we spent up to two hours washing and cutting vegetables, cooking, spicing, and plating, and then eating together like the new soul brothers that we were, all the while swapping stories about our day's workroom extravaganzas. Never before had I eaten vegan, but these new homemade meals, recommended by Clay and following one of his recipe books, were anything but plain. We had Chinese feasts with miso soup, pickled radish, rice noodles, and chow mein with freshly peeled ginger and crisp sprouts; whole-wheat pastas with organic carrots, broccoli and sun-dried tomatoes; "chicken" burgers and "fish" fillets both made from tofu, everything smothered in almondaise. And desserts: mocha parfaits, chocolate carrot cake, or warm gingerbread teacake with cashew whipped cream (our favorite).

After dinners and dishes, the three of us went for walks, one in front of the other like Buddhist monks, the hoods of our newly acquired matching purple sweatshirts drawn up over our heads. At the beach we talked openly about how we'd finally "come home to our new soul family" and that we never wanted to leave ever again.

Back at the Styx, our day's activities were completed with meditation. One member would ring a bronze gong, at which point we'd all focus quietly on a candle in our rooms. The maze of my mind led me mostly through alleys of sex in cars and public washrooms. Thirty minutes later, the gong was sounded again and we all returned to the incensed living room, sipped herbal tea and warmed ourselves before a crackling fire as we shared whatever thoughts or images had arisen during our time alone.

Brent usually shared a variation on the same theme. "During meditation tonight," he said once, "I really understood how my mother held me back my whole life from loving other women. It is just a matter of time before I have a relationship with a woman, I'm sure of it."

Brent's "acknowledgments" were always dissonant, considering the life-sized casting of Michelangelo's "David" that he'd positioned next to his canopied bed, not to mention the framed male nudes hanging on the walls of his bathroom. Staring into my own future, on the other hand, was seeing neither women nor men, so I talked about how grateful I was to Dr. Alfonzo and the members of the Styx for providing me with a war-free zone to call home.

Finally, someone would read a passage from *A Course in Miracles*, a book that Alfonzo had instructed us to read nightly before we all went to bed.

If any one of us needed more medication than our prescriptions allowed, the others offered up their own, like shared candy-colored goodies amongst siblings: "I'll give you two Rivotrils for one Surmontil."

Following our days of gut-wrenching primals, dreamless, medicated sleep was all we desired, and knew, without doubt, we deserved.

||||||||||

As I stepped off the bus near our home one night, I heard the thumping of primals from a block away. No matter how much junk we piled on the opposite side of our workroom's exterior wall—four gothic columns salvaged from a nearby demolition site, metal travelling trunks, flattened cardboard boxes, rolled up used mattresses—nothing seemed to fully insulate the outside world from our primals inside. By the time I neared our front door, pained howling from inside our house mingled with the joyful cries of children playing in the schoolyard next door.

Before entering the house, I walked to the schoolyard. I stood at the swing set, and then the monkey bars and slide, and waited, listening for the usual sounds. Nothing.

Clay and Brent were already upstairs in the kitchen when I entered the house.

"Come in here," I heard Clay call out. "We have a surprise for you."

When I entered the kitchen, I saw that both he and Brent were bald. In the middle of a sea of black hair sat a chair, and on it, electric clippers.

"What are you doing?" I asked.

"Dr. Alfonzo shaved his hair today, too."

"He did?"

"He said it would be a good idea if we shaved ours, so we did. Now it's your turn."

I had been growing my hair for years, and it was long, an inch below my shoulders, tied in a ponytail. The thought of having it cut off, like Samson, scared me.

"It will only help your regressions," Brent said, coaxing me into the chair.

"How so?"

"To connect to the child self. After all, babies don't have hair."

Clay aimed the clippers near the base of my neck. "Ready?" he said.

"Do I have a choice?"

When he flicked the on switch, I heard its motor buzz through my ears. The razor's cold, steel teeth slid up against my skin as long, dark curls floated down to a sea of encircling hair.

"Next we do your beard and mustache," Clay said. "Then all three of us will be like babies."

10

Soon after moving into the Styx, I arrived home from school one night to a letter from my mother. I had spoken to my parents only infrequently since beginning therapy when I sent them a letter "demanding" that they mail me money. If nothing else, batting and screaming for nearly a year had at least armed me with some sense of entitlement.

Brent was home when I opened the letter. My mother wrote that they were just about to start their retirement, were leaving for a seven-day Alaskan cruise, and had no money to send. The letter sent me into a rage. My parents hadn't been able to protect me as a child, and now they could not even support me financially while in therapy. I told Brent I needed him to come with me to the workroom, since we were strictly forbidden to primal alone, and we disappeared downstairs.

Often at the start of a primal we moved to the batting station only if and when emerging anger, always a defense, interfered with our pain on the mattress. I didn't even lie on the mattress this day, but picked up the bat and began beating it into the punching bag. My mother couldn't help me now, just as she had not helped me in my elementary-school bathroom as a child or when I was walking the downtown streets as a teenager. My mother could not help me, and her inability to help, I screamed, had walked me straight into the arms of every man I had ever met in a bar, in a bathhouse, in alleyways, and in parkade stairwells.

After twenty minutes and a hundred swings, exhausted and sweaty, I returned upstairs with Brent. We sat at either end of our new dining room table that we'd constructed out of a ten-foot sheet of stained plywood.

Brent asked me to tell him the circumstances around my "coming out." I told him about The Letter to my parents, the conversation with my mother in my old bedroom, her confession to me, and my secret about her.

For several minutes after, Brent said nothing. Then, finally, he spoke. "I told my mother I was a fag when I was ten."

"*Ten*?"

"I was doing up her bra, you know, the type with the snaps in the back? I said I thought I was gay, that I was a fag. I think I still have that bra in Bea's trunk."

"What did she say?"

"She asked me to pass her her lipstick."

"So . . ."

Brent and I had never been in a group together, so his admission confused me.

"I'll tell you another secret," he continued, smiling. "Alfonzo told me to leave all of my porno magazines behind when I moved into the Styx, but I didn't."

"Really?"

"Throw out all my pictures of Richard Locke and Jeff Stryker, gay icons extraordinaire? I don't think so! They're all in a box in my bedroom. Just in case."

Clay arrived home and so our conversation came to an abrupt end. But, afterward, all I could think about were those magazines. The moment I was alone in the Styx, I went in search of them, like mining for gold. When I found them, on the top shelf of Brent's closet, I rushed to the bathroom and I masturbated to the photos, as I'd done throughout my childhood, terrified that someone would arrive home and punish me for my transgression.

||||||||||

Weeks later, Alfonzo called one night and asked Clay if we could housesit his pet cat, a Siamese Persian named Fred, while he was away on vacation at Club Med. Clay covered the phone and asked Brent and me what we thought. Since Brent was allergic to cats, Clay told Alfonzo that we were sorry, but could not oblige his request.

I could hear Alfonzo's raised voice through the receiver. Clay said nothing, looking stunned as all three of us listened in disbelief to Alfonzo's tirade, telling us that we were "spoiled children" and that he was "sacrificing" his life for the betterment of our "souls"—how could we "deny" him anything? The conversation came to an abrupt end; Clay hung up the phone.

"He just threw us out of therapy," Clay said. "He said we were ungrateful brats and that we needed to be taught a lesson."

Confused, we finished our evening's chores in a daze, feeling as through our dad had just thrown us out of the house—which, in a sense, was true. And if we were no longer in therapy, did that mean we were no longer patients? That we should not go to the office for our sessions? And what about the Styx? What about the other patients who were about to arrive at the house for their three-week intensives?

Two hours later, close to midnight, someone pounded on our front door. Brent opened it and Alfonzo walked in, wearing dark sunglasses and a long beige trench coat. He said nothing, but proceeded past Bea and up the coiled metal staircase. He sat in a heap near a corner of our living room floor, next to the fireplace.

"I've thought about the Fred situation," he began, "about your unwillingness to help me in my time of need. I want you to know that I forgive you for everything."

We said nothing, too afraid to open our mouths.

"I should never have asked for anything from any of you. It was my fault, and I'm sorry. It will never happen again."

His face turned in my direction. I looked to see his expression, to see if what was happening was all some kind of joke. Dark Armani sunglasses hid his eyes.

"What?" I asked, uncomfortable by his blinded glare. "I didn't say a word."

"No. You didn't. That's just the problem."

Clay spoke up and reminded him that two of his other patients were arriving the following week for their three-week intensives. We had purchased furniture and beddings—out of our own personal savings—to furnish the spare bedroom in preparation for their arrival. We had done all of it because he asked it of us.

"Would you like to see their room?" Clay asked.

"That won't be necessary," Alfonzo said. Then he stood, and, without saying goodbye, disappeared down the stairs and out our front door.

"What just happened?" Brent asked.

Both he and I looked to Clay and waited for an explanation, for some insight that might explain such irrational behavior.

"What can I say? He can get a bit crazy. It's the therapy that's important. I believe in his therapy."

At the office the next day, no one said a word about our late-night visitor. Maybe if we didn't talk about it, we reasoned, we could all just pretend like it had never actually happened.

‖‖‖‖‖‖‖

Our first two intensives arrived the following week, as scheduled. The plan, Alfonzo had told us, was for them to have access to our workroom while continuing with their daily sessions in the office. Clay, Brent, and I would be responsible for their meal planning, shopping, and cooking. We'd guide them through their evening meditation and emotionally support them during, and after, their primals in the house.

No sooner had the intensives arrived than they were in our workroom, milking their therapeutic stay, and the three hundred dollars that we charged them. Later, we explained that all communication with family and friends would be discontinued during their three-week "retreat," and that evenings would be focused on our communal vegan meal, followed by meditation.

Corporate executives, mothers and fathers, students of all ages: every three weeks the routine was repeated as Bea, Bea's half-sister, Brent, Clay, and I all welcomed two new patients with open arms and a copy of the Styx charter in hand.

Witnessing a patient's "primal," especially for the first time, was always, without exception, voyeuristic. Whatever pleasantries we'd exchange outside the workroom were quickly replaced, once they were batting or lying on the mattress, with the sight of a gutted animal howling by the side of a road. Sooner or later, everyone looked and sounded the same. Everyone yearned for the same lost childhood. Everyone cried, while lying belly up on the mattress, for the love of the same absent mother. Everyone raged, while batting and screaming at the red "X" marked on the wall, against the same disapproving father. Eventually, no matter what their tax bracket, everyone bled red.

A sixty-five-year-old divorcee told everyone she was a mother of two, even though her youngest son, a promising sculptor, had committed suicide the previous year, which was what had sent her into therapy.

"He'll always be my son," she told us her first night in our candlelit living room following meditation. "His last piece was of his own hands, a bronze sculpture of his two hands reaching out for help. A week later he hung himself in his bathroom. He was calling out for help and I didn't see him. I didn't hear him. I wasn't there for him. I'll never forgive myself for that. Never."

A mid-thirties mother of six with fiery red hair and a spirit to match was with us only hours when she received a phone call from a friend, advising that her husband was killed while away on a business trip in New York. She called Alfonzo. He told her to go to our workroom and "work it," to "take it back historically," to the first time she had felt this kind of grief. After ten minutes on her back, though, she stood and left the workroom. There was no "history" to work, she said. "My husband just died. I'm a widow. I have six children. This is bullshit."

She left the house and, a week later, the therapy.

One man, a wealthy businessman who said he once had worked with Donald Trump, arrived at the Styx amid the crumbling of his twenty-year marriage. No sooner had he started to unpack than we were all being called to the workroom to support Clay while he let off some steam toward his father.

"Part of your intensive means joining us in the workroom whenever we work," I explained to him, "regardless of whether or not you need to work. The idea is to use our sessions as a trigger for your own."

For someone with chronic fatigue, Clay's rages were legendary. On this particular day, not seconds after we shut the workroom door, he grabbed the bat and began swinging it up and down against the bag, as though his life depended on its beating.

"DIE, MOTHERFUCKER, DIE!" he roared for twenty minutes, his face turning various shades of red, his forehead's veins popping like webs surfacing through his skin.

I glanced at the businessman, whose face had turned its own shade of deep purple. The minute Clay had finished, and we all streamed out of the workroom, he beelined to his bedroom, repacked the few pieces of clothing that he'd unpacked, and headed back out our front door, panic-stricken, clothes still dangling from his half-opened suitcase.

"Where are you going?" Brent and I asked him as he jumped into his lavender Porsche.

"I can't do what you guys are doing," he mumbled as he sped off. Apparently, wheeling and dealing with Trump had been easy compared to Clay's primal rages.

Another patient, a mid-fifties man with only a crest of graying hair left on his otherwise shiny head, identified himself as Alexander Scarborough and spoke in a perfectly enunciated British accent. "My wife and I have been struggling for years," he told Brent, Clay, and me that first night at the house.

"In what way?" Brent asked.

"With various . . . private matters. Related to . . . well, copulation. More precisely, the lack of any real desire, at least on my part, to engage with anyone, not only my wife mind you, but anyone at all, on that level. The fact of the matter is we have not had sexual relations in over fifteen years. She's asked me for a divorce. I agreed to go into therapy to try and salvage what is left of our marriage. If, in fact, there is anything left to salvage. I thought Alfonzo's unorthodox practice might help steer me away from the safety of words. Truth be told, I've made a career out of avoiding my feelings through language."

"What do you do for a living?" Clay asked.

"I'm a psychiatrist."

During a phone call with Alfonzo the next night, he told the three of us, Brent, Clay, and myself, that we should "handle this one with kid gloves."

"Our arrangement is for him to have his sessions only at the office, with me," Alfonzo said. "No primals at the Styx. I only want him to witness you working at the house. To wet his feet. This one is sensitive. It's a deal breaker. Be careful. I'm relying on all of you. Do not disappoint me."

Some intensives were mortified by the words Clay, Brent, and I used during our primals at the house; descriptions that, with every syllable, tore flesh, spoke blood, raised bile, aborted fetuses. Many intensives ran from our workroom midstream, called Alfonzo at the office, said that they refused to sit through primals that they considered "far too graphic," "disturbing," "cruel." On the phone, Alfonzo, chuckling, told us to "tone it down a bit in front of intensives. Keep the big ones for the office." Still, there were others who relished in the explicitness of our sessions, used us as emotional triggers, fertilizer to the gardens of their own pain, took up arms at the batting station the moment we concluded and raged with all their might.

A late-twenties socialite sent us a list of food requests a week before arriving: whole-wheat bagels, nonfat cream cheese, lactose-free skim milk, rice cakes, and organic, creamy, peanut butter.

When we told her she'd have no contact with her family shortly after she stepped out of her black Mercedes convertible, wearing a white tennis shirt and sneakers, she went into a tailspin.

"Dr. Alfonzo never told me I couldn't call my husband!" her shrill voice yelled at the three of us. "Dr. Alfonzo would have told me if I wasn't allowed to call my husband—and what about my four children? If you think I can go three weeks without talking to my children, you have something coming to you. And of course I'll have to leave every afternoon. I can't be expected not to live my life simply because I'm staying here for three weeks. This isn't supposed to be a jail, is it? *Is it*?"

On the mattress, however, her metamorphosis from diva to fragile little girl was alarming. Her voice dropped two octaves, and when she slammed the bat into the punching bag, beating her overpowering father down into a pulp, a ferociousness that had not been apparent "upstairs" toppled through her slim, waiflike figure.

In this young socialite, Clay had met his match.

Days later, she asked that Clay, and Clay only, accompany her to the workroom.

"I won't require anyone else but Clay, thank you," she instructed Brent and me, as if we were her "hired help." And then they'd disappear, the two of them like teenage suitors, into the workroom for hours.

Sounds of giggling could be heard in the house several nights later after everyone had gone to bed. I peeked out of my room and there, in the middle of the living room, were four bare feet sticking out from under a large woolen blanket. I recognized two as Clay's. The other two, I soon discovered, were hers.

"Clay?" I whispered.

Both pairs of eyes peered out from the top edge of the blanket.

"Oh," Clay said. "Peter. Hi."

He tucked his head back beneath the blanket, and together they giggled.

The following morning, we returned her money, with a request to leave. She did. The moment after she left, Clay walked straight to the workroom.

"You got me again, Mommy!" he screamed, batting and staring at the red "X." "You seduce me again and again through every woman I meet and I just want you out of me, get your stinking slimy teeth out of me, GET OUT OF ME GET OUT OF ME GET OUT OF ME!"

Yuen was a thirty-five-year-old Chinese Canadian whose parents had immigrated to Canada from Jamaica in the 1950s. After several failed suicide attempts and an episode where she'd locked herself in the bathroom of her large, two-story home, gripping a baseball bat, certain that her husband of ten years was trying to kill her, she arrived on Alfonzo's doorstep. Following her three-week intensive, Yuen decided against returning to her husband, opting instead to become a permanent member of the Styx family, a sister to our brothers, thereby increasing our core family unit by one sibling.

|||||||||

We were nearing our first Styx Christmas, four months into our new cohabitation and just over one year from when I'd left my hometown behind, and I felt like I was marooned on a deserted island with three orphaned strangers. I missed my real family, I told Alfonzo. I had doubts about all of it, the therapy and the Styx. I wanted to go home.

"You *are* home," Alfonzo told me after a session in the office. "Think of this as an opportunity to create a new one with your siblings at the Styx. It would be unwise for you to see your parents right now."

"Why?"

"Because they'd set you back. All the progress you've made in therapy—it would be like undoing months of work on the mattress or at the bat. What you need is to bond with your siblings. Your *new* siblings. You're at a crucial juncture. You have to trust me."

Because the "joyful" season triggered issues with his maniacal father and had sent him into a rage-fueled primal, Clay spent Christmas day in his bedroom.

"If I come out of this room I'm going to kill someone," he warned us from the other side of his locked bedroom door. "You don't want me to come out; trust me."

We left him alone.

Christmas dinner proceeded in his absence. Because meat was prohibited, Brent bought and cooked a turkey-shaped tofu loaf instead.

"Maybe I didn't cook it right," Brent confessed as the three of us picked at our individual servings.

"It tastes like sawdust," I said.

Outside it was snowing, and so Brent, Yuen, and I left the tofu disaster, dressed in padded layers, and ran next door to the fenced-in playground.

"Look!" Yuen called out, giggling, falling backward and then waving her arms and legs up and down like windshield wipers in the snow.

"I'm an angel!"

Brent and I fell back, too, and then all three of us were orphaned angels, playing and numbing ourselves on the frozen earth.

||||||||||

Claude, another original Styx member from Quebec, visited the house several weeks after Christmas to lead us through our first official Styx meeting.

"In order for a house like yours to succeed," he said, "you will all need to trust each other implicitly. I suggest you do a bonding exercise." He walked to the landing of our metal staircase, and then told us to each stand at the top step, facing into the living room, close our eyes, and fall backward down the stairs, trusting that one of our housemates, standing two steps below, would catch us.

All the others stood at the top of the stairs, closed their eyes, trusted, and fell back into the arms of someone down below. When it was my turn I started to laugh. Such a silly exercise, I thought, and yet the fear that my trust would be betrayed caused my heart to race, my palms to sweat, and my laughter to turn hysterical. With closed eyes, my back faced to the stairs, I heard the others encouraging me, saying they would catch me, not let me fall, that I was safe. My laughter gave way to tears, and I opened my eyes.

"I can't," I said to Claude, moving away from the stairs. "I can't do it, I can't. Please don't tell Dr. Alfonzo, please . . ."

I disappeared into my bedroom, still crying. Claude followed me in, asked me how I was. For some reason I started to tell him about my struggles with men, that I had sex with men, but that I wasn't gay, or that I didn't want to be gay, or that maybe I was gay but that I might have been "made gay," and the rejection I'd experienced by my family. He smiled and put his hand on my shoulder. With straight white teeth, marble blue eyes, and blond hair parted to one side, he looked like a French Canadian Boy Scout. A tingling sensation moved through my body like the first spark of hunger catching fire in my belly.

"If you can just hang in there for a little while longer," he said, squeezing my shoulder, "Alfonzo has big plans for you."

"What type of plans?" I asked, drying my tears with the back of my shirt.

"What he's going to do with you he's never done with anyone else before. And when he's finished, he's going to write a book about you."

||||||||||

Brent, Clay, Yuen, and I all began spending more and more time with Alfonzo and Yvette outside of our therapy: during late-night meetings at the office or in phone conversations, where we discussed the role of the Styx and the organization of the intensives. Though Alfonzo and Yvette lived as a couple in a separate house, we were told to consider ourselves one family with one goal: the evolution of our souls.

Privately, Yvette told each of us that Alfonzo was ailing. The stress of caring for our souls, she explained, on top of maintaining a home and a functioning office, was too much for even him to bear alone. For this reason alone, she said that we needed to start cooking their meals and deliver them to their home on Hampstead Street, a forty-five-minute bus ride to a ritzy part of town where I'd heard a lot of lawyers and doctors lived.

"We can't run this office without your help," she told us on the phone one night. "We're all in this together. We're relying on you."

Within weeks, Yvette provided us with lists of foods that Alfonzo liked (yams, carrots, leeks, anything with rice) or disliked (eggplant, kiwi), spices that we should include (saffron, cumin, oregano, basil, paprika, but only the Spanish kind) or altogether avoid (garlic—caused "excessive flatulence").

Within days, we were delivering so much food to "Hampstead" that we all just referred to the name of the street itself, as Morse code for the demands of Alfonzo.

"I have to go shopping for Hampstead today," Clay told Brent and me, on his way to the market.

"I'm taking this lasagna over to Hampstead," Brent said to all of us, rushing out the door.

"Hampstead needs this split pea soup before six p.m. tonight," I said to the others, ladling the hot soup into Tupperware containers.

Several weeks later, Yvette called again with another update about their food. "The doctor has decided that all his food must now be fat-free. He needs to watch his weight. His blood sugar is through the roof."

"Fat free," of course, did not mean "no desserts." In fact, when Alfonzo discovered I liked to bake, he called the Styx specifically to speak with me. "I want you to figure out a fat-free recipe for cheesecake for me. But without graham wafers as the crumb bottom. Try dates."

"Dates?"

"Mixed with a little oatmeal and honey. Do you know Splenda?"

"The sweetener?"

"Just no white sugar. I understand there's a way of making cheesecake with fat-free yogurt. Talk to Yvette, she'll explain how." And then he hung up.

If anyone at the Styx felt angry or overwhelmed by their requests, Alfonzo told us to use our feelings in the course of our therapy—"Ride the feeling on the mattress," he'd say, "or the bat. Work the feeling in private. Take it back historically to the first time you felt this type of anger. Who bossed you around as a child? Milk the feeling for all it's worth. This is an opportunity for growth."

Yvette warned us never to work the issue of our "house chores" in front of patients who weren't "part of the family," such as during a group session with mixed family and non-family members. Nor were we ever allowed to discuss them with Alfonzo, since he didn't like to get involved in house logistics.

During a session one morning before my writing class at school, I mentioned to Alfonzo that it didn't seem fair that he expected us to cook his meals.

"I don't want to hear about your little problems," he said, standing up from his squat chair near the mattress. He walked out of my session and slammed the door to his private office behind him. On the other side of the wall, I could hear him mumbling in Spanish. Seconds later, the door swung open and he stormed back in.

"Didn't Yvette talk to you?" he said, looming over me. "Didn't she tell you not to bother me with Styx logistics? You do as you're told or else you're out. Do you understand me? Out." He stepped an inch closer, lowering his voice into a deep, threatening growl. "I'm carrying the weight of your fucking soul, and you want to talk to me about the meals? You should try doing my job for a week and see how you like it. Now get out of here and tell the others that they'd better not talk to me about logistics or else you'll all end up on the street. Every last one of you. Got it?"

We never talked to him about the meals again. Instead, we did as we were told and worked our anger at the house, all four of us spending hours in our basement workroom, a dungeon, batting and screaming that Alfonzo seemed "just like Daddy."

||||||||||

Several months after moving into the Styx I received a letter from Pearl, my "past life" friend. Worried that I'd been sucked into a cult, she wanted to see me.

I discussed her letter with my Styx housemates, all of whom cautioned me against our meeting. Pearl would surely try to lure me back into my old life, they warned. We decided as a family that I should go only as a means of ending our friendship. I would have one final hour with Pearl, and then return home to my family at the Styx.

When I entered the ferry terminal café that afternoon, Pearl looked at me in shock. In addition to my buzz cut, I also had gained more than fifteen pounds since we'd last seen each other, most of it as a side effect of the medications Alfonzo was prescribing.

"What happened to all your hair?" she said, as I approached her table.

"I shaved it."

"I can see that."

"Babies don't have hair."

She laughed. I didn't. I sat down across from her.

"How have you been?" she asked.

"I can only be with you for a few minutes. They're waiting for me back at the Styx."

"Who are? At where?"

"My family. My new family."

"Peter, I've been worried about you. Don't your housemates give you your phone messages?"

"I've been busy."

"Busy? Peter, *what's going on*?" She leaned in closer, reached over to grab my hand.

"Don't touch me," I said, recoiling.

Pearl said nothing as I opened the menu. Page after page, I saw only blurred letters, distorted images. I folded the menu and placed it back on the table.

"I only have a minute. They're waiting for me at the Styx."

"Have you talked to your parents?"

"I'll never talk to those two criminals again."

"What do you mean by that?"

"I wouldn't have spent years having sex with men if it hadn't been for them. Just thinking about it makes me sick. They should be in prison for what they did to me. They crucified me." I looked across the café to hail a waitress.

"Are you seeing anyone?" Pearl asked.

"What do you mean?"

"Dating. Do you have a boyfriend?"

I looked away. Her question nauseated me. "To say that I'm a homosexual would be to say that I am what my mother and father did to me, that I've become the symptom of their abuse. I haven't. I'm not. There's nothing gay about being gay, you know. And I still haven't figured out what they're all so damned proud of. All those homosexuals out there—who do they think they are? Fighting for the right to live out their lifestyles of sickness and perversity. They should look at their own histories. All homosexuals have been sexually abused."

"I don't think that's true."

"What do you know?" Her ignorance disgusted me. "You don't know anything. Why did you want to meet with me anyway? What do you want?"

"I . . . I wanted to see you."

"Why?" I said.

She stared at me and said nothing.

"Do you love me?" I asked.

"You know I do . . ."

"No matter what?"

"What are you asking me?"

"Do you love me unconditionally?"

"Unconditionally? All friendship has conditions . . ."

"So you don't love me."

"Of course I do."

"You just said you don't."

"I don't think that's what I said."

"I don't think we should be friends anymore."

"Peter . . ."

"I came here to tell you to stop calling me at the house."

"What's happened to you?"

"I have no time for you. I have new friends now, a new family. They love me. Unconditionally."

The waitress arrived to take our order.

"I should go." I stood to leave. "They're waiting for me."

11

THE STYX WAS, IN Alfonzo's eyes, a huge success—so much so that in early 1991 he announced plans to open two more houses, which would become known as Styx 2 and Styx 3. Eight other patients, handpicked by Alfonzo as psychological "best fits," soon moved into the new houses, four patients to each house. Members of my house, Styx 1, continued cooking Alfonzo's meals and delivering them to Hampstead. Talk of our "chores" quickly spread throughout the other two houses, and all the other patients refused to follow suit. We'd been "brainwashed into acting as the doctor's domestic servants," some of them commented. Alfonzo was infuriated, and still they would not concede. All of us at Styx 1 viewed the others as traitors, unworthy of Alfonzo's love. We, after all, were Alfonzo's "family"; everyone else was just a "patient."

"Let's leave them alone," Alfonzo finally told us on the phone at the original Styx. "We know our priorities. We're a family."

After a four-year therapeutic hiatus, Claude returned to active primal work, moved out of Hampstead, where I discovered he'd been living with Alfonzo, and into the Styx. Gradually, I learned about his past as well, if not from Claude himself then from Clay when the two of us were alone.

Like Clay, Claude had begun treatment with Alfonzo years earlier in Quebec during a stressful time in his own life. After waking from a drunken haze in which he'd blacked out, he'd chased his then-girl-friend through his dream home with a rake, then tried to strangle her with a telephone wire. Beneath his calm, French-Canadian Boy Scout exterior, Claude was not at all what he appeared to be. His therapeutic relationship with Alfonzo had quickly turned to friendship, as it had with Clay, when he abandoned his career as a promising young architect to manage the minutia of Alfonzo's personal and professional life, including car repairs and house renovations, dry cleaning drop off and pick up, medical licensing and insurance matters, shopping, cleaning and banking, and, of course, overseeing the planning and construction of the new office, and organizing our new Styx house.

Soon after Claude moved in, in mid-1991, I arrived home one day to the news that Brent had moved out. Apparently, while we were out of the house, he had packed up his belongings, including Bea and Bea's half sister, informed Alfonzo by telephone of his decision to leave, and then all two-and-a-half of them had left the Styx for good.

"He's moved in with another man," Clay told me, shaking his head in bewilderment. "Another florist that he met at work, I think."

Brent's departure was unexpected, but I was secretly relieved. With his plastic fruit and life-size cacti went all of his pornography. Temptation, any and all reminders of my past life, had been eliminated.

As if orchestrated, Brent's departure provided a vacancy for Sebastian, another long-term patient and a member of the original Styx house, who arrived the following week.

"I've just driven across the country," he announced, suitcase in hand. His French accent, like Claude's and Yvette's, was pronounced.

"From where?" I asked.

"Montreal. I'm here to continue with my therapy."

The next day Sebastian met with Alfonzo at the office, who called us that night to tell us Sebastian would be living at the Styx while continuing with his sessions at the office. Sebastian was "a lifer," he said, "a dedicated brother."

Yuen and I went to the basement that night for Sebastian's first session, an experience that proved anticlimactic, at least for me, because he worked in French. Though I may not have understood his words, however, his tears, while lying face up on the mattress, were all too familiar. After he finished he sat up and faced Yuen and me, his two new siblings, still crying.

He apologized for working in French, his "native language," then said he wanted to tell us something about himself since "I guess we'll be living together."

The story was grim and hard to believe.

When Sebastian was seven years old, he told us, his father sodomized him in his bedroom late one night. Afterward, he tried to strangle Sebastian so he wouldn't talk. Sebastian ran away from home, but was returned by the police. He kept running until his grade-nine math teacher offered to let him live in his home.

"I was so happy," Sebastian told us. "He made me dinners and took me camping."

Then his teacher raped him in the middle of the night. He couldn't go home, so he ended up on the street, pulling a shopping cart "like a vagrant," sleeping in bus terminals.

"Before I met Dr. Alfonzo in nineteen eighty-five," Sebastian continued, "I had pretty much decided to move to LA and start treatment with Janov at the Primal Institute." He was desperate. He considered shock treatment and met therapist after therapist, until finally he found Dr. Alfonzo. "And only because I looked in the white pages under 'P' for primal, and there he was." Dr. Alfonzo with his very own primal institute in Quebec.

"Dr. Alfonzo is the only person alive who understands my distress, who understands mental illness. Dr. Alfonzo is the only therapist I know of who practices anything close to what I need, not 'talk therapy,' but something deeper that'll get inside my gut. The truth is, I'm lost without his therapy. I'm lost without Dr. Alfonzo. He's the only family I've ever known."

By the time Sebastian had finished talking, twenty minutes later, Yuen was crying along with him; it was impossible not to be affected by his honesty. We hugged him, first Yuen and then me, and then all three of us together, bound in arms and tears.

"I don't even know you yet, but I already love you," Sebastian told us. "I love you both, I love you like the family I always wanted, that I needed . . ."

Our Styx family had increased to five, three of whom—Claude, Clay, and Sebastian—had known Alfonzo for many years. Soon after and without warning, Alfonzo began shuffling patients like a deck of cards from one house to another, rearranging us according to what he saw as psychological "best fits." Every couple of months, a core family member from Styx 1 was also invited to live with Alfonzo, "Papa," in his private home, with him and Yvette, which was viewed as a privilege and a great honor.

He never invited me, and when I asked the others why, I was told I had years left in my therapy. I wasn't yet "clean enough."

Then, suddenly, in late summer 1991, Alfonzo told us that Yvette herself would be moving out of Hampstead and into the Styx with us, presumably because of "daddy issues" that had arisen in her own therapy.

I had known for some time that Yvette and Alfonzo were a couple. Initially referred to him when she was a nurse and he was the practicing psychiatrist at a university hospital, she also had lived in the first Styx house with Clay, Sebastian, and Claude. There were many nights, Sebastian had told me, where she would leave the house after therapy with Alfonzo, and everyone would find out days later that she had driven to Alfonzo's house and spent the night with him. They started living together after the house disbanded. Becoming his secretary, she told me, was a natural progression, though difficult at times because he'd never stopped being her psychiatrist and even "reparented" her as a surrogate father during nurturing sessions.

We were alone after dinner one night when I asked about her early years with Alfonzo.

"When I started with Dr. Alfonzo, primal was nothing like it is today."

The batting station hadn't existed "back then," she said. They had a mattress, but the process of regression was "much more primitive" and not at all as effective as what Alfonzo was doing with us now. "You know, Peter, this process was not handed over to anyone. It was etched in blood from other people's failures—the doctor's, and many others', as well as mine."

Her words, it seemed to me, were a warning.

"I had a lot of trouble connecting with my primal pain when I started," she went on. "I acted out a lot, talked back, argued, challenged. Like you. After several months he locked me in a padded white room where I stayed for twenty days."

"Why was it padded?"

"So we couldn't hurt ourselves. On the twentieth day, I broke through my defenses and submitted to my pain. That's when my real therapy started. You've got a long way to go before you get there."

"Isn't it confusing to you? Your relationship, I mean."

"Of course it is. He's therapist to me. He's Daddy, lover, and employer to me. It's a lot to get straight in my head. Sometimes the lines start blurring, and I still act out. Which is why he sent me to the Styx."

"To punish you?" I prodded.

"To work through my 'stuff.' Otherwise our relationship won't survive. This is my last chance. This is everyone's last chance."

||||||||||

Alfonzo called me to the office one afternoon. He said it was "a private matter."

I sat on the floor in the workroom, as usual. Other than Alfonzo and Yvette, who sat in her regular spot whenever she'd take notes, the three of us were alone.

"Do you know why you're here?" Alfonzo said to me.

"No . . ."

"Yvette?"

Yvette looked scared. "I have asked you here," she said, "I mean we, we have asked you here, because I want to work in front of you. I have witnessed your primals, and now it's only fair I share with you."

Yvette lay on the mattress, closed her eyes, and started moving her legs and arms, breathing gutturally from her diaphragm. With the rest of us, it usually took several minutes to "get into the feeling," but with Yvette it was instantaneous. Her neck arched up off the mattress, tears spilled out over the corners of her eyes, her arms thrashed the mattress, she howled. If everyone else had been in primal school, we were all in kindergarten, and Yvette was primalling a dissertation. The walls to the office shook.

Alfonzo sat, as if on the sidelines of a boxing ring, watching. By the look on his face as he leaned forward, I expected him to cheer.

As with Claude and Sebastian, everything Yvette said while on the mattress was in French. The little I could decipher told me she said something about father, *père*. She was pleading or begging—for his love, I was sure, because I recognized the desperation.

Alfonzo called out in French, mentioned *père*. Yvette choked back words, she gurgled, tears swelled out of her as if being pressed up from within. Then Alfonzo ran out of the room and I heard commotion in his private office, rummaging through his desk drawers. He returned with a large crumpled paper bag. "*Ici, maintenant!*" he screamed.

Yvette sat up and moved to the end of the mattress on her knees. Clearly, they had done this all before. Alfonzo opened the bag and pulled out a large prosthetic dildo. It must have been over a foot long.

He screamed something more in French, ordered her down as if heeling a dog. And then he held the dildo with one hand, forcing her face over it with the other. She gagged. The entire motion was violent, and I realized I'd been holding my breath. Yvette was crying; her face was red and puffy. She looked nothing like the woman, Alfonzo's secretary, I had known till then.

"Okay, enough," Alfonzo said. He stuck the dildo back in the bag, and Yvette rolled over onto the mattress again. She had stopped crying but was panting like a wounded pet. Alfonzo disappeared into his private office again, then returned and plopped back down on his squat chair.

"I'm sorry . . ." I said. "I don't speak French."

"Details aren't important," Alfonzo said. "Yvette? Do you want to add anything?"

Slowly, Yvette sat up, still in the middle of the room on the mattress. "I was a barmaid in Quebec. I had sex with many of my customers. Many times. For love . . . for companionship . . . for Daddy's affection. To all of them I was just a whore with a hole. It's Daddy I really wanted. My father. I think you know what I'm saying, don't you, Peter? You and me . . . we're not so different."

||||||||||

The heartbeat of our house, like that of any family's, fell quickly into place. Alfonzo and Yvette relied on Clay for their office bookkeeping, so most days, after his individual or group sessions, Clay worked with Yvette at the office before busing to his accounting courses at community college. Then he came home and detoxified his body for up to two hours in Epsom salt baths, which resulted in a constant skunk-like body odor that seemed to follow him from room to room like Pig-Pen's cloud of dust in *Peanuts*. After particularly intense primal sessions, he skipped school and slept all afternoon.

When Sebastian and Claude weren't talking in French, like impassioned characters from a foreign film I could not understand but loved to watch, Claude played tunes by Joe Satriani on one of his four electric guitars displayed on pedestals in his bedroom. Alfonzo had said Claude's father, a blue-collar worker from a small town in rural Quebec, had emasculated him of any passion, but it wasn't evident when he played his guitars, or even when he drafted his next "dream home" on his slanted architect's table beneath the ledge of a window in the corner of his yellow room.

Sebastian, on the other hand, had always wanted to be a successful businessman—the "father" that he'd wished his own to be. Resume-writing, job-hunting, meetings with executive personnel at various agencies around town: Sebastian was forever on the lookout for his next "big break," but seemed instead to return home every night broken, hapless, and headed to the workroom where his tears and rage, on the mattress and at the batting station, subsumed him completely.

"You're still a baby who wants to be a man," Alfonzo would tell him. "Maybe you need to stay a baby for a while and not engage too much 'out there.' But maybe you need to get punched down for a while before you figure it out yourself."

Without mentioning it to anyone, I often wondered how it was that Sebastian's childhood sexual abuse had "left him heterosexual," whereas mine had "made me homosexual." The question was a knot in my mind that I could not untie. Still, Sebastian's love of women never stopped me from imagining us a couple: his dark, brooding eyes and velvety lips, the way he'd wave his arms through the air while speaking French. Imagining us in love and out on a date was never much a challenge.

Yuen, a wannabe artist, organized her studio in the small living room on the ground floor of the house, oil painting Black Madonnas on life-size canvasses, throwing slabs of clay till all hours of the night, sculpting one black, pregnant Goddess after another. For a time I joined her with the clay, listening to Peter Gabriel's "The Rhythm of the Heat" while sculpting the bust of a man in full primal scream, his tongue like a slithering snake jutting from his gaping mouth. I dripped liquid cement over another sculpture, a large, twelve-legged spider, so that once dried it seemed to be encased in its own venomous goo, like one of the creatures from the film *Alien*. This one I named "Mother."

The charter, and Alfonzo's repeated reference to it, kept our priorities and all of us firmly on track. "Just read the charter," he would say. "Refer to the charter." At the top of the list was "Formal Acknowledgments of Emotional Triggers." Two people sat face-to-face, one told the other how they triggered their "historical pain," and the other received the words without comment. A primal session in the basement typically followed ten minutes later, after an obligatory "cooling-off period," in which both parties and maybe even everyone else in the house "took it all back historically," one at a time at the bat or on the mattress, until our bodies and the air inside were all depleted. We were never to go to bed resentful, concealing unacknowledged triggers, and if that meant demining our childhoods all night long in a padded basement cell, we knew where our priorities lay.

On Sundays we brunched at Mirabel's, a sixties-style diner with red vinyl booths, 45-rpm's of one-hit wonders hanging like earrings from the ceiling, film and television memorabilia from *The Godfather* and *Annie Hall*, and tin lunchboxes of *Charlie's Angels* and *The Partridge Family* plastered on all the walls. No matter what Yuen ordered, she always ended up mashing it to a pulp, as she did with almost all her food at the Styx.

"Why do you always have to do that to your food?" Sebastian asked her one Sunday, staring at her bowl of gray goop resembling something like lumpy papier-mâché.

"I like my food to look like pabulum," she said, picking up the blackstrap molasses to pour over her dish. "I like baby food."

"You like to stay a baby."

"Whatever. What's the point of growing up if I have to regress all over again the next day in my primals? Besides, I feel more like a baby than an adult—why shouldn't I eat only baby food?"

If Yuen preferred pabulum, Claude ate only the highest fat count possible. Every night before bed he slurped back at least two bowls of sugary granola drowned in 6% yogurt and whole milk. In all the time we'd lived together, I had also never seen Claude chew any of his food. At Mirabel's, he poured enough maple syrup over his stack of buttermilk pancakes until they floated like caramel clouds on his supersized plate, cut a large, pie-shaped slice, stuffed it in his mouth, and then swallowed it whole, an almost violent-sounding *kerplunk* emanating from the back of his throat.

Clay's ailing body, as he often reminded us, required him to eat only organics to help cleanse his system of all toxins. Systematically, before putting anything in his mouth, he cut whatever was on his plate into bite-size pieces, and only then would he chew each piece of food, slowly and purposefully, at least fifteen times per mouthful, until, as he also often reminded us, "the saliva breaks down all food compounds in my mouth in order to make it easier on my digestive system. Mastication is, after all, the most important step in a healthy diet."

On some occasions we all piled into Claude's beat-up 1984 Plymouth Sapporo after brunch to drive out to a national park and swim in the waterfalls. There was freedom in the country, if only because we were nowhere near Alfonzo, his ego or his office, the workroom and intensives. Toward the end of one afternoon, I noticed Claude and Yuen holding hands and kissing on the lips, just as I'd seen them do on many other occasions late at night at the Styx after dinner or a movie. No one ever commented on their obvious transgression of "charter rules"—that there never be sex, or sexual relations, and never between house members, while living in the Styx. On the contrary, allowances always seemed to be made for their coupling.

"Theirs is the best kind of union," Alfonzo had once commented about them during a house meeting at the office, "because they come together as spiritual brother and sister, emotionally naked and able to see the other for who they are. Only from this kind of nakedness can one receive another."

Watching Claude and Yuen embrace and kiss by his car, I yearned for that same kind of union—the same, only different. If real love truly was based on a kind of "nakedness," I thought, then there was no logical reason why two men, whose souls were neither male nor female, couldn't experience it as well. I thought all of this, and then just as quickly tried to turn my back on it and, by extension, myself. I'd not yet returned to my "innate heterosexuality" everyone, and even I, rationalized, as if my homosexuality itself were just a brief sojourn from where I was still meant to depart.

Some nights Sebastian and I drove around town in his white Chevy van that he'd purchased to start a new business painting houses, stopping at large charity bins set up at various residential street corners near our house. We had done this for months so our routine was down pat: Sebastian stood guard for passersby as I reached down into the large slotted openings and fished out anything in arm's way: records, cassette tapes, books, clothes. One enormous charity bin, several blocks from the Styx in an alley behind a K-Mart department store, was our last stop of the day; small pieces of furniture were often left in the open: kitchen chairs, ripped ottomans, scratched and rickety wooden night tables. A bonanza of a day meant finding something, anything, we could lug back to the Styx and possess as our own.

I didn't need Sebastian to go fishing for other people's discards, though. Nearly every afternoon I was out on my bicycle at the downtown Value Village, scouring the moth-ridden aisles for something to buy for under five dollars: teapots, vases, artificial flowers, books, or used LP records, all of which I brought back to the Styx to fill an emptiness my therapy seemed to carve out of me, one session at a time. Browsing for hours, I didn't have to think about my primals, all of them like grenades in my gut. I didn't have to think about the medications, a daily grind of pills that served only to combat rising infernal pressures. My parents, my childhood, my blood family—all was out of mind. I had a new family, and if I wasn't happy, at least I was distracted.

No matter what our activities the night before, though, every workweek morning I was up before the crack of dawn, dressed, and on my bicycle to the university campus, where I served up smiles and stews at its student union cafeteria, intermittently hiding in a nearby bathroom stall to pop an extra Rivotril and breathe through waves of panic. The university's drama department had chosen my play, *Off the Wall,* for production, and so after my writing workshops, my afternoons were consumed by rehearsals and discussions and rewrites, all of which I savored like delectable midday meals I wished never to end.

But they did end, and by early evening into every long and dark night, I was once again a primal patient at the Styx: preparing gourmet vegan dinners for intensives, joining my soul siblings in various house meetings, meditating by candlelight in our bedrooms, and reading passages from *A Course in Miracles* as a group in the living room—and most typically, almost always, swinging a bat in our basement dungeon: raging at my parents, sweating and screaming and crying on the mattress, resurrecting myself like a sunken ship from the wreckage of my childhood.

12

I was sitting in Alfonzo's waiting room when a slight mid-forties woman, another patient, I assumed, emerged from his office. The moment our eyes met, she stopped dead in her tracks.

"Oh, I'm sorry," she said, "it's just—you look exactly like an ex-lover of mine from twenty years ago."

"Oh . . . well, I'm not," was all I could say.

The woman continued through the waiting room, then turned around again. "The resemblance is uncanny," she repeated. "You look exactly like him." She continued out of the waiting room and down the hallway to the bathroom.

I waited for Alfonzo's office door to open again, for him to invite me in. This had been the day he'd told me about for months, the day I'd meet my new surrogate mother. I dried my sweaty palms against my pant leg, closed my eyes and breathed.

I thought about my mother. I remembered us together when I was a child, the way she sat on the edge of my bed, singing "Que Sera, Sera," lulling me to sleep; and then the night terrors, waking to her naked body with three breasts, an apparition beside my bed.

"*Peter?*"

I opened my eyes to Alfonzo, motioning for me to follow him into the workroom. "So you know what we're doing today, right?"

"Yes . . ."

"There isn't going to be any nurturing. Not yet. I've explained all of this to Alice."

"Okay . . ."

"I just want you two to meet. Talk. Get to know each other. Sound reasonable?"

He'd hardly finished talking when the woman from the waiting room reentered and was introduced to me as Alice, my new surrogate mother. That I appeared to look like my newfound "mother's" ex-lover was the worst possible introduction Alice and I could have had, and we both knew it. Alfonzo left us alone and before another word, she tried backtracking, telling me that she hadn't had her glasses on when we first met, that I looked nothing at all like him. But it was too late: the spell had been cast, and I was terrified of my new mother.

Alice and I sat face-to-face on the mattress, as I studied her wiry, shoulder-length brown hair, the way she spoke with gentleness in her blue saucer-eyes that both surprised and scared me. At least she didn't look or sound like my mother, I thought, as I started in on my family history, beginning with my mother.

"I was an emotional acrobat around my mother," I told Alice. "I don't want to do the same with you."

"You don't need to protect me. That's not your job."

I told Alice about our father's rage, about the night Kriska ran away from home, my own escape through sex. I said I wasn't sure that I was gay because I liked attractive women, although I didn't want to have sex with them, and that I didn't like men, but was sexually aroused by them. At one point, Alice tried to take my hand, but I jumped back and told her not to touch me.

My most childlike feelings emerged when I talked about how much I loved my mother, wanted her to sing me to sleep each night, but feared the moment that she did because of the way her nightie draped wide open and I'd glimpse her breasts. Even though I talked openly about disturbing memories, I never cried. Instead, whenever I felt my most vulnerable, I laughed. Alice seemed to understand, and sat and listened through it all without interrupting.

At one point I began to shiver. Without missing a beat, Alice found a nearby blanket and tucked it neatly around my sides, took my hand in hers and rubbed my chest with her other hand. I could feel the muscles in my body constrict, and I had to make a conscious effort to breathe. All I wanted was to suck my thumb and lapse into baby talk, while familiar feelings of shame and need cloaked me in a deadening silence. Through it all, Alice sat by my side, her warm eyes drawing me into her world of compassion.

Our subsequent sessions were consumed with heightened emotion. All week long, at work at the student union cafeteria or during my writing workshops, I looked forward to my nurturing sessions, or else I dreaded them. I liked Alice; then I resented her. If I arrived at my session excited to see her, as soon as she asked me what I wanted to talk about I became depressed, anxious, angry without apparent cause. I didn't want to think about what I wanted to talk about: I wanted her to take care of me.

Alfonzo sat in on our early sessions and explained that it would take some time for me to know the "mother space," that my own mother's seductiveness had totally unbalanced me, which had led to my fantasies about men.

"You need to let Alice touch you," he explained, "and then use your emerging feelings by taking them back historically on the mattress or at the bat, by making the connection between how you felt as a child and how you feel as an adult."

If I resisted Alfonzo's advice, he became angry and threatened to throw me out of therapy unless I complied with all the rules. After he left the room, Alice would hold me and I'd remember my father screaming at me, at all my siblings, that it was his house, his rules, and if I didn't like it, I could leave.

Sometimes Alice's mirroring of my pain contrasted so sharply against my mother's refusal to do the same that I had to physically separate myself and move to the batting station. And then for twenty minutes or longer, I would bat and scream at my mother about all the years she'd reflected back to me not who I was, or what I was feeling, but who she wanted me to be, what she needed me to feel in order that her own pain not be reignited. The disorientation of never having had my truth reflected back to me had left me reeling through years of anxiety, fearful that I was imagining things, going crazy, or with a rage too large to call my own. After exhausting myself at the bat, always I was more able to feel Alice's love for me without my mother coming between us.

Whether Alfonzo was present in my sessions or not, I talked about how much I loved and trusted him, that I wanted my new parents to take care of me, to love me unconditionally. Once, while Alice was shouldering me in her arms, I said that I would give my life for Alfonzo.

"No," she said, physically separating us so that she could see me, and I her, as she spoke. "You should never trust anyone that much."

This confused me, and secretly I wondered why Mommy didn't trust Daddy.

Progressively, though, I resisted Alice's bodywork less and became more and more relaxed while cuddling in her lap. My mind was calmer and clearer than it had ever been before, as if the hard drive of my brain were being reformatted back to its original state of love and peace. Sometimes, during her bodywork, my lungs felt like they were being constrained. But I always pushed through it, and if our sessions ended with my head nestled in her gentle hands, I'd feel her butter-soft skin against my cheek and smell a familiarity that made me safe and childlike in her arms. If terror stabbed through me, like ripples surfacing from the hauntings of my childhood, I'd call out for Alfonzo.

"*Papa!*" I'd scream.

He'd rush in, then both he and Alice would reassure me that everything was okay and that it was just my biological mother, like a parasite, forcing her way back inside of me.

"Just make contact with the mommy space," Alfonzo told me as I breathed and lay with Alice, heard her coo me back into the comfort zone. "Keep in contact with Mommy . . ."

||||||||||

I returned to Vancouver for one night to attend a new, all-female, production of *Off the Wall,* as part of an arts festival for dance, music, theater, and multimedia.

Two local acting students had also recorded my fifteen-minute piece for sound that I'd written the previous year, called "Deluge." Each evening, after *Off the Wall,* the audience filed into a smaller, darkened theater where they played "Deluge" over speakers with another artist's sculpture of a candlelit coffin at the front.

Primal was an assault on my senses, and my goal with "Deluge" had been to convey that same sense of overwhelming cacophony. Based in part on psychiatrist R.D. Laing's slim book *Knots*, as well as my own childhood night terrors, overlapping voices, like mental tapes, looped back in on each other from different times in the narrator's life, a disorienting, sometimes "psychotic" experience I was becoming more and more familiar with, considered "normal" in primal.

At the end of the play, not one of the roughly forty-member audience moved, spoke, or clapped. Slowly, after several minutes, everyone filed out of the room.

||||||||||

Therapy continued four times each weekday afternoon: two groups, one nurturing hour with Alice, and an individual with Alfonzo to keep me "on track."

In bed at night I spent hours crying for "Mommy," visualizing Alice instead of my biological mother. At the batting station, I called out for "my soul mother, Alice," at times sounding as though I were exorcising a demon, and not my mother, from within. Switching between little-boy Peter, who was sucking his thumb while lying in his mother's arms, to grown-up Peter, who was a university student while working to pay his bills, became increasingly difficult. Countless sessions were spent with me crying, fearful and anxious at going back out into the "real world." At these times, Alfonzo would tell me to "sit up and pay attention" as he outlined the whole deal.

"Everybody has these feelings of not being able to function in the outside world while going through primal," he'd reiterate. Regardless, the disparity between my child and adult selves continued to mirror my boyhood years, when I'd felt myself forced out of childhood innocence in order to protect my parents from their pain.

Game-playing became an integral part of my nurturing sessions. When I asked Alice if she could be my mother, and I her baby, she always said yes. The sounds of her breaths, rhythmical waves, calmed my mind as I lay in her lap and listened to her paint a picture of the two of us by the windows in our house. There were plants all around, and sunshine. Warmth and security. We were cuddling, and I was just a toddler, age three. Later, the two of us went in search of chestnuts. All was well. Then lions and wolves surrounded us, backing us deeper into a clave of fear. But Alice squeezed tight to my hand, never letting go, and together we shouted at them to go away, to leave us to our chestnut outing, and as soon as they did, the spell was broken.

The love and safety that Alice created was unlike anything I'd ever experienced before. At the batting station, I drained the emotional poison from within; in her arms, I was filled back up, like a balloon whose air would one day carry it away.

Details of my sessions were always relayed back to Alfonzo through Alice's and my weekly mandatory written "reports," after which Alfonzo always reinforced in me just how much progress I was making.

"You have recovered the need for the need," he told me. "Soon you'll be getting better, and only then will you grow up and go back out into the world."

|||||||||||

Eighteen months into my therapy, I attended my first weekend "marathon"—an intensive group session held at the office: ten hours a day, two days in a row. Like an elite club, only select patients were invited: Styx members and intensives. Because British Columbia's government-administered Medical Services Plan prohibited the billing of ten patients over a two-day period, Alfonzo scheduled the marathon prior to his vacation so he could bill for each patient throughout the two weeks that he and Yvette were away at Club Med. Alfonzo's billing methods were no secret amongst "family" members at the Styx.

Saturday morning began with a guided visualization led by Yvette, who, in addition to acting as Alfonzo's secretary, co-facilitated many of his group sessions.

We all picked a spot on the floor and lay on our backs. Candles were lit, lights dimmed, soft music with the sounds of chimes and light rain played in the background.

"I want everyone to close their eyes," Yvette instructed, stepping around limbs like rungs on the floor. "Take a deep breath through your nose, slowly. In . . . then out. In . . . out. Feel your stomachs rising and falling like waves on a sea. In . . . out. Good."

Our visualization lasted thirty minutes, after which everyone sat in a circle around the room and was encouraged to work on the mattress or at the bat as many times as possible. The process was relentless, offering little respite between primals. For two days the world outside would cease to exist as ten of us dove deep into ourselves, like un-swum oceans, waiting to be chartered. The stated goal: to break through our defenses and submit to our "primal pain."

Saturday night was spent as a group at Ludo's house. Ludo was one of the marathon's members and a past Styx intensive. Originally from Denmark, Ludo was an architect and had designed his multi-million-dollar dream home, inspired by Frank Lloyd Wright, on the crest of a wooded property. Everyone ended up in pairs after dinner, taking turns playing their favorite LPs from one of Ludo's hundreds of records or enjoying a few minutes of banal conversation following our day of intense "body work." I went out to the house's veranda, closed my eyes, and breathed the scent of pine deep into my lungs. Inside I heard the Moody Blues' "Isn't Life Strange." After a minute, Ludo joined me on the veranda.

"Beautiful, isn't it," he said.

"How long have you lived here?"

"Ten years. It was my present to my soon-to-be wife."

"This was your wedding gift?"

It was always strange talking to someone outside of therapy. On the mattress we bared our souls, our histories of loveless childhoods, of abuse or neglect, but in reality, no one knew much about anyone's "real" life of wives and children and daily trials. All I knew about Ludo, from his session that morning, was that he'd been profoundly affected by his father's inability to express any sort of physical affection, his "wall of silence."

"Are your parents still alive?" I asked.

"My father is," he said, slowly, as if each word were a painful effort. "My mother died three years ago. I hate saying it . . . but I think it would have been easier if my father had gone first."

"Why?"

"At least then I would have a parent I could talk to. I have never been able to talk to my father. He refuses to talk to me. I became an architect to please him. I thought maybe then he would be proud of me. Now all I think about is how he'll die and I won't know what to say at his funeral. Once he even said to me, out of the blue, he said . . . 'What will you say during my eulogy? You don't even know who I am.' He's my father, but he's a stranger to me. I worry sometimes about my own children."

"How many children do you have?"

"A boy and a girl. Everyone expects you to be a good parent to your children, to hold them and to love them. You're expected to do for them what no one did for you. Sometimes it feels like too much to learn in one lifetime."

Yuen poked her head out of the house and said that meditation was about to begin. The scent of frankincense wafted onto the veranda as we slid open the Japanese partition and returned to the group.

Within the hour we were all in bed, some of us in shared rooms, or on the floor in sleeping bags. I ended up on the bottom of a bunk bed, curled like a peanut in the child-size frame the shape of a toy truck. Blurry white elephants filled my vision as my nighttime medication, 350 milligrams of Elavil, smothered me to sleep.

||||||||||

Alfonzo joined the group Sunday morning. I was the first to volunteer to work on the mattress, but before I could, Alfonzo told me to lie on my stomach on the floor.

"What for?" I asked.

"You want a good trigger for your session? Just do it."

I followed his lead, nervously, and lay on my stomach on the side of the room.

Alfonzo told Claude and Clay to lie on top of me and to pin me down. I glanced over as one held my arms above my head, the other pinned my legs to the floor.

"Now," Alfonzo said, "try and break free."

I turned my head and glanced up at him: he was standing next to me, above me, arms folded, smiling.

I did not move.

"Feel familiar?" he continued, bending down to where I lay, staring me in the eyes. "How many times have you been fucked in this position? Huh? Fucked up your ass by some man you didn't even know. And you just lie there and . . . take it."

He must have motioned for Claude and Clay to release the prisoner, because their hands let go, their bodies lifted off me, while the weight that bound me, the shame inside me, was heavier and more powerful than any man who had ever held me down before.

I rolled from my stomach onto the mattress and immediately I started to work: closed my eyes, moved my arms and legs like I was walking, then running, sank back into the endless pit of shame. Within minutes, I was using my screaming, pounding, and writhing on the mattress like an ice pick to chip away at my defenses. My internal scale had tipped to one side, and the conflicted feelings over being gay that I had struggled with for years had given way to the militant conviction that homosexual acts were unnatural, abominable, and disgusting, and that homosexuality itself was the result of historical pain.

My homosexuality, moreover, was the result of the sexual abuse. Or so I screamed while lying on the mattress. Like a cartographer, I was involuntarily mapping out my life through primal, one word at a time. Promiscuity was the nature of homosexuality. All gay men dissociated while having sex. Shame and a lifetime of lovelessness were synonymous with homosexual desire. There were no shades of gray. My life was black and white.

Better yet, there was someone I could blame for my life's unhappiness: my parents. If it had not been for my parents' poor role modeling, their lack of intervention, I would not have spent my teenage years in public toilets and bathhouses, behavior I still equated with homosexuality. My parents were the cause of my misfortunes, as surely as if they'd walked me downtown and into the arms of every man I'd encountered. My body was a grave, and I was falling deeper into it, word by word, as I talked without interruption about the sickness of my homosexuality, digging myself deeper into the pit of my self-hatred.

After an hour on the mattress, something inside me cracked wide open. I hit bottom, or center: tears flooded out of me, overwhelming me with grief, clouding my vision. The next thing I knew, someone was guiding me by the arm, leading me into Alfonzo's private office. The door slammed shut and I collapsed, sobbing, in Alfonzo's arms.

"One-quarter cc," I heard him say to someone in the room.

Then I felt a cold prick like a bee sting near my bicep as Alfonzo injected me with something. The next thing I felt were his powerful arms as he wrapped himself around my middle, squeezing the screams out of me like a blow-up doll wailing out its pain.

Everything blurred as the boundaries of my body dissolved and I floated up. Up and outside myself, I looked down upon my body. I had given up the fight, let go, and released into his containment. I had surrendered.

"Ssshh," he whispered in my ear. "Papa's here now. Baby's safe in Papa's arms. Everything's okay . . . Papa caught you."

||||||||||

The walls to my "self" took hold as I returned from wherever it was I had gone. I was a body again. Peter. Eyes opened, fingers stretched wide, the world was seen anew. Structures and boundaries became evident. Wetness was tears and sweat and snot. They were wiped away by a cloth Alfonzo handed me.

"Thank you," I said.

"Go slow," he said. "Drink this. You may feel slightly dehydrated for a while."

He handed me a glass of water. I sipped and my parched throat, a tunnel, opened.

"Stand up slowly."

I did, and like my parent, he was watching me take my first steps. Then I heard the bat in the adjacent office and I remembered where I was: at a marathon. The others were still working, sweating, pounding, crying.

"What time is it?" I asked.

"We've been in here about forty-five minutes."

"Oh. Okay. I guess I should go back . . ." I stumbled toward the door, weak and disoriented from our session.

"Wait a minute."

He moved to his desk and pulled a bottle of cologne out of its drawer.

"Come here."

"What's that?"

"Papa's scent," he said, spraying the pungent odor over my shirt. "So baby feels safe. Now you have me on you wherever you go."

13

I ATTENDED A FRINGE Festival production of my play, *Off the Wall*, in Vancouver, with the same cast as from the previous production. Recurring regressions had taken possession of my body and I was infantilized, constantly on the verge of tears. One local reviewer wrote that I was "a playwright to watch," but I could not enjoy my success. I was a child in need, five years old and away from my parents, Alice and Alfonzo. All I wanted was to return home to the Styx.

In Victoria, my radio play, "Deluge," was broadcast on the university's radio station, following which I was briefly interviewed. Near the end, the interviewer, a graduate student, asked me what I was working on now.

I thought for a moment.

"Myself," I said. "And then, maybe, another play."

||||||||||

Ketamine hydrochloride, most commonly used as an animal anesthetic, was the drug Alfonzo had injected in me that first time.

"I use it only in very small doses," Alfonzo told me upon his return from vacation, weeks later, "mostly during the nurturing sessions to help remove the patient's observing ego. I've been waiting for the exact right moment for your first injection."

"What would happen if you didn't use it?"

"Your therapy would be jeopardized. You don't want that to happen, do you?"

"No . . . no, of course not."

"The medication helps the child self bond directly with the surrogate parent during your regressions. It's in your own best interest to use it. Without that bond, the parent loses the child to despair. That's where you've been the last twenty years of your life. It's imperative we create that bond."

Weekly injections of "K" followed that first one, and were always administered immediately prior to a nurturing hour with Alice or Alfonzo. Like a schoolboy about to get his flu shot, I would roll up my sleeve, but within minutes, the fog of K had flooded my body and I was curled up with Alice or Alfonzo, regressed to pure need. For sixty minutes, all sensation became intensified as I floated, formless, through a pool of black terror or a sense of timeless euphoria. Then, as if guided by a stream that swam me back into my self, I returned to the brick-and-mortar of my body as the medication waned.

Although I was aware that others in the Styx were also receiving this "mild hallucinogenic," I was privately instructed never to talk about its use to anyone, not even with my housemates. At times, I slipped and referred to my use of K. Looks were exchanged, I knew I was doing a "bad" thing by talking about it, even tangentially, and then I changed the subject.

After one of my nurturing sessions with Alfonzo, still buzzed and "outside myself," Alfonzo took me to a nearby dessert shop for frozen yogurt, then later, for a ride in his shiny new black Mercedes Benz. When he opened the sunroof and sped through the winding city streets, I felt like I was out with Daddy, and I laughed like a child for the first time in years.

Back at Hampstead, I stepped out of the car like off an amusement park ride: disoriented, but every bit alive, tingling with excitement, joy.

"You're getting fat," he said, looking at my stomach. "How much weight have you gained?"

"I don't know . . ." I said, aware that I had gained a lot of weight due to the water retention brought on by the medications he was prescribing.

"Well you should watch that."

My heart sank.

||||||||||

As the dosages of my medications increased, so too did their side effects: dry mouth, labored breathing, heart palpitations, involuntary twitching, constipation, and weight gain of more than forty pounds. I learned to walk through dizziness. Stopped reading books because of blurred vision. Tried to pee but nothing came out. Concealed from the world the dead weight of my penis as it pulsed inside my pants, heavy but lifeless, like a broken limb. A shell of dry, flaky skin crusted over my scrotum, yet I couldn't dig deep enough to reach the itchiness inside. I did try, however, scratching my scrotum with a wire hairbrush until the sores cracked and bled fire.

Whether triggered by too much medication, a contraindication of medications, or a trapdoor that prolonged regressions had dropped me through inside myself, threat of annihilation appeared around every corner. Demons rattled beneath the floorboards of my soul, and helplessness overwhelmed me. Passing faces on streets were like Francis Bacon nightmares, cadaverous, moribund, and doomed.

Once, convinced that someone "out there" was trying to kill me, I locked myself in the Styx bathroom for hours, tucked in the corner beside the toilet, waiting, barely moving or breathing, praying a Styx mate would arrive home soon and save me.

Fantasy and all erotic sensation receded. My imagination was being whitewashed. One day, in desperation, I bought a gay pornographic magazine and masturbated, less an act of eroticism than a fight against the currents of my physical decay, and as I did, in order to take me over the hill of orgasm, I pierced needles through my nipples.

The next morning, caught in the familiar grooves of desire mixed with shame, regret, and then despair, I confessed the entire ordeal to Alfonzo during an individual session in his office. He rose from where he'd been sitting and started pacing about the workroom.

"Why didn't you go to one of your housemates?" He looked down at me with that familiar, menacing glare.

"I don't know . . ."

"You think sticking needles through your flesh is productive, *is that it*? What sort of dysfunctional house are you guys operating there, anyway?"

I couldn't answer, was scared and infantile, could barely look at him.

"You think this is a game? *Is that what you think?*"

"No . . ."

"You lie in bed and jerk off to pictures of men, acting out your historical neuroses, and then you stick needles in your nipples? Is that all you care about, getting off? *Why don't you just move back to your hometown and fuck another man in a car? Pick up another trick in a washroom or a bathhouse?* What do you think this house is for anyway? This type of behavior is grounds for eviction!"

His final threat scared me most of all. If I didn't change my ways and do as I was told, I would be thrown out of therapy and the Styx, lose my new family, and be exiled to the life that had almost killed me. I began to cry.

"Oh stop pouting. At the least you should have woken one of your housemates and worked in the workroom, even if it was two in the morning."

Alice had been waiting for my nurturing hour to begin. Alfonzo stormed out of the workroom and into his private office.

"Don't listen to a word he tells you," she said, positioning my head in her lap. "The man's a homophobe. A lot of men are. That's their own stuff, though, it has nothing to do with you."

"I try and let go of my fantasies," I told her, "but sometimes I can't control myself and I still think about men."

"Of course you do. And there's nothing wrong with that."

"But there is; there *is*. I'm supposed to be letting go of my homosexuality, not reinforcing it."

"Says who?"

"Homosexuality is wrong. It goes against nature."

"Why would you say that?"

"Sex with men has never brought me any kind of pleasure."

"Maybe it's not the sex that hasn't brought you pleasure, but your *feelings* about the sex. What part of love between two men goes against nature?"

I had no answer to that question.

"Besides, you are not just your sexuality, my dear Peter. You are a child of God. And you're loveable, gay or straight. I'll love you no matter what you are."

"Can we just lie together?" I was more confused now than before we'd started talking. "No talk, just lie together?"

"Of course."

Alfonzo reappeared at the close of my session fifty minutes later, dropped into the stance of a sumo wrestler, and stared me in the eyes. Alice had moved to the side.

"Your homosexuality is an addiction that must be given up if you want to go anywhere in your therapy. Do you understand me? You need to carry your cross with dignity, Peter. Not act on your insanity."

His anger had shifted to a gentleness that confused me more.

"No one but your mommy and daddy can give you the deep primal love that'll relieve the pressure you feel inside. No one. That awful feeling of having had your lovability rejected by your biological parents? . . . It's our job to fix that."

Again, I began to cry. Alfonzo wrapped his arms around me. "You need to hang on," he said, rubbing my back. "You need to hang on."

I had drilled a hole down toward the center of me, and the earth above, I feared, was filling back in on me like a grave.

||||||||||

My all-consuming primals continued unabated. There seemed to be no limits to the depths of my anger toward both my parents—"my crucifiers," as I now called them. A recurring theme that I was "not homosexual" also overwhelmed my regressions to the point that I became convinced of my "non-homosexual" identity. "I am not a homosexual!" I'd scream out in full primal, lying on my back in the middle of the dimly lit therapy room, eyes shut, neck craned, back arched up off the floor. Afterward, as I'd wipe the tears from my eyes, Alfonzo would reframe everything I had said about being "not a homosexual" as proof of my "innate heterosexuality," reiterating time and again that "primals don't lie"—the fact that I could articulate my "non-homosexuality" during a regression was proof that my false homosexual self was slipping away, soon to be replaced by my underlying, inalienable heterosexuality.

"You're in a classic place of primal rage right now," Alfonzo would say. Only after I felt the pain of never having been loved, he'd reinforce, would my integration into the outside world become possible. For the time being, however, all I needed was to allow myself the right to feel what I'd suppressed as a child.

One early evening at the Styx I grabbed the phone after dinner, hid inside a crawlspace beneath the coiled metal staircase, and called my mother after not having spoken with her for over a year.

She was overjoyed to hear from me. I interrupted and reminded her of our conversation in my old bedroom, the day she told me she'd been raped. Horrified, she denied ever having told me about the rape.

"That never happened, she said. "I never told you that."

I continued, reminded her of all the times my father had chased me and my siblings through the house with his black leather belt, asked her why she'd smothered me in her breasts every night before bed, accused her of turning her back on me instead of wanting to hear the truth, told her that she had no idea of the damage she'd caused.

"*Damage*? Son, you don't know the meaning of the word 'damage.'"

She told me what I knew, what had kept me from saying any of this in the first place: that she and my father were orphans from the war, that they couldn't speak English when they'd arrived in Canada, had no money, or jobs, and that if they'd made mistakes it was only because they didn't know better. She begged me to understand. I understood, I told her—I had been in therapy already for years. I understood, but understanding did not change the way I felt. The best thing I could do now, I said, was stay with my anger.

"Anger is a flame that burns itself out," she said. "Anger will destroy you."

"My anger has saved me."

Then I told her what I had been encouraged to repeat a hundred times over at the batting station: I told her she was no longer my mother, and that her husband, "that pathetic excuse for a man," was no longer my father.

Again, she begged for me to stop, but I raged on, said that she had been poisoning my mind and body for my entire life, and that I gave it all back to her. I did not want a birthday card from her or a Christmas card or an Easter card; I did not want to have anything more to do with her, with either of them, ever again.

"But we love you!"

"You don't love me—*you crucified me. I was your fix!*"

"Oh my God . . . you really are cracking up, aren't you? I don't think there's a doctor alive that could help you now . . ."

Before I hung up the phone, there was a shard of a moment where my heart throbbed with compassion through a fissure in my rage. But then the moment passed, the rage again possessed me, and I smashed the phone down like a lead gavel onto a cradle, leaving behind my parents and everyone who had known me before.

||||||||||

Alfonzo upped my doses of medication.

"It's normal for a person to need more medication the deeper they go in primal therapy," he said. "You're nowhere near what I was taking when I had my own breakdown, my dark night of the soul. Don't worry about it."

But I did worry about it. In addition to weekly injections of K, I was now taking 4 milligrams of Rivotril, 550 milligrams of Elavil, plus Surmontil and Sinequan daily. Nothing helped. Nothing stopped the panic and the fear; nothing stopped grief and despair. The more medication he prescribed, the worse my symptoms became and the faster my fear intensified about ever stopping the medications at all. There was no rational thought, no trying to figure out whether my worsening symptoms were the result of extended primal therapy, or the medications. No energy was left to think. Crawling out of bed every morning and bicycling to school or to work or to the office: every act, thought, movement, conversation, sound, syllable required more from me than I could give, became a chore, an endless weight, like chains wrapped 'round my body, dragging me down deeper, every day, down deeper.

Then one day my body would no longer sleep.

"Five hundred-and-fifty milligrams isn't working," I told Alfonzo at the office. "I haven't slept in days."

"Well, I can't prescribe more than five hundred-and-fifty

milligrams. The pharmacist won't fill the prescription. But I sometimes take more myself. Just take an extra fifty milligrams, if you need to. We'll renew your prescription a bit earlier next time."

So that's what I did. The 550 milligrams turned into 600 milligrams. Still sleep eluded me, like the sexuality that remained always beyond my reach. Every morning I crawled out of bed earlier and earlier for work; it was that or lie awake, drenched in icy sweat, immobilized by fear. By the winter of 1991, I was bicycling to my job at five in the morning, over snowy roads, numbed by the blizzards. For three hours until my shift began, I would sit alone in the half-lit, empty university cafeteria, smoking and drinking endless cups of coffee in an effort to awaken my body from its medicated stupor. And I wrote: about my mother's escape from the camp and my own body's imprisonment. Like an emotional bulimic, I was attempting to purge from my insides with pen and paper every last thought and feeling that had possessed my mind for years.

Then, one winter morning, the moment I crawled out of bed, something inside of me unhinged. I collapsed, feeling the air rush past me as if I'd plunged down an endless elevator shaft. Clay found me sometime later, conscious, lying motionless on the floor beside my bed, still feeling as if I were falling through space, the endless landscape of my shattered mind, rootless to myself and my surroundings. He fed me a dose of his antipsychotic, Nozinan, and called Alfonzo to the house.

The days and weeks that followed were a jumble of events. I imagine someone called my employer at the university's student union and told them I would not be back to work; I never returned to school. Alfonzo placed me on medical disability and added Nozinan to my regime of daily medications. Elevators, escalators, even cars and buses—any and all involuntary movement of my body—exacerbated the sense that I was plummeting down inside myself and toward my own untimely end. Only walking, remaining physically active, counteracted the dread and so, every day, all day, through parks, inside shopping malls, down streets, I walked. Clay walked with me. I could not be left alone.

Sometime later—weeks, months, I don't remember—Alfonzo told

me to start working in his office. With blurred vision and short-term memory loss, I could barely see let alone concentrate, but was given notes to type and did my best. Mostly he talked to me between patient visits. My collapse had been "a close call," he told everyone in the Styx. He wanted to keep a careful eye on my recovery.

For months, time ceased to exist. My days were clocked by experiences, not minutes: feeling the jigsaw puzzle of my mind break apart; repeating entire conversations because I'd forgotten I'd had them already; hearing all sounds, traffic, wind, and voices swirling around me as if I were locked in the eye of a storm; carrying the weight of my body around like a suit of armor I wished only to remove so I could sleep. Maybe I slipped away for an hour or two, inconsolably exhausted, and yet I always surfaced again by three or four in the morning and lay panic-stricken in my bed till dawn.

Arriving at my sessions zombielike, my speech was sometimes incomprehensible.

"I'm in so much physical discomfort," I told Alfonzo once, "I don't know how much more I can take."

To which he repeated what he'd said so many times before. "You need to feel the bond with Mommy. Just be in the mommy space."

My body was an earthquake that I was trapped inside.

||||||||||

Then one day, we were moving. Alfonzo must have told the others that we needed a bigger house, "more rooms for more intensives," because everyone was packing, and movers were arriving. Conversations I could not follow overwhelmed me with fear.

The first time I saw our new neighborhood, I thought we'd stepped into the movie *Futureworld*. Prefabricated houses lined a treeless, dead-end street near a dank and gloomy swamp at the outskirts of the city. The inside of our split-level house was vacuous and drafty, like a barn. Within days of arriving, patients I'd never met before began moving in, converting an upstairs, enclosed sunroom into an additional bedroom and the downstairs' expansive living space into three tiny sleeping quarters large enough for single-sized cots.

Wooden stairs that creaked like bones popping in their sockets led down into a gutted basement, with cement flooring and overhanging cobwebs. In one dark distant corner, behind the steaming furnace, was a tiny crawl space just large enough for our newest workroom. Two-by-fours were raised, gyprock was attached, and a portable door was secured to the loosely hanging frame. So poorly constructed was our newest dungeon that it often tipped from side-to-side, like Dorothy's house in the cyclone, as we thrashed about inside, batting and screaming and calling out for the love of our mommies and daddies. Sounds of exorcisms had long since become the norm at the Styx.

We'd been in the new house only days when I heard the shrill cry for the first time, followed by a thunderous reverberation. I went out back, near our neighbor's dilapidated property. Standing knee high in a sea of overgrown grass, mice scurried underfoot. Next door, through a dangling wire fence, I watched in horror as a fat older man with a yellowing beard decapitated chickens. One by one, he hurled their blood-soaked torsos inside enormous, rusty canisters, where the convulsions of their still-alive bodies echoed like a drum.

Awaking each morning in my cell-like room in the basement of our barn, the reality of my life shifted slowly into focus. There was no waking from the nightmare I was living. Then I heard the chickens' squeals from outside my bedroom window, as if each were calling out to me for help.

||||||||||

"How are you feeling today?" Alfonzo asked me weekly.

I understood his meaning. He could have just as easily asked me if I was still thinking about or attracted to men. The truth was I had never stopped finding men attractive, clocking in at about a six on Alfonzo's revised "Kinsey scale" of one to seven, and my inability to "flip to the other side" was feeding into my obsessions about the possible "causes" of my homosexuality.

Viewing my obsessive-compulsive thinking as one more symptom of my pathology, Alfonzo reminded me that I would never be able to make the "switchover" if I continued to obsess about "the gay side." Anafranil, my fourth tricyclic antidepressant, was prescribed specifically to deaden my sex drive. The medication made me feel numb, lifeless, passive. Any light that had remained alive in me was now switched off. Erections were eliminated; fantasy and arousal, eradicated. Fear of the world, my vulnerability and dependence on Alfonzo, increased. On a number of occasions when we'd discuss my increasing passivity, he told me that homosexuals were passive by nature.

"You need to push through your passivity. Remember: your unexpressed anger is what's keeping you from your heterosexuality."

If I talked about my ongoing fear of the world, Alfonzo said that there was only one fear, and it was of not being loved. Repeatedly he told me that if I ever didn't know what to do, I should just talk to my mom (Alice) or dad (himself).

"Papa has your best interest at heart" were the words I heard so often, as I picked myself back up and headed out the door.

||||||||||

"How are you feeling today?" Alfonzo asked during one of our sessions, as usual.

"I still think about men."

"We may need to try something new. Through the years you've learned that homosexual relations are pleasurable. This is incorrect data. Homosexuals have confused their sex organs. Why else would they stick their penis where they shit? We need to correct your brain's faulty wiring. I want you to go home tonight and bottle some of your feces in a little film container. Every time you're attracted to a man— if you're out on the street or on a bus—I want you to open the bottle and sniff the contents. You need to be reminded where homosexual men stick their penis. You need to be reminded that homosexual relations are not pleasurable."

Listening to Alfonzo, I was free falling into space, falling backward from the top of the stairs, trusting he would catch me.

If the film container did anything, it reminded me of how often I still thought of men. Whereas before I had always unconsciously noticed a man on the street or the bus, now I had a means of counting every last one that caught my eye: I'd reach into my shoulder pack, pull out the container, my firearm, discreetly hold it up under my nose, open it and take a deep, powerful whiff, like I was back snorting poppers in a bathhouse. Only this time its perverse stench was a bullet to my soul, silencing, but not killing, me.

One night after sniffing the container three or four times on a bus, I caught the evening's front-page headlines: *Persian Gulf War: One Man's Story of Torment*. Yes, I understood. Alfonzo was my commanding officer, and I, his enlistee, had been sent to wage the war of my life, the war within. Desperate times required desperate measures. Or so I told myself.

Some weeks later, he asked me again how I was feeling.

"There's no change," I told him.

"You're still sniffing the vial?"

"Yes. And I'm still attracted to men. Only now I smell shit all the time. It's confusing me."

"Well, then . . . ordinarily I don't like gimmicks, but we may need to begin hooking your genitals up to electrodes. We may need to help retrain your penis."

14

IN EARLY 1992, YVETTE called us down to the office for an "urgent family meeting." In the past, meetings of this nature had typically meant that one of us wasn't pulling our weight with chores or that Alfonzo had a new idea for a family-run business that would allow us the freedom to withdraw entirely from the "outside" world while earning enough money to continue with our therapy in the Styx. No one knew just what to expect this time.

Once seated in the workroom, Alfonzo explained that he had just received a letter from Kirsten, an ex-patient from Styx 2, and that he wanted to read it to his "spiritual family." Together, he said, we would decide on our next course of action.

The letter began with Kirsten apologizing for her precipitous departure from her house and treatment, but that she'd been wrestling for some time about whether or not to stay in the therapy. The tone of her letter shifted when she described her conflicted feelings toward Alfonzo, the way he'd been injecting her with ketamine for well over a year but telling her never to discuss the drug with her housemates, since none of them were considered "lifers"—they weren't receiving injections and did not know about its use. This "culture of secrecy," she wrote, was "deeply troubling" to her, as she felt it just "reinforced the dysfunctional, compartmentalized patterns" from her childhood.

She considered Alfonzo's use of ketamine to be without informed consent, since by the time patients were told about it they were already "vulnerable, childlike, in a bonded state of mind, had given up their entire lives, associates, spouses, families, children, and were already deeply invested in the therapy." She wrote that if Alfonzo did not tell her ex-housemates about his use of ketamine within a matter of weeks, she would tell them herself. She would also have to consider what to do about the fact that other healthcare professionals continued to refer new patients to him for treatment. She might need to report him to the College of Physicians and Surgeons, the governing body of all registered and licensed physicians in the province of British Columbia.

After Alfonzo read us the letter, no one said a word. There, in black and white, were all the words that we could not admit to ourselves, let alone write down. Kirsten had said what we could not even allow ourselves to think.

Finally, Alfonzo turned to Yvette. "We need to draft a letter of informed consent. Everyone needs to sign it." He scanned all of our faces, one by one. *"Got it?"*

Two weeks later, the morning of the day he and Yvette were leaving for vacation at Club Med, we were called back to the office for "a follow-up meeting." Once seated, with Alfonzo in his squat chair as usual, Yvette handed all of us a form titled "Informed Consent for the Utilization of Ketamine Hydrochloride."

"You need to sign it and pre-date it from before your first medicated session," he said. "Ask Yvette if you don't remember the date, she'll look it up."

I read through the form. One phrase in particular caught my attention; it stated that I had "prior knowledge of the drug." Because this was not true, at least not for me, before signing the form I penciled in a clause. *Dr. Alfonzo did not tell me about this drug before injecting me the first time during a weekend therapeutic marathon.*

I handed it back to Alfonzo.

"What's this?" he said, staring down at my handwritten note.

"I just added a statement about not having prior knowledge before—"

"You just—*what*?" You think I can use this now? I can't use this once you've scribbled on it." He ripped up the form and threw it on the floor. "Yvette!" he called. Yvette! Give Peter another form. *Vite!*"

Alfonzo charged out of the workroom as Yvette rushed over.

"What are you doing, "Peter?" she said in a hushed tone. "You know we're trying to get away on vacation."

Alfonzo reappeared from his office.

"I don't have time for this bullshit, Peter. Shut up and sign the form. *Or else.*"

I did as instructed.

||||||||||

A letter from the College of Physicians and Surgeons was waiting for Alfonzo at his office upon his return from vacation at Club Med, several weeks later.

In sum, the letter stated that Yuen's husband claimed that his wife had moved into a residential facility in 1990 following what was supposed to be a three-week therapeutic intensive overseen by Alfonzo; that she had refused to return home and was now working for the doctor without pay; and that the therapy as a whole was "a cult." The College cited Alfonzo's inappropriate involvement with his patient as "a boundary violation" and told him to terminate the relationship immediately. They requested a letter from Alfonzo, confirming he would follow the board's direction within three weeks.

Alfonzo was infuriated. He despised having to deal with "the outside world," and was angry at Yuen for not taking care of her "other world business"—divorcing her husband before committing herself to the therapy—and for forcing him to get involved with that world. The week after receiving the letter, he recruited Yuen to help him write his response to the College. Every day, after the office had closed for regular business, they reviewed her medical files and listened to all her primal sessions on reel-to-reel recordings. Yuen had "severe borderline personality disorder," he wrote back to the College; she had attempted suicide twice before being referred to him for psychiatric intervention, and in an effort to help improve her low self-esteem, his secretary (Yvette) had asked Yuen to "help her out" around the office, which had nothing to do with him. Still, he agreed to discontinue the relationship.

The entire situation—the letter from her former husband, as well as the response she was now helping Alfonzo write to the College—humiliated Yuen. Following every one of her "writing sessions" with Alfonzo in the office, she lay on the workroom mattress and worked at the batting station to, as Alfonzo so often instructed, "take it all back historically." Any anger Yuen felt over having to help write his response to the College, he told her, had everything to do with her father, and nothing to do with him.

The day after mailing his response to the College, Alfonzo told Yuen to start work in the office early enough in the day, or else arrive late at night when the other psychiatrist who shared office space was absent. Two weeks later, Yuen asked Alfonzo to be paid for her "services." He said that she was acting out her historical anger toward her father and refused her request. Soon after, Yuen called her own house meeting at the office. She even asked that Alfonzo attend.

"I've decided to move out of the Styx," she said, once we were all in a circle on the workroom floor. "I want to get my own apartment, try living on my own. I wanted to tell you all together, as a family."

Yuen seemed genuinely excited by her news, but a hushed silence fell over the group.

"What are you going on about?" Alfonzo responded, squinting his eyes and shaking his head, as if something inside had come loose.

"I just thought—" Yuen began.

"You just thought—*what*? Is this what you wanted to meet about? You want to move out? You want . . . you *want*. If all of us did as we want, nothing would get done around here."

Claude spoke up. Though no one discussed the fact, we all knew they'd been sleeping together for years. "If Yuen wants to live on her own I don't think we should stop her," he said.

"Oh we shouldn't, should we?" Alfonzo said. "What do you know? You're a drunk and a wife beater, and if it weren't for my therapy and this house, you'd be lying in the gutter somewhere, clutching a bottle of wine, drinking yourself into oblivion—that's where you'd be."

Alfonzo turned to Yuen. "And you, you'd be in that dead-end marriage of yours—no, you'd probably be dead if it weren't for this therapy. Do I need to remind you where you were when you came to see me the first time?"

"No . . ." Yuen said, her oval eyes hidden beneath the glare of her frameless glasses.

"Out of the hospital for weeks, that's where you were. How many suicide attempts?"

Yuen said nothing, but began to cry, softly.

"Paranoid and thinking that your husband was trying to kill you. I saved your life. *I saved all your fucking lives.*"

Sitting around a circle, I prayed Alfonzo would not include me in his review of failing lives: sex in public toilets, sleeping all day because I'd feared being awake. He would have plenty to say about my life, I knew.

"This is no time for any of you," he continued, scanning our faces like a floodlight, "for *any* of you to be moving back out into the world. I'm just about to begin writing my life story, I've discussed this with Yvette, and we will need all of your help. All. We need to focus our energies on the office, and my book. Especially the book. That's where your priorities lie right now: on the book. You think the world gives a shit about any of your little lives? This book is God's will, and it *will* be written."

"But . . ." Yuen started to say. We all turned to her. "I still want to move out."

"Yes," Alfonzo said. "And I want to retire, move back to Spain, and sit in the sun all day and drink margaritas. Now shut up and go home."

Back at the Styx, I passed by Clay's room before bed. "Can we talk?" I said.

"What's up?"

I entered his room and sat on the floor. In all the years I'd lived with Clay, he had never purchased a bed but slept on a one-inch foamy that he rolled up each morning and tied with a string, like a map. "Do you still want to kill your father?" I asked.

"If my father walked in here off the street today I *would* kill him."

"How long have you been in this therapy?"

"Ten years, not counting an eight-month break when Alfonzo closed his practice back and east before moving out west."

"Don't you ever think about leaving?"

"Where would I go?"

"Into the world."

"I've been in the world, Peter. It's crazy out there."

"Don't you want to fall in love one day? Get married? Have children? Even just have sex?"

"Of course I miss the sex, but I got a vasectomy years ago. I'll never have children."

"Why not?"

"Because I'd massacre them. I'd do to them what my father did to me."

"How do you know that?"

He smiled. "Listen, Peter, there's nothing that I want to do for the rest of my life but this therapy. Nothing. Primalling on the mattress, batting at the batting station, cuddling with Mommy. My life now is about healing the damage that was done to me. My chronic fatigue is a symptom of what my father did to my insides. The only thing that'll heal me are my Mommy sessions. Mommy's love is all I need now."

Downstairs, I found Yuen sitting alone, cross-legged, staring into a fire. I joined her on the carpeted floor. Though it was only eight o-clock, Yuen had already changed into her red silk Chinese pajamas, as if sleep could not come soon enough.

"Do you think anyone ends up living the life they imagined?" she asked, not turning away from the flames.

"I think it took courage to do what you did."

"What did I do?"

"Telling him you want to leave. That must have been really hard for you. Speaking up like that."

Yuen had never spoken up, not to Alfonzo, not to her ex-husband, definitely never to her parents. All her primal sessions that I'd witnessed had focused on one issue alone: overcoming the cultural taboos, as a Chinese female growing up in Jamaica, that had silenced her emotionally. Tonight, she had stepped up to the plate, and in one fell swoop, Alfonzo had shot her back down. There was something sadly ironic in the fact that he was the one person who had encouraged her assertiveness during therapy.

"I was sitting here thinking about the night my parents drove me home from the hospital. The third time they drove me home. The whole ride, my eyes were fixed on my mother's head in the front seat, at her long black hair, squeezed in a bun. She never moved, not once. She never even looked at my father, who was driving. Both of them: silent. Silence like if you close your eyes you'll disappear. Even after, at the house, no one talked about it. Asked me, anything. How I felt, why I did it. It was like it had never even happened. But in the car, the whole way home, all I kept thinking was *Next time I'll get it right. Next time I'll make sure I get it right.*"

Yuen hugged her bent knees up toward her belly. When she sniffled, I knew that she'd been crying, although I couldn't see her face, all wet and swollen like a baby's, no doubt, hidden beneath her long silken hair that was draped around her like a curtain.

I scanned our living room. A cable-reel table, reclaimed from an abandoned sugar-factory warehouse that we'd used as a coffee table for years. A green plaid sofa and a broken orange winged-back chair purchased secondhand at Value Village. Chalk-white walls, blank as the day we'd moved in. Recessed bookshelves without a single book. For a time, I'd filled the bookshelves in our first house with hundreds of my books of poetry and plays that I'd lugged around for years. Then, for some reason, I repacked them all up in boxes and shoved them in the attic. I don't know why. Maybe because by then I knew they weren't an anchor. At least not the kind I needed.

"When I was a child," Yuen continued, still staring into the fire, "I remember that I wanted to say and do so many things, but no one ever validated me for who I was and what I wanted to do. On the contrary: they *in*validated me and told me I'd amount to nothing. And so . . . I just stopped doing . . . everything. I have felt hopelessness and despair my whole life simply because I had no validation for who I was and what I wanted to do. For who I was."

I lay back on the orange shag carpet as heat from the fire pulled me toward sleep.

The next time Yuen spoke, minutes or an hour later, her voice snapped me back inside my body.

"I think we're all born for greatness," she said, the embers still reflecting off her hair, "but I think it needs to be kindled, inside us. Because if it's not, it just dies within us and we become something else."

||||||||||

In the months following my collapse, a ribbon of imagery spooled out of me faster than I could write it all down. During this entire time I wrote poetry, or sometimes it seemed like poetry was writing me, each line surging forth fully formed and with such velocity that it was all I could do to write them down before another charged forth, all of them, some 220 in total, like voices demanding to be heard and documented. If my collapse had felt like I'd fallen down and through my self, language held me up, one poem at a time.

> *I did not know, as a child, that even innocence was, for some, a meal.*

Or:
> *The grief the son feels when the mother wills to live, but feels despair, and takes him in her arms to keep herself sane.*

Or:
> *Even hails of prayer will not break silence when I, myself, inside, am still so loud.*

Or:
> *Revenge is a knife and there have been, already, far too many stabbings.*

Or:
> *I am, in the hands of the Sculptress, amazed.*

Often I brought all my week's poems to my sessions with Alice, eager for her thoughts and validation. Poem after poem, I read them all to Alice; poem after poem, she told me just how talented her boy was at creating images with words.

"You have a gift from God," she told me, "and once you work through your pain and confusion, that gift will shine through and help to heal."

I'd hang on to her every word, asking question after question, just as young children do with their mothers. And as soon as she answered my questions, a wave of relief would wash over me, and I would dive back into her lap, where she'd match her breathing to mine.

On K, I felt our bodies dissolving into one. I imagined us playing building blocks, and together we'd knock over all my little plastic soldiers. We'd walk to the park, and she'd push me on the swings. Later, we'd come back to the house to make dinner, and when Papa came home, he'd grab hold of me and toss me high up in the air, and I'd giggle and give him a great big bear hug, and when he laughed, I'd feel his belly jiggle. After dinner, I'd be bathed because I was still a "grubby-buggy" from the park, and there would be stories in bed as I twirled my fingers through my mommy's hair, then drift off to sleep, peacefully, as children should, without the slightest worry.

Sometimes Alice and I talked about going to the "big chair" where toddler Peter would lie with Mommy after his nap. Predictably, my biological mother appeared in the form of a giant scorpion, baring her teeth and snapping her claws, as if to want to eat me whole. Alice would talk to her, tell her to go away, that this was no longer about her, that she and I wanted time together to feel safe and loving and good. My mother would disappear for a spell, then after a while return again, lie on top of me, and press down into me. Alice suggested I feel her back and arms—to check that it was she and not my mother who was holding on to me.

Alice described our surroundings, reminded me that I was not in my old bedroom with my mother, perhaps sang a bit, then rubbed my back. I looked at her—this woman who was not my mother, but who I believed loved me as I knew my mother should have all along—and I felt such tenderness and comfort.

Some sessions were completely nonverbal, with Alice telling me to just be in the "mommy space," as we lay belly to belly while she sang me lullabies and rocked me in her arms until I'd fall to sleep. The emotional space we'd created was different and distinct from anything I'd ever known before. Sometimes I'd feel someone sucking my penis—sensory hallucinations brought on by K—and Alice would come to the rescue, telling the men to go away.

"We are strong and good people," she said to one of the men, "and together we can take on anything. You don't scare us, you don't have a chance, so bugger off!"

"I'm your one lung," I told her, all snuggled and warm in her arms, because at times I felt myself merging with her, even breathing for her. But Alice told me she had two lungs, that I had two lungs, that I could rest against her and let her carry me, but that our boundaries were clear and strong and that we were two separate people.

Near the end of my session, after I had surfaced from K, Alice took me in her arms and began to cry.

"Why are you crying?" I asked.

"I have something to tell you," she said, taking a deep breath. "I'm going to be leaving the therapy. My husband and I are moving away by the middle of next year. He got a job back east in Toronto, so . . . you know how much I love you."

For a moment I looked at her, as a child might when news of his mother's departure seems baffling. "That's okay," I said.

"And that I'll always love you . . ."

"I know, me too. I was scared when you told me, but only for a second. I know that distance won't change the love we feel for each other."

"Oh my boy," she said, clutching me tighter in her arms. "Do you know how proud I am of you, how far you've come since I first met you? You wouldn't even let me hold you, and now look at you. All soft and cuddly and loveable in my arms."

"Can I ask you one question?"

"You can ask me two."

"It's about my writing. What should I do with it?"

Without another word, Alice understood my meaning. "I think your writing is still a wounded passion. And when you're more healed, it will naturally find expression, and it will become powerful and positive. First heal thyself. Your writing will take care of itself."

"Funny. That's what Dr. Alfonzo said about my sexuality when I first came to see him."

We laughed; then we continued talking for the remainder of the session, at times cuddling, our bodies finding each other, all familiar and entwined, like branches from one tree that knows itself. She was Mama,

I told her, not Mommy or Mom, just Mama, and I knew that I would miss her but that I'd carry the love she'd given me around inside me.

"I keep thinking of a time with my mother," I said. "Can I tell you?"

"You can tell me anything."

"We were at the beach, all of us, my whole family, playing in the sand. Dad was throwing us up in the air, and we were swimming in the ocean like baby seals. Then we were all playing hide-and-go-seek. We were playing, and I was happy and free, and I ran away from the others and into a patch of forest. Something large and textured, like a piñata, crashed into the side of my head, and a swarm of bees exploded into me, my ears, eyes, nose. I started screaming, crying, flailing my arms. The next thing I knew someone wrapped their arms around me and pulled me into a clearing. I opened my eyes, and I saw her face. My mother. She kissed me on my cheeks, and she wiped away my tears, like you do during our sessions. She told me, like you tell me sometimes, she told me to lie quiet because Mommy was there, that now I was safe and sound."

When I looked up from my story I saw that Alice's eyes were moist with tears.

"How could she have loved me like that, and yet I felt so violated by her? It doesn't make sense."

"You mother was a hurt little girl, she was hurt in the concentration camp and God knows where else, and sometimes that hurt spilled out and onto you. It shouldn't have happened, I'm sure she never stopped loving you when it did happen, she probably didn't even know it was happening, but it happened."

Afterward, Alfonzo came into the room and saw us there, in bliss. I told him that I'd just felt real mommy love for the first time in my life, and that it felt like what I'd imagined great sex would feel like when the energy was open and loving and honest and safe.

"The old introject of your mother is vanishing," he said. "The crazy period is over. I'm sure you'll continue working your primals, but the madness and chaos are spent."

Instinctively, I knew not to divulge my continued interest in men. I was "noticing women," I said. To which Alfonzo reaffirmed that all my hard work and perseverance were truly garnering a reward.

15

ALFONZO MUST HAVE TOLD Claude he wanted the Styx closer to the office, "more accessible," because Claude arrived home one day and told us we were moving again.

And so in the summer of 1992 we packed up our meager belongings, mostly used and reclaimed furnishing, and moved from our barn in the 'burbs to a 1930s Victorian cottage on a shady, oak-lined street near the downtown core, and Alfonzo's office and home. The house, as I discovered while bicycling to the office early the day after we moved in, was also around the corner from a large city park where, in the midst of a cluster of trees, men were known to cruise for sex.

Yvette called late one night the same week. Alfonzo had gone into a primal, she told Claude. He wanted all of us, "his soul family," in the office workroom. "Pronto."

Everyone at the Styx knew that Alfonzo had been continuing with his primals, as well as his K-enhanced nurturing sessions with Alice. We knew, but did not discuss it.

"He's nearing the big one," Yvette had told us all, privately, several times, then left it at that.

Anxious at the opportunity to witness our master working his primal pain, we jumped in Claude's car and rushed to the office.

We sat in a circle on the floor of the workroom, as we did for all our groups, and waited in stony silence for close to an hour. Then the door to Alfonzo's private office creaked opened. Yvette entered and, without a word, sat next to us on the floor. Seconds later Alfonzo stumbled in: groggy, disoriented, pupils dilated. He dropped to his knees on the mattress at one end of our circle.

"I wanted my family around me tonight," he said with a slur, looking at each of us through watery eyes. "The only family I know . . . my brothers and sisters: I have no one else . . . no one . . ."

He raised his arms to his side, like a cross, and turned his palms, and face, up toward the ceiling. "The world has become a maze of insanity since the last time I was alive. And my book, what humanity named the Bible . . . it has been misinterpreted by all. Distorted by everyone to serve their own agendas."

I glanced quickly at the others. Everyone's eyes were fixed reverently on our leader.

"The end of the world is upon us. This is the world's last chance . . . the world's last chance to hear my message. Don't they know who I am? They crucified me the last time I was here. I am . . . I am . . . the Christ."

His arms dropped to his sides, his chin fell forward. Only then did I notice he'd been crying. Or else maybe tearing from a shot of K. Yvette stood, helped him to his feet, then back into his private office and behind closed doors. Transfixed by what we'd witnessed, as if we had slipped through time's corridor and glimpsed a sacred secret, no one moved. Were we to leave? Was there more? Should we wait?

Minutes later, the door creaked back open and Yvette reappeared. I heard Alfonzo mumbling, softly, in French. "You need to go home now," she told us. "He needs his rest."

One by one, we filed out of the office and back into the car. All the way home: no one spoke of what we had seen. Back at the Styx, preparing for bed and in the morning: not one word passed between us. It wasn't until that night that I spoke with Clay in our dining room, a dark wooded chamber with a beamed ceiling and built-in leaded cabinets.

"I'm almost scared to talk about what happened," I said, "to say it aloud."

"Go ahead," Clay said.

"Alfonzo . . . he's . . . Christ. Isn't he?"

I heard my own words, which frightened me, but I believed them absolutely. After two years in the Styx, sequestered from all former friends and family, the outside world in general, without television or radio, newspapers, books, medicated to the hills with major psychotropics and regressed to a near-childlike state of submission, there were caves in my mind inside which everything, whether true or false, seemed real.

Clay took a deep breath.

"We've been chosen, Peter. You think it's a coincidence we're all in this house together? It's no coincidence. We've been chosen to do the work of God. We're his followers. We're his Apostles."

The truth of what we'd spoken silenced me. Alfonzo was Christ, or he was a reincarnation of Christ, or a Christlike figure. He was to be followed, and obeyed. And we, his Apostles, "the chosen ones," had been graced by his presence. That Yvette had been promiscuous could have also only meant one thing: She was Mary Magdalene.

The following day I was back in the office with Alfonzo for a nurturing session, which began like all the rest: I rolled up my sleeve. Alfonzo injected me with K. He sat in the corner and waited for me as I lay on my back and breathed the drug into my system, and only then did I crawl over to him, across the room as if through a swamp, and nestle my body in his lap. After a spell, I managed to pry open the steel doors of my eyes, peer up at his wild brows, and his dark, muddy eyes, staring down at me.

"Papa . . . you're Christ. You're Christ . . . aren't you, Papa?"

He rubbed my head, affectionately, and smiled.

Before the doors of my eyes slammed shut again and everything went black, as they did each and every time Alfonzo injected me with K, I recalled thinking that his silence meant that I was right.

||||||||||

Alfonzo's dream of purchasing a retirement home, where we could all live communally, grow our own vegetables and continue our therapeutic process undisturbed, came true in 1992 when he found an enormous, two-story log house on a remote wooded property. The house required substantial renovations prior to Alfonzo's and Yvette's move from the city, so every weekend Styx members piled into Claude's Plymouth, traveled to the house, pitched tents on the lawn, then hammered, sanded, and painted for days.

"You can break now for a bowl of soup," Yvette would call out, middays, "but then it's back to work!"

Alfonzo knew all about my past writing, so he asked me to help him write his life story. He imagined the book, which everyone at the Styx soon referred to as "the Bible," would serve as a manual for psychotherapists, while documenting his life's journey with primal therapy and the evolution of his present-day reparenting sessions with surrogate mothers.

"Of course I'll pay you for your time," he told me after one of my medicated nurturing sessions, "for any work you do on my behalf."

I had barely recovered from the dissociative effects of the ketamine when he said the words. The prospect of such an intellectually demanding undertaking as to work with him on a book intimidated me, but Alfonzo was in charge.

Yvette handed over the keys to Hampstead, where I began reading, or squinting through blurred vision in a strained attempt to read, hundreds of ex-patient files, all stored in his garage. My goal, he'd explained, was to locate patient reports that dealt with surrogacy and the use of ketamine, and then bring them back to him for his own perusal.

I was in his garage, scanning one of his personal journals written in the 1960s while he was under Janov's care in Los Angeles, when a small, black-and-white, passport-type photo fell out and landed in my lap. It was of Alfonzo as a young man, before he'd grown his goatee. There was something eerily familiar about the photo, a darkness in his eyes that I recognized. Then it hit me: I looked remarkably like him when he was my age. The photograph could have been of me.

For weeks, in between only his most pressing patient sessions at the office, Alfonzo barricaded himself inside his Westfalia Camper, parked facing out to sea, and then handed me a draft of his "private recollections" and asked that I streamline the facts of his life into a cogent narrative. He was, as he'd told me, "recovering memories and remembering the sequence of events" of his life, but when I read his drafts, his thoughts were confused, confusing, and nonsequential. They demanded the acuity of a highly cogent, medication-free mind to sort out and reconfigure, and I simply couldn't understand what he had given me. And, secretly, I did not understand how Alfonzo could not have known that I didn't have the ability to comprehend what he had given me.

One day he passed me a handwritten note with his draft. *God bless you, brother, for helping me to retrace my steps*, it read. *I know He is pulling hard to see this work done. So be it. There are many ways to score sanity points and sometimes it involves the apparent relinquishment of our own progress to help others.*

I could only take his note to mean that helping him with his book, at the expense of my own therapy, would make me "saner," in effect, "correct" my "loveless mind." Or at least that's how he'd always interpreted *A Course in Miracles*.

We started meeting at Hampstead. For hours, I listened and tried to follow as he explained what he referred to as "the three levels of error" to the human mind: the biographical and the cultural errors, correctable only through psychotherapy; and the transcendental error, correctable only through the love of God. Like a father to a son, he told me more about his childhood, living under the dictatorship of Franco, his marriage and his son, his early years with primal, his years of self-medication, and his "dark night of the soul."

"In all of recorded history," he explained during one of our meetings, "only the mystics have had the same type of experience as what I went through. Like St. John of the Cross. Only his dark night was self-induced as a means of reaching spiritual enlightenment, whereas mine was a reaction to ongoing primal regressions. It's hard to return to the world of man and play doctor after you've felt the love of God."

He stopped talking, like he'd forgotten his thought mid-sentence, lowered himself to the floor, crab-like, and looked beneath the round coffee table.

"Where's Fred?"

"What?"

"The cat," he said, jolting upright. "Where's Fred? He was just here. Yvette!" he called out, "*Où est Fred?*"

"*Il est avec moi,*" she answered from the kitchen. "Don't worry."

Alfonzo sighed in relief.

"Where was I?"

"You felt the love of God."

"Right. For a person, any person, to feel lovable, totally and absolutely lovable, they have to have their lovability mirrored back with perfection. Only God knows how to do that. Only God is perfect. Only God can mirror back your intrinsic lovability. Nothing but the love of God can repair the transcendental error, the first, perhaps only real error of the human mind: the illusion of separation. Everything else pales in comparison. And you either make that connection yourself, *like I did*, or you work with someone else who's made it for you."

He looked to make sure I was listening.

"I'm your ladder to the love of God, Peter."

His final words made me uneasy. I turned away.

"You'd be dead today if it hadn't been for me. Now it's your time to help *me*. I need you. Just like you need me. This family is not going to survive unless we all pitch in and help each other. This is your time to repay me. And while we're on the topic . . . I've been thinking about our little arrangement."

"Our arrangement?"

"When I said I'd pay you for helping me write my book. I've decided against it."

"Oh."

"It would not be right. You're learning from me, gaining experience as a writer, listening to me share my life. Why should I pay you for that?"

||||||||||

A short time later, Alfonzo announced to all his patients that he had decided to close the three Styx houses.

Members of my house were then called to Hampstead for a private house meeting. Alfonzo confided that after the recent complaint from Yuen's husband, as well as Kirsten's earlier threatening letter, he was concerned the College of Physicians and Surgeons might become aware of one of his twenty-plus patients living "in residence," or the many more that continued rotating through the houses as intensives. He didn't want to draw undue attention to his therapy. While patients from Styx 2 and 3 would disband and go their separate ways, he told the five of us that we would continue living together because we were "family." Longer-term patients, who had known and visited our Styx for years, saw us as "spiritually advanced souls," or "lifers," so they would also continue to visit for dinners and evening meditation at a cost of seven dollars, or weekend retreats at a cost of fifty dollars.

"However," he said, "I want to be very clear about this. Your living together does not mean that I am involved in this house. I am not involved in your house. It is your choice to live in the Styx. *Got it*?"

Though Alfonzo considered himself no longer involved in the Styx, our involvement in Alfonzo's personal and professional life increased to that of a full-time job without the pay. In addition to the ongoing renovations to Alfonzo's new house, Claude and Clay helped run group sessions in the city, especially during the doctor's increased absences. While we all took turns cooking his meals, labeling all the ingredients on each Tupperware container, I was the only one to bake the fat-free cheesecakes, varying the ingredients, as directed by Alfonzo.

"Try freshly squeezed lemon juice instead of lemon extract," he reported back to me on the phone one night after tasting my latest cake. "And cut back on the dates, the crust is too rich. By the way, the stroganoff you made was delicious, but the meat was tough. You'd better watch that next time."

Since the Styx "family car" belonged to Claude, he was responsible for delivering food to Alfonzo. The rest of us took turns raking his lawn during the spring and shoveling the snow during the winter, taking out the garbage, washing dishes, and cleaning the office and bathrooms. Nightly, I edited, or tried to edit, drafts of Alfonzo's book. And Fred, his Siamese Persian cat, became our full-time responsibility while he and Yvette vacationed, every six months, at Club Med.

||||||||||

"Where are we going?" I asked the others as we loaded into Claude's car.

"We're going to look at a dog," Clay said.

The four of us—Clay, Claude, Sebastian, and I—drove for over an hour until we reached an old, shabby country farm on one side of a dirt road. We weren't just going to *see* a dog, I'd been told in the car.

We were going to *steal* a dog, or at least scout out the dog's property and mastermind a plan to steal it. Alfonzo had discovered the half-wolf animal "by accident" and decided he wanted it as his own. The dog's owners were neglecting it, he'd told Claude. We'd be doing the animal a favor by bringing it back to Alfonzo in the city.

Even from across the gravel road I could see that the animal was emaciated, its mane dull and patchy. But that didn't stop it from jumping up against the barbed-wire fence, barking and snapping its fanged teeth as we stood at a distance.

"We'll have to come up with a plan," Claude said as we climbed back in the car and returned to the city. Part of that plan meant not involving me in the final capture—I was too drugged, too confused by details, of no great help. But later the next day Sebastian did show me their black ski masks, wire cutters, and a large steak to be soaked overnight in a sedative provided by Alfonzo.

The next time I saw the dog, while cleaning Hampstead two weeks later, he was caged inside a new, enormous, fenced-in kennel that Alfonzo had built in his spacious backyard. Alfonzo also wasted no time injecting the animal with ketamine and administering a nurturing session to expedite their bonding process. I could easily imagine the session, because at one time or another we had all been like that animal—drugged and lying in the arms of Alfonzo, its new owner.

|||||||||

At some point Alfonzo told me that I needed a "passport." Maybe we were in his office, after a primal; maybe we were at Hampstead, editing his book. I know we had the conversation, because I asked him what he meant by a "passport."

"Some way of earning a living in the outside world," he said. "You don't want to live off of Social Assistance forever, do you?"

And then he said something about my need to find steady employment, move back out into the world, earn a proper wage, and think about my future, all of which left me reeling. Primal had plunged me backward into childhood, trauma. I was much too "young" to work, too medicated even to think.

Through my anesthetized stupor, however, I did manage to find my first job since my collapse, nearly eleven months before. Each mid-afternoon I bussed to my job as a cook in a busy, uptown restaurant, armored with pills, and there was Candy—a tall, slinky, unsmiling waitress with a black bob, like a crusty Kit Kat girl from *Cabaret.* While Candy waited tables, glancing back at me through a painted-on face that looked like it had covered up her own, I worked the line in the pit with the blood from the beef on my whites and a mist on my mind that could no longer think, that could no longer reason, could no longer follow the breadcrumbs of conversations and orders down the paths of their meanings. Some nights all I could do was hide inside the bathroom at the back of the kitchen, door latched, crying, staring in the mirror, emotionally still back on the mattress, talking baby talk.

Only weeks after I started, the head chef took me aside and said calmly: "This isn't going to work, Peter."

He fired me. My relief was so instantaneous that, without stopping to think or consider, I told him, blurted out of context, all about the meds, the antidepressants and antipsychotics, the therapy and the primals, the Styx, and the doctor. He said nothing, stared at me, mouth agape.

"Well . . . perhaps it is best you not be working right now. At least not here."

Luckily, the home-care agency that hired me next said that all of my elderly clients suffered from some sort of dementia, which also meant, to my relief, that none of them noticed my own short-term memory loss brought on by the medications. Mostly I cooked meals and cleaned homes, bathed my male clients, and reminded all of them to take their medications as I took my own, furtively, and then sat with them, often well past my shift, as they talked about their lives and their children, many of whom had abandoned them in their old age. It was January 1993, when, as I watered plants during one of my shifts, Bill Clinton, the forty-second president of the United States, delivered his inaugural speech on a TV in the background:

> Today, a generation raised in the shadows of the Cold War assumes new responsibilities in a world warmed by the sunshine of freedom but threatened still by ancient hatreds and new plagues.

||||||||||

The pain, radiating from the middle of my lower back down my left leg and into my big toe, had started months before. I'd even seen a chiropractor several times, who'd "snapped" me back in place and sent me on my way. But as I was moving a male client in and out of his bathtub one day in late summer 1993, the streaking pain intensified, as if I'd been knocked from behind with a sledgehammer. I made my way back to the Styx, and by the next morning, I could not stand. I could barely breathe.

The final diagnoses, once I'd been driven to a doctor and completed a battery of tests, was a ruptured disc at L-5—a "slipped disc," as it was more commonly called. As with my breakdown at the Styx, I never returned to my homecare clients. All therapy, even visits to the office, came to an abrupt halt. Clay brought me all my prescriptions. My new physician placed me back on medical disability, the same as what Alfonzo had placed me on after my breakdown, totaling, once again, barely enough to cover rent and food. I could not stand and crawled from room to room; ate all my meals from the floor; only stood, half bent like a sideways "U," when I had to move to my bed, get dressed, use the bathroom. For the most part, I lay on the floor in the living room of the Styx, my feet elevated on a bolster. I slept. The pinched nerve, as well as the sciatica that moved in waves of excruciating pain from leg to leg, required yet more medication, anti-inflammatories, and painkillers, this time prescribed by my physician.

After six months of convalescence, slowly, I began rehabilitation, mostly swimming at the local pool. I walked with a cane, not yet even able to stand upright. Walking, however, was good. This time I walked by myself, around the block and home, clutching my cane, hunched like an old man. Sometimes I thought about my friend Pearl, because we'd loved the poet Anne Sexton, and I could still remember the line from one of her poems: *I am standing upright but my shadow is crooked.*

||||||||||

In early 1994, we received news that Ludo, the architect whose house we'd stayed in during a weekend marathon two-and-a-half years earlier, was dead. According to Clay, Ludo had bought a gun, waited until his wife and two small children, a boy and a girl, were out of the house, and shot himself in the head. We were all in shock.

I thought of how Ludo had welcomed us into his home, high above the city. The thought that he was now dead, dead because he had chosen to not live, left me with a sullen emptiness.

The next day I waited in Alfonzo's private office as he filled my prescription. Though I'd not yet returned to active therapy, I had returned to see him for periodic "check-in" sessions at the office, and, of course, to pick up my prescriptions.

"I heard about Ludo," I said.

Alfonzo said nothing, but continued to write.

"Do you feel sad about his death?" I asked.

Alfonzo turned to me. "Why would I feel sad?"

"Well . . . he's dead."

"So?"

"He killed himself."

He stared at me.

"You don't feel responsible?" I asked.

"Why would I feel responsible?"

"Well . . . for his therapy. He was obviously in despair. That had to have at least contributed to his death."

"Ludo killed himself, and that was his decision."

He turned back to his desk and continued writing my prescription. "In fact," he said, "I think that what he did took courage."

Courage? Alfonzo's aloofness, his lack of caring, frightened me. For years I'd fought to stay alive, to not succumb to my own despair. How could ending one's life take courage? Choosing to live seemed to me far more courageous, if for no other reason than to risk the certainty of pain for the possibility of love.

"I'm placing you on a therapeutic holiday."

"A—what?"

"You'll still live in the Styx and receive medicated nurturing sessions in the office, but as of today, I'm suspending your primals indefinitely."

"But . . . why?"

"I told you this before. You need to move back out into the world, focus on your future, figure out what you want to do with your life. You need to regain your strength. Then we'll start you on 'round two.' You're not going anywhere, Peter. You'll be doing this therapy for the rest of your life, in one way or another. You need to pace yourself."

There was no discussion: a decision had been made.

Consequently, as my medication dosages were lowered, my thoughts became more lucid and independent. A veil was being lifted from my brain. One day in spring 1994 I was out alone on the street when I noticed a man walking toward me. From twenty feet away our eyes locked. His were blue and bright, contrasting against my own, which I was sure looked dull and drugged. His lips were full and moist. I noticed his one-day's stubble; tufts of chest hair reaching out near the top of his unbuttoned Polo shirt. When he brushed past me, the touch of his shirtsleeve and the musky odor of his cologne sent currents of excitement through the grave of my body and lingered like a ripple of sensuality long after he had disappeared around the corner.

That night I caught the reflection of my naked body in my bedroom mirror. I had always avoided looking at myself this way, but that night I did not. I stood and stared at a sad reflection of my former self—at my body, pale and bloated from years of overmedication, and into my twenty-eight-year-old eyes: dark, sunken, unhappy. There was no heterosexual in me waiting to emerge; there was not even a homosexual from which I could escape. There was just me, my body: now more like a shell with its innards scooped out.

When I asked a stranger, several days later on the street, for a cigarette, I knew I'd turned a corner. As the fog in my mind cleared, desires in my body intensified. I spent longer hours away from the Styx: in bookstores, searching out gay literature; in coffee shops, writing in my journal, documenting specific conversations I'd had with Alfonzo, Alice, and various members of the therapy and at the Styx.

By late 1994, nearly five years had passed since the day Alfonzo compared my homosexuality to a chocolate addiction and said that the sex must be given up if I was to get anywhere in his therapy. While walking home one night from Alfonzo's office, where I'd been working on his book, I didn't go home and instead chose a path leading deep within the wooded city park and back into the world I'd denied.

Out of the shadows the figure of a man appeared.

"My name's Bill," he said, extending his hand.

"John," I said, extending mine.

And then the two of us, as if on cue, stepped off the path and into a clump of trees. Without another word, we started kissing. He was carrying a bottle in a brown paper bag, and the taste of his breath, cigarettes and liquor, mixed with the smell of his body, dried sweat and urine, reminded me of all the men I'd kissed in public toilets and in cars throughout my youth.

There I was, again, as if I'd never left. Nothing had changed. With just one kiss, the passion I'd denied out of guilt or confessed out of shame had been rekindled. *Stop, I have to stop.* But then we were feeling each other's hardness, and I was down on my knees, pulling him out of his pants, taking him in my mouth. He moaned. I closed my eyes.

"Let me feel you," he whispered.

I stood and we stroked each other, faster, as our breathing quickened. When the orgasm came, it was deep and dizzying, a whirlwind of desire, like the high from a drug I'd shot deep in my veins.

Then it was over like a downward spiral, and all I wanted was for it to be as if it had never actually been: to go back to before, before I'd met him, succumbed to my desires, turned right instead of left, turn around and never look back. He tried to kiss me, but I told him it was late and that I needed to go. He turned around, and in an instant the nighttime swallowed him whole. I tried to follow, but became disoriented, lost inside the forest with tree after tree like the bars of a cell out of which I could not find freedom.

Twenty minutes later, I emerged, panic-stricken, and ran home, through the streets like a child who'd scraped his knee and wanted only to be comforted. Yuen was alone in the living room when I arrived. I told her what had happened, confessing the sex as if I were still that child.

"Honestly," she said, "I don't know how you've lasted this long. I couldn't go five years without sex, without that kind of intimacy."

"I guess you have to tell everyone."

"I wouldn't worry about it."

The next morning, at a secret house meeting that I was not per-mitted to attend, she did tell everyone. Unanimously, they decided that my acting out should result in immediate discharge from the Styx. Yvette was consulted, but she suggested I not be thrown out of the house since I was also organizing her and Alfonzo's move. I would be given a "second chance." More importantly, Alfonzo would not be told of my "lapse."

During one of our many visits to Alfonzo's new property in prepa-ration for his relocation, Alfonzo and I left the others to their reno-vations inside the house while we went for a walk with his dog, the same dog we'd stolen for him, which he'd since named Loba. Like Joshua to his Moses, I followed closely behind, through his property's trails and up the side of a mountain. He started talking about his daily meditations, of how he'd made direct contact with God.

"He has special plans for you," he said, leaning heavily on his tree-branch-turned-hiking staff that he'd been whittling down for months. "God has instructed me to watch over you. Only with my loving guidance will you be shown the way. We all have crosses to bear. Some are heavier than others. Yours is particularly heavy, one that you'll have to bear for the rest of your life."

"What do you mean?"

"You know too much, Peter: about yourself, your homosexuality, where it came from. For you to act on your homosexuality now would be like a drug addict consciously shooting up. Your only hope is to remain celibate. Only then can you go back out into the world—once you're strong enough to resist temptation, to not act on your drug of choice."

He stopped along the side of the path and turned to look at me.

"You think anyone else out there will understand you the way I do? I'm your last chance. Without my help you'd probably just get AIDS and die."

|||||||||||

The ten-ton moving truck arrived bright and early one Saturday morn-ing to cart Alfonzo's possessions to his and Yvette's new home—a

5,000-square-foot, fully renovated retirement home. Everyone from the Styx—Clay, Yuen, Sebastian, and I—arrived sometime later with Claude in his Sapporo.

All day we unpacked: rearranged sofas, organized bookshelves, hung clothes in bedroom closets, filled kitchen cupboards with food and supplies. Early before dusk, after vacuuming the hard-wood floors, dusting the entire house, and cleaning the glass patio doors, Alfonzo gathered us all in his newly constructed, sound-insulated basement workroom for what I thought was a house meeting. The oblong room was twice the size of his downtown office workroom, windowless, with cream, pile carpet; a king-size, sheeted foam mattress in the middle for primals; and a brand-new punching bag and aluminum baseball bat at one end of the room to use as a "batting station."

For several minutes we discussed the distribution of house chores and the operation of his office: who would stay overnight at his new home and when; how his downtown office would remain functional while he lived and practiced part-time in his retirement home. Then Alfonzo knelt in the middle of the mattress and started talking about the heaviness of his cross, that he could not bear its full weight when others did not carry the weight of their own.

He turned to look at me. "Do you have something you'd like to tell us?" he asked.

Everyone turned to me, waiting, as if they'd all expected his question.

"No . . ." I said.

Alfonzo breathed in deeply through his nose, closed his eyes, and craned his neck back, like a wolf, about to howl at the moon. "I know what you've done," he said, exhaling through his mouth with a grunt, as if already primaling on his back on the mattress. "Did you think I wouldn't find out?" He opened his eyes. They were larger than before, pupils dilated. "I have ears and eyes that watch you at the Styx, I know everything you do. Don't you know that by now?"

"I don't know what you're talking about," I repeated.

"Don't lie to me, goddammit! You got fucked up the ass! Do you deny it?"

"Well . . . technically, I didn't get fucked."

No one laughed. No one moved, or blinked. Alfonzo's eyes squeezed shut, the skin around them, crinkling, as he dropped on all fours. When I heard the growling, I looked toward the door because I thought a rabid dog had entered the room. The dog was Alfonzo. With his claws, he ripped the sheet off the mattress and sunk his teeth into the foam, biting and ripping it apart as if it were a slab of flesh. Then he spat it out. Over and over, he bit into the mattress and spat its pieces about the room. I glanced at the lineup of bodies leaning back against the wall. No one appeared surprised or the least bit bewildered.

Alfonzo's hands clawed at the floor, anchoring him—a wolf in full rage. His spine arched, and he raised himself back up to a kneeling position. His belly grew large as he filled his lungs with air, and then he let it out, all as one extended roar. His stomach, after he'd collapsed again, rose and fell with every pant.

"Do you think for a second that this is easy for any of us?" he said, still down on the floor. He crawled to his knees and faced me. "Look at everyone. Do you know how hard we're all working to keep this family alive? When one family member acts out, that throws the entire family off balance. If I were living with you I would have thrown you out of the Styx. *Out.* I would have bought you a one-way ticket back to your hometown and told you to go live with your parents for a year. Maybe that would remind you how bad it was before you met me, before you moved into the house. Maybe you need to be reminded. Maybe you need to get *fucked* a few hundred more times in that parkade before you understand what you've just thrown away. Do you have anything to say?"

He waited for my answer. Everyone waited for my answer. I nodded no.

Slowly, he raised himself to a standing position, and headed for the door, muttering something to Yvette in French and signaling with a wave in my direction.

Moments later, I heard his upstairs bedroom door slam shut. The rest of us filed silently from the workroom as Yvette walked over to me.

"You need to leave our house right now and return to the Styx tonight. I don't think the doctor wants you in his home."

I turned to gather my things.

"Tonight was for your own good," she said. "You deserved this."

16

FOR MONTHS AFTER THE confrontation, Alfonzo refused to see me. He passed my prescriptions through someone at the Styx, or Yvette, who met me at the office every few weeks for a "check-in" session. During one, as we sat in the dimmed workroom, she asked me to update her on my "feelings around men."

"What's the difference between how you feel now as opposed to when you started therapy? Is there change?"

"Change?"

"Are you doing anything destructive to yourself?"

Acts of "self-destruction," like piercing my skin while masturbating, had always been conflated with my "homosexuality." Questions about one were like a barometer reading into the other.

"I did do something, this week." I hadn't planned to tell her, or anyone. But now it was too late.

"What?"

"I pierced one of my nipples with a needle. As I masturbated."

"So . . . you stayed in your dirty diapers. Feel good?" She shook her head. Her eyes narrowed. "Jesus Christ, Peter, I have never met anyone as irresponsible. You *still* don't take responsibility for your choices."

"Choices?"

"Why don't you leave?"

"Leave?"

"The Styx. Therapy. Only *choose*. Stay or leave, but make a choice."

"You're saying I should leave?"

"Go if you want to go. You're discharged, go, live on your own, live your own life, just take responsibility for your choice."

The idea that I could "leave," pack my bags and return to the "outside world," had never been something I considered as an option. Leave and return to—what? To whom? A life that had almost killed me before the therapy? Besides, I had seen what happened when Yuen wanted to leave.

"For Christ's sake, you can be a *man*, you know, Peter? You can be a *fucking man*. You don't have to be Mommy's little boy for the rest of your life. You know what I'm talking about, don't you? Jesus Christ, *she crucified you, she blasted you, she killed you*! How old are you now anyway?"

"Twenty-eight."

"You're not going to stay in the middle your whole life, are you? I would be kicking and screaming if I were you, kicking to get out: 'Help me, please, tell me what to do.' Instead I see you sitting, waiting—waiting for what?"

She looked at me for a response. I said nothing.

"I could just kill your parents—*kill them, cold blood*—for what they did to you. They steal you from the most wonderful thing a man and woman have the chance to share: the possibility to get together and feel what *real* love is all about, *the vehicle of love*, and they steal that away from you? That is about the only thing worth living for in this fucked up fucking life, and they steal that away from you? They robbed you of your masculinity."

My silence seemed to aggravate her even more.

"Look at you. You're not a man *or* a woman. You're sitting on a fence, like a passive little boy. *You're about as homosexual as I am a lesbian, Peter, so it's time you wake up and you kick that fucking shit out of your brain and you start looking in the other direction.* Because, I'll tell you, this is a *disease*. And you know *that*. Don't you. *You were not born a homosexual*, Peter. *You know bloody well . . .*"

She was right about one thing: I did feel passive. But the idea that my passivity could have been the result of the helplessness I felt at the futility of trying, for almost five years, to "correct" my desires would never have been considered, let alone tolerated.

I looked over at her. Hanging on the wall above her head were the same words from *A Course in Miracles* that had stared back at me for more than five years:

This is a course in miracles.
It is a required course.
Only the time you take it is voluntary . . .

"So what if I choose men?" I said. "What if I say that I'm a homosexual . . . that I choose men . . . that I'm gay?"

Clearly, this was not the response she expected.

"Then you'll be dead within the year."

‖‖‖‖‖‖‖

Dizziness swept through my body as I floated up toward consciousness one Saturday morning.

"Something's wrong," I told Yuen in the kitchen.

"You're probably just coming down with the flu," she said, feeling my sweaty forehead.

The first blister appeared on my face within the hour. By mid-afternoon, my temperature rose to 101. A dozen pus-filled welts appeared across my torso by early evening. When my temperature reached 104, someone called 911.

Inside the ambulance, on the way to the hospital, my mother's naked body with three breasts floated toward me as I slipped in and out of consciousness until I lost all track of whether I was asleep or awake.

The next thing I knew, my stretcher smashed through the doors of the emergency room and a crowd of white-jacketed bodies swarmed around me beneath the blare of overhead fluorescent lights. When I awoke again, there were cold plastic tubes stuck up my nose and in my arm, and a young, pimply-faced doctor was leaning over me, asking if I'd ever been tested for the AIDS virus.

AIDS? Did I have AIDS? Oh God oh God oh God was all I could think until there was not even a me only thoughts and then not even thoughts just a sinking, drowning fear in the fire of my flesh.

Sebastian was holding my hand when I opened my eyes, sometime later.

"Am I dying?" I asked, as the doctor reappeared from around the curtain, stethoscope dangling around his neck.

"No, no, you have chickenpox," he laughed. "We'll have to keep you overnight until you're out of danger. For a man you're age, that was a close call. But you'll be fine."

I was home in days and lay in bed for weeks, with cool, damp cloths stretched across my blistered body. After my recent back injury, chickenpox was one more obstacle to overcome, as if my body knew something that I hadn't yet figured out. The only time I didn't sting was when I slept. And so I let my body heal itself, unconsciously, as scabs fell off, and in their place, beneath the wounds, my skin grew strong.

Like a snake, I was shedding dead skin.

||||||||||

Still too weak to go anywhere, I spent days in the Styx office, a small room at the front of the house, trying to edit Alfonzo's book on our house IBM. Mostly, I stared at words, too confused by rhetoric or nonlinear life stories to make much sense out of any of it.

One day Sebastian arrived home with a friend. It was still unusual to bring anyone other than another patient to the Styx, and this person, I knew, was not.

"This is Shane," Sebastian said, as I shook the man's hand. He was about my age but taller with intense, chestnut eyes and short, sandy, wind-blown hair.

"I met Shane at work. We got to talking, and, well, he was hoping to talk to you. Privately . . ."

"Oh?"

"Shane has been . . . how shall I say . . . he's been going through some 'issues' lately. With his sexuality." Shane blushed, glanced at the floor. "I told him about the work you've been doing in the therapy. I thought you could help him."

The work I'd been doing? *Help him*? I felt like an imposter.

"If we could just talk some time," Shane said. "I'd really appreciate it."

"Sure," I said.

||||||||||

We met a week later. By then, Sebastian had told me about Shane's mental breakdown one year earlier, brought on after he'd recovered memories of being raped by his father as a child. More recently, he'd been struggling with his increased same-sex attraction, which, as he told his current therapist, he'd denied for as long back as he could recall. Then his therapist told him that the rapes had created those sexual feelings. This confused Shane even more. When Sebastian mentioned my abuse, and that Alfonzo was helping me "correct" my desires, all Shane could think about was joining the therapy.

"I never used to believe in repressed memories," Shane confided in me during one of our walks by the ocean, "until it happened to me. Out of the blue, I started having dreams, waking up sweating, screaming, terrified. I don't know what I would've done if it hadn't been for my AA meetings. Start drinking again, I'm sure."

"What sort of dreams?"

"About my father, and the rapes. I remembered everything, not just in my dreams. It was like a veil protecting me from the events had dropped away and now I could see what had always been there, in the background to my life. Everything made sense."

Shane expressed his desire to join the ranks of Alfonzo's therapy.

"I want to reclaim my true identity," he said. "I don't want to live in the shadow of my father's abuse."

Like the private who'd yet to go to war, he wanted nothing more than to face the enemy, his same-sex desires, and blast it to pieces.

"Do you think Alfonzo can help me the way he's helped you?"

"I don't think you should jump into anything. Until you know more."

"I agree. Which is why I've set up an appointment with him."

"You're going to see him? Dr. Alfonzo?"

"Next week. Seriously, I don't know what I'll do if he can't help me. This is my last chance, Peter."

||||||||||

Shane and I met again at a bustling courtyard shopping bazar.

"I'm really damaged," he said as we walked in and out of Middle Eastern clothing shops. "At least that's what Dr. Alfonzo told me. He said I'm one of the lifers, that he's the only game in town."

"What did you say?"

"That I want his help like he's helped you."

"You said that?"

"I hope that's okay."

"And then what did he say?"

"He said he's still considering me as a patient for his therapy, but that I wasn't supposed to tell anyone. His one condition is that I do the therapy in his home. He said he's trying to get a group of men together. In the meantime I need to start on medication."

"What sort of medication?"

"Clomipramine. Clonazepam. Amitriptyline."

I recognized the names as Alfonzo had prescribed the same brand names to me: Anafranil, Rivotril, Elavil.

"He said he makes all his patients take the same medications. I'll do whatever he tells me. I have to; there's no one else."

Shane was entering into something that was beyond a simple explanation, but I didn't know what to say, where to begin, how to help. Nothing about my own years in the Styx was clear yet to me. He wanted to be fixed, and Alfonzo, it seemed, offered a cure.

We sat on a bench in the courtyard.

"All those nights I lay in bed," Shane said, "too afraid to close my eyes. I used to think that as long as I kept my eyes open he couldn't hurt me. But . . . every night at midnight, like clockwork, there he was. I couldn't move. He'd peel the covers back . . . take me in his mouth . . . rub my belly with his hands . . . tell me to lie on my stomach. Once he had to stitch me up."

"What do you mean, stitch you up?"

"What do you think I mean? He poured a shot of whiskey and told me to drink it down."

"You were how old?"

"Five . . . six . . . seven? He did it to my older brothers, too. He went from bed to bed and made us watch as he did it to all of us."

"Where was your mother?"

"Not there. The last twenty years of my life, all I could think about is that my father made me into something that I'll never be able to change. And since I can't not be who I am, what I've become . . . I might as well not even think about what he did to me. And now . . . now it's all I can think about. I don't want to be gay . . ." He started crying as shoppers wove past us, some glaring, others ignoring, many numbed by the drug of their own addictions. "I don't want to be gay . . . *I don't want to be gay* . . ."

I looked at Shane, but through him, the window of his suffering, I saw myself, recognized the familiar illogic, the years I'd tried not so much to even become heterosexual, but to not be myself. For Shane, "not being gay" still meant undoing his past; it meant not being what he thought his father had made him into.

Two weeks later, he called me at the Styx.

"I'm calling from the payphone in the hospital . . ."

"Why are you in the hospital?"

"Because I'm in the psychiatric ward."

"Why are you in the psychiatric ward?"

"Because I had a psychotic breakdown."

"You—*what*? Are you okay?"

"I'm better, now that I'm off most of all the meds, except for clomipramine, my psychiatrist here said I still have to take clomipramine, at least for a while, oh and he knows all about Alfonzo, he says he's a wacko and I should stay as far away from him as possible—"

"What's his name?"

"Who? What?"

"Your psychiatrist, in the hospital."

"Scarborough, I think. A Brit."

"Wait a minute, I don't understand, what exactly happened?"

"The medication, *he prescribed too much medication*, or the wrong medication, or a combination of—"

"Who? Who prescribed too much medication?"

"*Alfonzo, who do you think*? And then I started taking the Nozinan . . ."

"He put you on Nozinan? But why?"

"He said he needed to plug up holes in my defenses . . ."

"What does that mean?"

"*I don't know, Peter.* I don't know anything right now; all I know is I took what he told me to take until I went psychotic and now I'm in the psychiatric ward and, Peter, can you come and see me? Please? *Can you? Please?*"

For weeks I visited Shane at night next to a dumpster in the parking lot outside the back door of the psychiatric ward. We smoked. Janitors came and went. I said that I'd do what I could to help. And as he talked about how Alfonzo was a wacko and that he did not need his help to reclaim his true, heterosexual identity, because he would do it alone after the hospital, I thought about how much I wanted to kiss him.

||||||||||

Within the week, Yuen shared news of her own.

"I want to live on my own," Yuen announced to Sebastian, Clay, and me in the kitchen one night as we were preparing dinner. "Maybe go back to school."

Sebastian and Clay exchanged a knowing glance. They'd heard it all before.

"And then what?" Sebastian said.

"What do you mean? *Live.*"

"Yuen . . ." Clay said, the hint of a smile sneaking in around his lips, the way he always looked right before ordering any one of us to the workroom for "acting out."

"What about your therapy," Sebastian continued, "or the Styx?"

"I am forty years old. *Forty*, and I have nothing to show for it. No house, no marriage, no husband, no formal education. No *family*."

"You're just acting out again," Clay said.

"*We're* your family," Sebastian said.

"You are not my family."

We all stopping chopping and looked at her.

"You're a bunch of people I met in therapy after I left my husband. Now I want to leave."

She started to leave the kitchen, but Sebastian grabbed her arm. "Wait a minute," he said.

"*Don't touch me!*" she screamed, swinging free.

"What's going on here?" we heard Claude say, from behind, as he entered through the side door.

When we turned back, Yuen was pointing a chopping knife in our direction.

"Yuen, *what are you doing*?" Claude said.

"Yuen, we're going to the workroom," Sebastian ordered. "Now."

Clay opened the basement door.

"I don't want to work."

"Stop acting out, Yuen," Clay said.

"If she doesn't want to work . . . " I said.

"*Now*, Yuen," Sebastian repeated.

"I think you'd better," Claude said, guiding her gently toward the door.

Yuen dropped the knife on the counter, and then all five of us, like schoolchildren filing in from recess, marched down to the workroom.

Word of Yuen's "break" must have reached Alfonzo, because Yvette called a house meeting at the office the next day.

"Yuen was right in one regard," Alfonzo told us the moment we sat in a circle on the floor. "You all need to deal with your anger upstairs in the house, not down in the workroom. Continuing to run downstairs every time you have a feeling is no longer feasible, or practical. Somewhere along the way, 'working' your feelings replaced your real life of feelings. All of you have a disconnect between the anger you express in the workroom and how you conduct your lives upstairs. Unless you correct your life patterns, *now*, by practicing more tough love on each other outside of the workroom, none of you will survive in the world out there. Frankly, I don't want you living with me if you haven't corrected your life patterns at the Styx. Yvette and I don't go running to the workroom every time we have a lovers' spat. We confront each other in the moment: every day, everywhere, no matter what. Either you learn it now, or you go back to the world and you figure it out on your own. End of story. *Got it*?"

We took his words to heart. In the safety of our dungeon, we had summoned our demons through the Ouija Boards of our bodies; now, in our upstairs living room, the kitchen, or our bedrooms, we had nowhere to project our near-constant state of primal rage but on to each other. Caged primates were what we became, as *"fuck you, me first"* supplanted the governing rules of the charter. No issue was now off limits, and all of our issues were now fair game, including my homosexuality.

In all my time at the Styx, in fact, the moment I ever mentioned anything about sex and men in general, the others had always ordered me to the workroom. "Work the issue downstairs, or shut up about it," they'd command. Usually, I would start down a path in my mind about the sexual abuse as a child, the fat man in the bathroom stall, but before long I was talking about all of my one-night stands over the years—in alleyways, bathhouses, parked cars, and toilet stalls—mounting desperation fueling my every word as I gleaned some sort of inadvertent pleasure out of mentally revisiting all the sex I'd had but did not think I should have enjoyed, until, finally, exhausted, I'd blurt out, "*But I am not a homosexual.*"

After all, if I was a homosexual then the fat man and I were the same.

Except we were not the same. I was not the same as my abuser.

My own contradictions left me in knots, and the others enraged.

"I don't want to hear it anymore," Sebastian interrupted one such frenzy, midstream, while I was in the Styx office. "I don't want to hear any more about your neurosis, Peter. It's *bullshit.*"

Clay and Yuen appeared from around the corner. "You are not the same as your neurosis," Clay said. "Getting fucked up the ass when you were a kid: you act out whatever crap was from your parents, but that was not you. We don't want to hear it anymore."

"*You are not a faggot, Peter,*" Yuen added, the others joining her seconds later. "*You are not a homosexual,*" they all repeated, each time louder than the last, and every time like I was the red "X" marked on a wall and they were letting me, their projections, have it. "*You are not a homosexual.*" It seemed the same words used by them meant something else entirely—my negation, perhaps—and not at all what I had meant when I had said them. The incongruity of it all left me spinning.

"Fuck you all!" I pushed past them, ran up to my room and slammed the door.

Seconds later, I heard them pounding up the stairs. Then the door swung open.

"This is my room," I said, backing in a corner. "*Get out . . .*"

"It's not your room," Sebastian said for all three, blocking my exit. "It's our room, too. This is *our* house."

I covered my face with my hands and started to cry. Trapped, I was back in my childhood bedroom and my father had broken through. "Please get out," I begged. "*Please . . . please . . .*"

When I looked back up, the door to my room was closed, and they were gone.

‖‖‖‖‖‖‖

Days later, Claude arrived home with news from the office.

"We're closing shop," he announced to us all. "I've talked it over with Alfonzo and Yvette, and we feel a break is what we need. It doesn't mean we can't come back together down the road, but for now, it's over. The Styx will end."

There was no discussion. The decision had been made. We would all leave the house, but like when Alfonzo closed the other two Styx houses and then reinforced how we, at Styx 1, would still be a "family," closing the final Styx now had nothing to do with leaving the nest. He was still my doctor, he told me in private, and as far as he was concerned, I would need to return for an indefinite period of time for regular "check ins."

Over the next several weeks before we left, on September 1, 1995, Alfonzo called each of us to the office for a tailor-made version of the same speech.

"The house failed," he told me during my meeting, reclining in his leather chair. "The Styx failed, and it's your fault. I'm really disappointed in you, Peter. But I know you'll be back. None of you will survive away from this therapy. Once you've lived in the primal world for a while, the secular world becomes intolerable. Just wait, you'll find out on your own. You will all wind up needing to come back. You won't survive on your own, that's for sure. All those homosexuals out there? The threat of AIDS? You're not going anywhere. You're a lifer, Peter, and this is the only game in town."

Each for our own reasons we had entered the Styx; now, for one reason only we were calling moving trucks and pretending, as grown-ups often did, that we would all remain the best of friends.

Claude and Yuen said they might cohabitate.

Sebastian said he might return to Quebec.

Clay said he might move in with Alfonzo and Yvette so he could maintain his medicated "daddy sessions" in Alfonzo's basement work-room, and sleep on his rolled-up foamy in a pup tent in the forest.

I said as little as possible.

|||||||||||

I moved from the Styx into an attic suite on the top floor of a sub-divided Tudor mansion. From my desk, positioned in a bay window, I faced down onto a finely manicured lawn ensconced with twelve-foot hedges. A recent financial settlement with my former homecare employer over my lower back injury provided meager earnings so I didn't have to find employment right away. I had time and the means to recover—from everything.

Within days, I resurrected my Smith Corona typewriter, packed away since I'd dropped out of the university, and started writing another play. *Scenes from the Life of a Homosexual* focused on the relationship between a young man named Joshua; his child self, Little Boy; and a woman known only as Healthy Mother, modeled after my relationship with Alice. Through a series on nonlinear but interconnected scenes, the three revisited key moments in Joshua's life in an effort to disentangle his history of sexual abuse and subse-quent homosexual identity from Little Boy's fear of Joshua's "inner sickness." Ultimately, Joshua's relationship with Healthy Mother, as a guiding principle in his own healing process, became the play's central focus.

For weeks I stopped writing only long enough to visit Shane at the psychiatric ward, eat, and sleep. That I could even translate the last several years of my life into a play was victory, but I wanted "Daddy's" feedback, so I left a copy of the play in the office for Alfonzo to read, still believing that he would applaud my creative venture. Several weeks later, I met him for a "check-in" session, and prescription, as I was still being weaned off the last remaining medications. We said little throughout the session; then, near the end, he raised the subject of my play.

"I read your play," he said, turning to face me in his private office.

"And?"

He leaned forward in his chair. His eyes narrowed. "Do you have the faintest fucking idea of how long it's taken me to perfect surrogate mothering? How many years of my life I've *sacrificed*? If you show this play to anyone, I mean *anyone* . . . if you so much as *try* to get it produced, I will take you to court. I will do whatever is in my means to stop you. Do you understand me?"

Still under the spell of our weekly nurturing sessions, where I'd believed he loved me as a father should a son, his words blindsided me. Numb, I left the office. Once home, I packed my only paper copy of the play inside an envelope and stored it in a box.

||||||||||

I waited until after Shane's discharge from the hospital, three months later, before I arrived at his apartment one night, unannounced.

"We have to talk," I said, leading the way into his living room while trying to breathe my way through the anxiety. Instead of furniture, he had yellow milk cartons. I sat down on one. "It's about the therapy. This whole idea that we can 'correct' our desires."

"What about it?"

"Sebastian should have never told you about this therapy, that I was trying to be heterosexual."

"Why not?"

"Because . . . it's a *lie*. It doesn't work. I've wasted the last six years of my life trying to make myself into something that I'm not. I should have told you sooner, but . . . I've been lying to myself."

Shane looked at me, but said nothing. I stood back up.

"I'm attracted to men. And there's nothing wrong with that. And so are you. I know you are. You know you are."

Then I did what I had wanted to do since meeting him at the Styx. Stepping closer to him than I had ever dared, I took his hand in mine, and I kissed him, gently, on his lips. When I opened my eyes again, moments later, his confused expression stared back at me. I pulled away, afraid I'd made a terrible mistake.

"No . . ." he said. Gently, his free hand graced the small of my back. Chest to chest, my eyes fell shut as his lips pressed up against my own: a joining of our breaths.

We fumbled with our shirts, unbuttoning each other's as our fingers spread across chests, through hair, over nipples, firm, then up toward shoulders, like the peaks of mountaintops we'd fought years to summit. We gave our bodies to each other, consciously—gave them because in the other each had found himself.

Later, while lying in his arms, I thought of Alice's words that maybe it hadn't been the sex but my feelings about the sex that had caused me so much pain. With Shane I'd felt no guilt or shame, no regret. For the first time in my life, sex, this mingling of limbs and saliva and semen, was not an act of clutching, but one of giving: an expression of love, a communion of gratitude. A dialogue beyond words. Perhaps love, then, was the answer. "The vehicle of love," as even Yvette had told me. Never before had I felt love.

17

BEFORE EACH OF MY remaining visits with Alfonzo, I continued to fluctuate between feelings of outrage over what had occurred in the therapy and a great deal of loyalty toward Alfonzo, my "surrogate father." The Styx had been too much like my home life to see it for what it had become.

Then I'd sit across from him in his private office during all of my periodic "check-in" sessions and he'd continue to make derogatory comments about anything to do with my life without the therapy, or him. If I talked about wanting to travel one day, visit Europe, maybe return to university, he'd say that I would "learn" that all of those ideas were only childish pipe dreams. "Why would you want to travel the world when you can travel to the moon on the mattress?" he said, once. All roads—whether literal or figurative—would lead back to him, and he told me so. Eventually, my best defense was to say as little about my life as possible, get my prescription—if he wrote me one—and leave. No sooner was I out the door, however, when I'd start crying.

Finally, I called Natie, from one of my former groups, and arranged to meet. I'd always remembered the way she'd challenged Alfonzo during groups and spoke disparagingly about him behind his back. Her attitude had scared me at the time, yet later confirmed that she'd always seen him for who he was.

"I thought he was saving my life," I told her.

"By doing what? Getting you to cook his meals and deliver them to his home?"

"I was drowning when I met him."

"Define drowning."

"Depressed. Miserable. Self-destructive. I hated myself."

"That's the point of oppression: fear of annihilation. Invisibility. Normalization of the oppression. Being a survivor of sexual abuse doesn't help."

Natie was five years old when a friend of her parents molested her while she was staying with relatives. As an adult, she'd made a profession out of counseling survivors. She knew what she was talking about.

"Alfonzo told you lies about yourself for years. It's up to you what happens in your life, how you interpret your homosexuality. You've just imagined a life of one-night stands and loveless relationships because that's what you learned it meant to be gay. But you can change that image. You can change how you want your life to unfold. We all end up living the life we've imagined, one way or another."

"I thought he was going to save me."

"From what? In the end, no one saves us but ourselves, Peter. Save yourself."

||||||||||

The last time I saw Alfonzo was in early August 1996. I dreaded returning to his office. Near the end of our twenty minutes, he turned and faced me.

"I'm concerned for all my children, especially for you," he said.

"Don't be," I said.

He looked at me, surprised, but continued. "The world is filled with homosexuals, Peter, and you've stepped back into it. How is that going? It must be difficult."

I was nearing the final withdrawals from the medications, taking 50 milligrams of Elavil and 1 milligram of Rivotril each day, but still suffering through sleepless nights. Just as my senses had been anesthetized for years, now they were heightened. His words sent a jolt through my body, as though I was hearing his hatred for the first time.

"I'm one of those homosexuals," I said. "And nothing's going to change that fact. I can't hide from the world my whole life, and homosexuals are as much a part of the world as anyone."

There was an electricity in the room, an anxiousness about what might happen next. I had stood up to the class bully and was waiting for his reaction, staring him in his eyes. He said nothing. A moment later, he turned back to his desk to write another prescription.

"Besides," I continued, "I've started dating someone."

"What do you mean?"

"Shane. Shane and I are—"

"You're *what*?" His bushy eyebrows looked wilder, more uncombed, than ever before as he leaned forward in his chair, jutted his chin, and placed one hand on either knee. "Do you know how fucking damaged that young man is? Do you have any idea what he's been through in his life? If you don't give a fuck about your own life, at least think about that, think about what he's been through." He handed me my prescription. "Now get out of here," he said, after making another appointment for the following month.

I didn't keep it.

||||||||||

Shane slept over most nights. Some days we stayed inside all day. One of the many books that I'd recently read was Larry Kramer's *Reports from the Holocaust*, a collection of essays during "the plague years," and so we lay in bed and talked about AIDS, the soundtrack to *Schindler's List* playing in the background.

Many had branded Kramer a self-hating homosexual, a loud-mouthed paranoid, because he wrote fearlessly about his own belief that AIDS had been intended as genocide of the homosexual population. Personally, I had no trouble believing it. Genocide had touched my own family history. If psychiatry could still convince us that we should try to change ourselves into something that we weren't, virtually kill ourselves by whatever means for the sake of so-called normalcy, the idea that AIDS had been intended as yet one more form of genocide did not seem like much of a leap.

Other times, I wrote at my desk while Shane lay on my bed,

188 / PETER GAJDICS

flipping through any one of the dozens of books about psychiatry or AIDS that I'd been reading.

"Who buys a copy of the *Diagnostic and Statistical Manual of Mental Disorders*?" he asked once, reading passages from the red, 886-page book.

"I did, obviously."

"Why?"

"I wanted to know what psychiatry was saying about homosexuality."

"They took it out over twenty years ago."

"We're still there, you just have to look. The whole thing is bullshit."

"What is?"

I turned to face him from my desk. "Psychiatry," I said.

One night in 1973, I went on, homosexuals all over the world went to bed still considered mentally ill, only to wake the next morning magically "cured" because the guardians of the gate of mental illness—the American Psychiatric Association—took a vote at some conference and agreed that gays were no longer mentally ill. Nothing about the health, or supposed "illness," of gay men and women had actually changed in reality.

"The only thing that changed was politics."

Another night, the moment Shane arrived at my apartment, I grabbed him by the hand and led him back outside, down the street, and to a nearby grassy field.

"Where are we going?" he said, laughing.

"Just come . . ."

Mounds of leaves encircled a large oak tree like a border in the middle of the field. And there we lay, spooning near the tree on a bed of leaves beneath a harvest moon. Our bodies, hot and tired, breathed in unison. The comfort of his body reminded me of my sessions with Alice. Intimacy knew no gender or sexuality.

At one point I pulled his hand up from around my middle and snuggled back against the curves of his flesh. Shell against shell, we fit together as if the two of us had once been one.

||||||||||

While lying at the beach one day, Shane raised the subject of monogamy. "Monogamy is antigay," he said.

It was a discussion—or an argument—we'd had before. Sex without love with as many men as I could find, or who found me, was what I'd done as a teenager, I told him; all I wanted now was to make love with one man. All Shane kept debating, given any opportunity, was the idea of an "open relationship"—remaining emotionally committed to one person while also being open and honest about having sex with any number of men.

"You don't think a person can be intimate with more than one person?" he said.

"It wouldn't work."

"But as long as you don't cheat on each other . . ."

"You sleep with someone else, you're cheating."

"Cheating is lying to each other; an open relationship is consensual."

"Is this a hypothetical situation, or are we talking about us?"

"Are you sure you're even gay?"

"Fuck 'gay.' A lot of people also use promiscuity to escape intimacy."

I asked him if he had sex in the park. My question was what I knew we were talking around, so I confronted him with it head-on. He squirmed.

"No. Not often. Sometimes. Yes."

"What do you do?"

"*Peter* . . ."

"What? You can do it, but you can't even talk about it?"

"I knew I shouldn't have told you . . ."

"You wait a lifetime to meet someone to love, and he wants to go fuck a stranger in the park . . ."

"I never fuck strangers," he said, grinning.

"Is that supposed to make me feel better? You would rather suck some stranger's dick in the park than find out what real love is all about?" As soon as I'd said the words, I heard someone else's voice inside me. I squirmed.

"You always get so angry at me."

"What's wrong with getting angry? *More* people should be angry. Maybe *you* should get angry. Then you might not need to go to the park for sex."

"Sometimes you sound an awful lot like Alfonzo. I can't live up to your ideals."

I was beginning to feel the weight of Shane's history, like a third body, lying between us in bed. Early on he'd told me, unequivocally, "I don't get fucked." I never questioned why, because I knew. During oral sex, even while we were kissing, sometimes he'd push me back, mid-act, and say, *Stop*, and then I'd think of his father, the stitches, scars that never heal. We were on either side of a revolving door, separated by the past, unable to connect in the present.

One day, he called and asked that I meet him near a city park. He was sitting on a bench at the start of a trail, but stood the moment he saw me.

"I can't do this anymore," he said, beginning to pace.

"Do what?"

"Us. A relationship. Whatever it is we're doing. I want my autonomy."

A rugged man wearing a plaid lumberman's jacket, blue jeans, and black work boots sauntered out of a nearby public washroom, glanced at us, and continued along the trail and into the woods.

"Our entire relationship has been a mistake," he continued.

"What are you talking about?"

"You lied to me from the start."

"I never lied to you."

"You told me you were straight."

"I told you what you wanted to hear. What's going on?"

"I had sex with someone, okay? In the park, here, last Tuesday, and then on Friday I was going to, I wanted to, but I didn't."

"You don't want your autonomy—you're scared of intimacy. And every once in a while you need to go blow your load."

"Why do you have to say stuff like that?"

"What would you like me to say, that I'm happy for you? I'm happy you want to get your dick sucked by a stranger in the park?"

"I can't talk to you when you get like this."

"Like what?"

"You talk to me like Alfonzo talked to you."

"Does this have anything to do with your father?"

My question surprised him; it surprised both of us.

"Why would you say that?"

"You are not gay because of what that man did to you."

Without another word, he turned and started down the trail. I followed. "Shane . . ."

He stopped and faced me. "You can't just tell me something like that and expect it all to be okay. I haven't done the therapy you've done."

"Thank God for that."

"Okay, *I get it.* Alfonzo was an asshole. You know maybe the guy was an asshole *and* he helped you. Did you ever stop to think about that? Whatever it is, I don't know what you know, what's been figured out in your body."

Shane was right: my body had managed to distinguish between the lies of my youth and the truth of my sexuality today—maybe even in spite of Alfonzo and his therapy. "All the more reason to trust someone who knows," I said.

"*Know*? *What* do you know?" His voice took a sudden turn. "You've just spent how many years in a therapeutic cult? Why did you stay with him for so long anyway?"

The question was like a wall I'd run up against inside my own mind, and I had no answer. I could barely face it. I couldn't face him. I turned away, but he continued.

"Hiding from the world, maybe? From men? Afraid of AIDS? *Playing the victim?*"

"That's not—"

"Just how many relationships have you been in, exactly? As opposed to getting your dick sucked in a bathroom when you were a kid."

"What about you? Crying you don't want to be gay, feeling sorry for yourself . . ." Now I intended not just to crush but to scar.

"Every time you kiss me, I see *his* face instead of yours. *Okay?*"

I was not expecting these final words. The pain on his face was sharp and real.

"Whose face?" I said.

"Who do you think? Forget it. I can't see you anymore. This isn't going to work. And don't call me."

And then he walked away. Before I'd said another word he had turned toward the forest.

Once, along the trail, he looked back and forced a smile. Just once. "I'm sorry," he mouthed. As if that would make it all okay.

18

FOR THE FIRST TIME since moving into the Styx, six years earlier, I was on my own.

With no medication to help me sleep, I'd lie awake for hours every night, wondering whether my love for Shane had been a delusion. Months of insomnia followed as my body fought to regain its natural rhythms. Memories of Alfonzo plagued me as I imagined him screaming down at me that I was an "error in need of correction," that I would "never be a man" as long as I was experiencing sexual feelings for other men, that gays were "incapable of emotional intimacy," and that leaving his therapy would result in my own self-destruction. Even Yvette's voice echoed back: *You'll be dead within the year.*

I knew, at least intellectually, that I was free to live my life, finally, but it seemed to me that there was essentially no life left in me to live, that I was on the outside looking in, going through the motions, putting in time. For almost six years I had believed that we, along with all my "soul siblings," were part of a "family"—that we were doing "God's" work, toward the end.

Far from feeling liberated, my life now seemed to have little purpose or significance, but was just an endless repetition of days. Nothing made sense. Everything seemed comparatively inconsequential. I was back in the world but not of the world. That I could be out in public, shell-shocked, and not have anyone notice the hole that had been blasted through my gut proved to me I really was invisible.

Even my vocabulary was more like the mother tongue from a lost country. "Triggers," "take it back historically," "acting out," "introjects," "primals." So many words and phrases that had been commonplace in the primal world sounded so strange in the "secular" world. Some nights I bought a bottle of wine, drank it down in ten minutes, and passed out on my bed. Sleep was lost to me. I had to be unconscious.

||||||||||

Gradually, however, I thawed out from the therapy. I started a part-time job as an outreach worker for a local AIDS organization, facilitating support groups for HIV-negative men and handing out condoms to "men who had sex with men" in public sex environments. I completed a three-month night school course on office administration, learned about something called "the Internet," and found a second full-time job as a civil servant in the province's Ministry of Attorney General.

In new friendships and in work relationships, I was accepted as a "gay man," and while this assisted in challenging my homophobia, the self-identity of "homosexual" that I'd clung to before the therapy, and still seemed to be the only way of describing my unwavering erotic desires, no longer made sense. It didn't quite "fit." I was like a refugee in a new country.

More therapy was the last thing that I wanted, one year after leaving the Styx, when Natie suggested I see a counselor friend of hers. "Think of it as a dialogue with your soul," she suggested over the phone. "The word 'psychopathology,' after all, originally meant 'suffering of the soul.' What you want is to better understand your suffering, right?"

Her friend, Eva, was a rotund, sixty-eight-year-old lesbian. Every Wednesday night at six o'clock, starting in late 1996, I sat on her cat-scratched burgundy sofa in the living room of her two-bedroom bungalow overflowing with antiques from around the world: engraved trunks, oversized sheesham dressers, mahogany bookshelves packed with first editions, crystal chandeliers, embroidered carpets, and various artifacts she'd salvaged from outdoor bazaars throughout Asia and India. When I finally told her about Alfonzo, three months into our sessions and almost as an aside, she had to stop and ask that I repeat my words.

"You were with this doctor for how long?" she said, sitting

adjacent to me in an overstuffed armchair, her characteristic turban perched upon her bundled graying hair.

"Almost six years."

"*Six* years? And you wonder why you feel anesthetized? Your body must still be in complete shock from the medications alone."

Once, out of nowhere, her fat cat, Sammy, jumped up onto the sofa and clawed his way onto my belly. I liked Sammy. I liked the warmth of his overfed body, the fact that he trusted me enough to make a bed of my stomach. When I rested my hand on his furry back and closed my eyes, everything about Alfonzo and the reason for my visiting Eva was out of mind. I was just a body, feeling the warmth of a cat lying on my belly.

Until I started talking about it with Eva, I had little insight into what had even happened during my years with Alfonzo; a storm had swept through my life, certainly, but my memory had not yet sorted out the past. If I viewed my time with Alfonzo as a journey, it also seemed to me as though I'd arrived back at, or perhaps had never even left, the exact same spot. I still had unresolved issues with my sexuality, and residual grief and anger over my parents' refusal to acknowledge not only my sexuality but also my sexual abuse. I had primalled on a mattress and shouted and beat a punching bag in the safety of a "workroom," but nothing in the "real" world had changed. All I knew was that Alfonzo had betrayed his most basic oath as a physician: *First, do no harm.* Not only had his actions been counterproductive to my overall well-being, they had most definitely caused enormous harm—to me and to those I loved.

|||||||||

After six months with Eva, I decided to document everything that had happened in my years of therapy—five pages of clear dispassionate facts—and mail it to the College of Physicians and Surgeons.

One week later, a man called me on the phone. He identified himself as Albert, a police officer and now chief investigator with the College of Physicians and Surgeons of British Columbia. He asked if we could meet.

A week later, I welcomed Albert into my apartment. Before even sitting down, he handed me a pamphlet; most of what it said I already knew, had learned beforehand. Protecting patients was considered one of the College's main functions, it read. The College's complaints committee, the ones who reviewed complaints like mine, consisted of three members of the public and six senior doctors. If a complaint was found to be valid, the committee either made recommendations to the doctor regarding his practice or conduct; reprimanded the doctor; asked the College to communicate its views on an issue or case to the profession at large; or referred the matter on for a formal investigation into the conduct or competence of the doctor. Only the most egregious complaints were ever referred to a formal investigation, resulting in a fine charged against the doctor, a suspension, or a revocation of the doctor's license.

"I should tell you right away," Albert said, "that Dr. Alfonzo has been given the common practice of fourteen days to respond to your complaint." By this time, we were sitting at my kitchen table and he had pulled a portable tape recorder from his briefcase. "Once the College receives that response, they will review your case and decide whether or not to penalize the doctor at the end of the summer."

For the next two hours I spoke slowly and logically, recounting much of what I'd already detailed in my letter. I told Albert everything he wanted to hear and more and, in doing so, felt not exactly happy but at least relieved that I was finally clear-minded enough to be able to talk about the therapy.

At one point, I realized Albert hadn't once asked about the allegation describing how Alfonzo tried to change my sexuality. When I broached the subject, he said that those facts seemed fairly clear to him, and that unless I had more details, there was no reason to discuss it further.

I explained that Alfonzo recorded all our primal sessions on reel-to-reel, which he'd said he wanted to quote as case studies in a book that I'd been helping him write. When I left the therapy he had hundreds of hours of me talking about "the sickness of homosexuality." If he ever wrote about homosexuality, I told Albert, I was sure that he would use my sessions as a means to his own end: to prove that homosexuality was a drug of choice, and that homosexuals' only hope was to remain celibate, to not act on their "insanity." Quoting those sessions would only perpetuate an attitude of violence toward gays, I told Albert, and I didn't want any of them used for that purpose.

The whole time I was talking, I noticed that Albert's eyes, his kind, blue eyes, either avoided my own all together or lingered one moment longer than they probably should have. I sensed his interest in my case cut deeper than a purely clinical fascination.

Our interview came to a close. Albert was up and almost out my front door before he turned and looked at me. "You know, Peter," he said, glancing at the floor, "some things just can't be changed. Being gay is not a choice. I hope for your sake you're able to put this whole thing behind you and get on with your life."

I smiled, shook his hand, and thanked him for his time.

19

I HAD BEEN THINKING of Shane while out walking one night, when suddenly there he was, not five feet ahead of me. I picked up my pace to meet him at a light.

"Shane . . ."

He turned around.

"Peter . . ."

I told him that I'd sent my letter of complaint to the College. He didn't seem surprised. Then neither of us said a word. The light was red and we waited. We were alone on the street, in the city, the world. For a moment I remembered us together, limbs like vines, wrapped around each other in bed, in bliss, in love. My stomach lurched. I wanted to kiss him. Nothing else mattered. I turned to face him, but he turned away.

"Would you like to grab a coffee?" I asked.

He turned back and faced me. "I'm glad you've reported Alfonzo, really I am. That man ruined a lot of people's lives. I hope he loses his license. But I don't think you and I should talk, ever again. And please don't call me. Goodbye, Peter. Good luck."

The light turned green. I stood at the intersection and watched as Shane stepped off the curb and walked ahead without me.

Before I could move, the light had turned red again.

||||||||||

I hadn't talked to Claude since leaving the Styx, but he was the first person I called to see who among those I once called "family" might support me in my complaint. And he did seem happy to hear from me, asked me how I was, where I was living, if I was working, felt stable in my life, was off medication? I asked him how he was. He said that he and Yuen were now living together as a couple. Then I told him about my complaint.

"You've got to be kidding!"

"I was wondering if you wouldn't mind talking to the investigator."

"Is that why you're calling?"

"Yes."

"Alfonzo and Yvette are personal friends of ours. We go on vacations together. All four of us."

"Oh. Well, do you know where Clay lives now? I'd like to call him."

"Clay lives with Alfonzo and Yvette. He won't want to talk to you either."

Then the call ended, abruptly.

I spent the next two weeks tracking down and calling more than ten former patients. One of them was Dr. Scarborough, the former intensive who had been Shane's psychiatrist in the psychiatric ward. He invited me into his office when I arrived for a visit.

At first I said nothing about my complaint, only that I'd left the therapy and was wondering what he now thought of Dr. Alfonzo.

"The man shouldn't be practicing," he said. "I'd go so far as to say that his form of treatment is unethical. It's counterproductive and highly problematic."

Then I told him about my complaint to the College, but before I could ask him if he'd support it, he opened his office door and, clearly alarmed, ushered me out, saying, "If you tell a soul what I just said to you, I will deny ever having said it."

Most of the other ex-patients I found were supportive of my decision to report Alfonzo to the College—as long as it meant not getting involved. But that didn't stop one woman from telling me that she left the therapy because she knew it was a cult.

"When did you know?" I asked her on the phone.

"The moment I walked into my first group."

"Then why did you stay?"

"All sessions were covered under my medical. Besides, I wanted to work with the surrogate mother. That was my real reason for staying as long as I did. I didn't stay for him, that's for sure. I left because of him. He got in the way of my therapy."

Another woman said she remembered Alfonzo telling me my mother made me gay and that I'd never be happy as a homosexual. She also recalled how he insisted that all his patients take medication.

"You especially. You were always drugged, spaced out, like a zombie taking orders from on high. We either took the medication, or our therapy was terminated. That's why I left: I didn't want to get addicted. When I left, he told me that there was no other game in town but his and it was just a matter of time before I'd be back."

She said that Alfonzo was a "megalomaniac, a monster," that he had "created a sense of hopelessness in all his patients." She said that she admired the courage it must have taken for me to file the complaint, but that she did not want to get involved—it had taken over three years to get her life back together and only now was starting to feel hope again. She suggested I call Brent.

Brent and I had not seen or talked to each other since he left the therapy to move in with his newest boyfriend in 1991. Finding him was difficult, as he'd moved three times since then, and, as I soon discovered, changed his name twice.

Bea and Bea's half-sister greeted me inside his apartment doorway the following week, an apartment, he explained, he shared with his newest boyfriend, who was three boyfriends past the boyfriend he'd moved in with after the Styx. Any excitement that I'd felt at seeing a former "family" member quickly vanished, however, the moment we started talking. I was not who I'd been while living in the Styx; neither was Brent. And without the veneer of self-deception that had brought us together and maintained the illusion of "family," we had little else in common.

"Leaving that therapy was the best thing I ever did," he said.

"But you left so suddenly. One day you were there, talking about maybe having a relationship with a woman, the next day you were gone and living with a man."

"I was a fag and Alfonzo didn't like that. I knew what to say and what to avoid. You were different, though."

"How so?"

"I could tell that you wanted to believe you could change. You accepted everything he said to you. You stopped fighting. You gave up."

Several minutes into our conversation I couldn't remember why I was there, why I'd filed the complaint with the College or would want to talk to anyone from the Styx ever again. When I realized I'd been staring at Brent's mouth but not hearing a word it said, I interrupted and told him that I had to meet another friend for dinner, and I left.

‖‖‖‖‖‖‖

In a follow-up letter sent to my home, weeks after our initial meeting, Albert wrote that Dr. Alfonzo had requested an extension for his response to my complaint, and that the College had allowed it. My concerns regarding the doctor had, meanwhile, become the subject of a formal investigation.

Near the end of August 1997, Albert sent another update. Alfonzo was preparing a detailed and lengthy response to my complaint, Albert wrote, which was expected to arrive at the College by October. According to Alfonzo's lawyer, my former medical file consisted of approximately 1,500 pages, which Alfonzo was reviewing, along with many old documents and records relating to my various group sessions, before writing his response. Because of these "extenuating circumstances," Albert wrote, my complaint was taking longer to resolve than the College would have normally expected. He thanked me for my patience.

October came and went with no word from the College.

In November, Albert called to tell me that if Alfonzo's response was not forthcoming in the next ten days, the College would make their recommendation to the board without it.

Ten more days came and went.

In mid-December, Albert called to tell me that Alfonzo had finally released his response to his lawyer, prior to submitting it to the College. "It's five hundred pages," Albert told me over the phone.

"*Five-hundred pages*? Do you know what it says?

"All I know is he's denied all of your allegations. We'll have to wait and see what's in those five hundred pages, though."

They'd have to wait three more weeks, Albert went on to explain, before Alfonzo would provide his rejoinder. But even in the absence of that response, the College had gone ahead and referred my complaint to their preliminary review committee—comprised of the president and past president of the College, as well as a public representative appointed by the Ministry of Health—for their consideration and advice.

"I don't mind telling you," he said near the end of our call, "that this whole situation is so completely bewildering to me. In all my years as an investigator for the College, even as a police officer before that, I have never once encountered a case as complex and bizarre as yours."

ıııııııııı

My sister, Kriska, and I were like strangers when I called to ask if we could meet, alone.

"Why?" she asked, cautiously. "Why now?"

"I 'remembered' you. I mean in my therapy. I was in the middle of a session and I remembered the love I used to feel for you when we were kids. It wasn't anything mental, no real memories or anything, just a feeling in my body. The truth is, I don't remember much about living with you when we were children . . . except I do remember the love. Can we meet? Please?"

In the thirty years since her final escape, Kriska and I had rarely been alone together. Once, years after she'd run away, my parents drove me out of town to meet her new foster family. I couldn't talk to her. I couldn't look at her. She frightened me. She was no longer one of us, part of "the family." She was the enemy.

Years later, when I was twenty, I saw her from the bus as she was walking down the street. Her hair, still golden, was longer, but every bit as wild, like weeds that could not be controlled. At first I thought she looked like the girl who used to be my sister. Then I realized that she was.

I traveled by ferry back to Vancouver and met with Kriska in her apartment.

"Were we close as children?" I asked her over dinner.

"Why do you ask?"

"In one of my therapy sessions I had this memory, in my body, that you used to hold me as a child. Did you?"

"When you were born, yes. Mom couldn't get out of bed for three months after you were born, excessive bleeding, I think—so it was me who held you mostly."

"The night you left, I cried myself to sleep. No one explained anything to me. I thought that there was something I had done. I blamed myself."

"My leaving had nothing to do with you," she said.

"Did something happen? I mean, why that night?"

"You know Mom got pregnant with me out of wedlock."

"It took me to the age of seventeen to count the number of months between their anniversary and your birthday, but, yes, I finally figured it out."

"Dad never forgave himself for what he did: having sex out of marriage. I'm sure he'd never admit it, even to this day, but I know it's true. When I was born, I became the personification of his mortal sin, his failing as a human being, a good Catholic. He could never forgive himself for that, or me, as his constant reminder."

"But the night you left, why then? Why that night?"

Kriska looked away. "There was this boy at school," she said. "The night before I left, he and I had gone out on a date. Just a date; it was all very innocent back then, in the early seventies, kissing and some heavy petting, but that's it. Dad was waiting up for me when I got home. He asked me where I'd been. I told him. He asked me if we'd had sex. Of course not, I told him. I had never had sex with anyone. He didn't believe me. So he told me to pull down my pants. He wanted to inspect me, my underwear. As if my body belonged to him. The humiliation. I was crying. When it was over I knew I had to leave."

"All through my childhood, whenever they talked about you, they called you troubled; you had the devil in you, they'd say. Mom once told me that I should stay away from you because you were evil."

Kriska started crying.

"I'm sorry. I didn't mean to hurt you."

"Not feeling wanted by them has been a part of my life for as long back as I can recall. I had anorexia and bulimia before I knew what to call it, before they had names. Speed was my drug of choice. I wanted to get as far away from the present as I could manage. I was a small size three throughout my twenties, and still I thought I was fat. I'd be out with friends and they'd tell me how thin I was, and I'd get really confused 'cause I'd go home and look in the mirror and all I saw was fat. Sex was difficult. Men were always telling me how beautiful my body was, but . . . I couldn't even walk around in front of them. Naked, I mean. It's taken me years to be able to do that and still I have to tell myself to do it and that it's okay, that nobody's going to judge me. I just tell myself that all these people, years of people telling me that I have a beautiful body, that they can't all be wrong. They must be right and I'm wrong."

Kriska could have been describing my own history with men, at least when I was a teenager. Men had told me I was desirable. But all that meant was I had something that they wanted.

"Where do you think your body dysmorphia came from?" I asked. "Do you remember anything specific?"

"I was talking about this with my counselor just the other week, about a time when I was ten, maybe twelve. We were eating dinner, all five of us kids. You were two or three, I think. Dad told me I was taking up too much space. I remember being really confused because I looked around and I wasn't taking up any more space than anyone else. So he took two paperback books and put one under each of my elbows and he told me to hold them against my body like that and if I dropped them I'd have to go to my room without dinner. I didn't eat dinner that night. It's taken me years of therapy, and even more failed relationships, to reconnect those types of dots in me."

"So the runaway kept running. At least for a while."

"Something like that."

"I understand," I said.

||||||||||||

I had not seen or talked to my parents in years when I called and asked if I could visit.

"Are you still in that therapy?" my mother asked on the phone.

"No," I said. "Actually, I've filed a complaint about the doctor; if it's okay with you, I'd like to send you a copy, so you can read it at your leisure."

My parents agreed to my visit, so back again I traveled by ferry and bus, the weekend after the weekend with my sister, to stay at their house, the house of my childhood.

They didn't mention the therapy or the copy of my complaint letter that I'd mailed ahead of time, and I didn't raise the subject. We ate dinner in the kitchen, watched television in the living room, an episode of *Highway to Heaven*. A young man, the prodigal son, had returned home to tell his parents he was gay, had AIDS, was dying. Angels helped son and parents reconcile. They cried. Hugged. Clouds parted, beams of light shone down. Lessons were learned; love healed all. During commercials my mother talked about baking, my father, gardening.

I stayed overnight in a spare room in the basement. For hours I lay awake, thinking. In primal, I had demonized them both: my father had been oppressor, my mother, seducer. Before me now I saw only a silenced little boy in the body of a tired old man, and the resilience of a woman who had survived against all odds to raise a family in a country not her own. Nothing about what I'd felt or believed in the Styx seemed clear or absolute, incontrovertible; everything was called into question, thrown into disrepute.

The next day I asked my mother if I could talk to her in her bedroom, privately. Once alone, I shut the door. We were standing next to her bureau mirror.

"I wrote a poem about you when I was in that therapy," I said. "About when you were in solitary confinement. I'd like to read it to you." I pulled out a piece of paper with the typed poem.

She said nothing.

"It's called 'Cell of Prayers.'"

She looked at me, waiting.

I began to read.

> *Each night I scrawl, with one hairpin,*
> *a poem, one prayer to God into the walls of my hard cell;*
> *and with the guards asleep, and*
> *rats beneath the floorboards of my feet,*
> *locked alone inside my cell of prayers with*

Terror, always suddenly from behind me,
stabbing me, I beg my persecutor, Despair,
to let me be alone with God,
and live.

I had barely spoken the last word, "live," when she broke out in sobs and fell toward me and into my arms. I held her, like the time years before in my old bedroom, only both of us now silent. No more words. Nothing more to say.

Later that evening, she cornered me, alone, in the kitchen. "I want to talk to you," she said. Her face was stern and cold.

She turned and walked back into her bedroom. I followed her in, watched as she shut the door behind me. We were next to her bureau again, side-by-side our reflections.

"I need to talk to you about what you said on the phone that night, when you were living with those people. Do you remember?"

Of course I remembered: *You have been poisoning my mind and body for my entire life, and I give it all back to you. You are no longer my mother. And your husband, that pathetic excuse for a man, he is no longer my father . . .*

"You don't honestly believe what you said, that your father beat you when you were a child. And the rest of what you said. I need you to take back your words, especially what you said about me—that I molested you."

She waited for my response.

I waited for my own response, to tell my mother anything that might satisfy us both. If by "molest" I thought my mother, who I now understood had also been a hurt child, had taken something from me, then I could not "take back" my words. Even while in the same breath of the word I also believed that she loved me, had always loved me, and all her children, wholeheartedly, and that her love, which I'd also experienced, had given me what I'd needed to survive most of what had happened in my life.

"We have all said and done things through the years that we regret," I said. "But none of us can undo the past or take back our words. It's what we live with every day."

She stared at me, still waiting. After a moment, I turned and quickly walked up the narrow wooden stairs to the top floor of the house, away from my mother and into my old bedroom at the end of the bookshelved hallway. Below the sloped attic ceiling, I sat on the bed in the room of my childhood: smaller than I'd remembered, less onerous.

My mother's request, that I "take back" my words, reminded me of the first time I showed her any of my writing. I was sixteen years old.

I had written a poem about the other boys and girls my age I saw night after night following my part-time job downtown, selling themselves for sex. In them I saw a part of me I feared might one day find expression—to act according to the value I had placed on my body as currency. Panicked, I wrote my poem and I handed it to my mother when we were alone in the den. If I could not say the words aloud to anyone, *I am scared that I will prostitute myself*, at least I could write a poem and ask them to read it.

I watched as my mother read it, grimacing, as though every word forced her to step with bare feet over jagged rocks. Then, with a slight wave of her hand as she left the room, she handed it back to me, saying: "Why can't you write about flowers or sunshine? Why always doom and gloom?"

|||||||||

Before leaving my parents' house, I quickly called Kriska.

"How did it go with Mom and Dad?" she asked.

"Dad will barely look at me, and Mom's clearly angry."

"Would you like to go for dinner one night soon? Maybe to a play? A production of *Rent* is coming to town."

"I'd love that."

"Me too, Peter," she said.

|||||||||

Later that night, when it was time to return home, my father drove me to the downtown bus terminal for my trip to the ferry and back across the ocean. His offer to drive me was, I suspected, an excuse for us to spend some time alone, to get to know each other. No sooner had we left their house than he was talking about Christ, Jesus's love for all his children, faith in God. Our conversation, his monologue, felt too much like my childhood. Then he started talking about praying before meals, about praying with the family before meals.

"Family nurtures faith," he said as we drove over a bridge, "and prayer is one such way to nurture each other's faith in God."

I listened to my father, but I could not tell him what I thought—that I had not prayed with him for years because I did not share his sense of family or of religion; that I'd felt estranged from the family, like an outsider, for as far back as I could remember.

"Life is so short," he said with a sigh. "I want you to talk to me. I'm your father. I want us to talk about what's important."

"You mean what's important to *you*," I said, surprising us both. "You have never wanted to hear about what's important to me."

"That's not true. You can talk to me about anything."

"Anything?"

A sullen smile curled at the edge of his lips. "Why are you so anti-Christian?"

"I am not anti-Christian," I said.

"Well you don't pray, and you don't go to church anymore."

"How do you know I don't pray?"

"Well, do you?"

"For years you weren't there for me when I needed you, now you want to know if I talk to God when I need Him? This has more to do with control, your control over me, than it does with whether I have a relationship with God. Frankly, that's none of your business."

"Do you go to Church?"

"Haven't we talked about this before?"

"You never answer the question."

"Why would I go to Catholic Church when the leader of your religion tells me that I'm an abomination, that unless I remain celibate for the rest of my life I am acting on an intrinsic moral evil?"

"What are you talking about?" he said, with a familiar grin I'd danced around for years.

"I'm gay," I said, for the first time, aloud, to my father.

"You are not gay. Your 'gayness' is learned behavior."

Part of me wanted to laugh. I didn't even know my ultra-Catholic father knew the word "gayness."

"You don't know what you're talking about."

"I'm your father."

"What does that have to do with anything?"

"Who else knows you, if not your father?"

"Know me?" Now I felt trapped inside his car. "You don't know the first thing about me. You don't ask, and I don't tell. Fine. But don't now say that you know anything about me, because you don't. You have never wanted to know the first thing about me, who I am and what I've been through."

I'd hurt him, I could tell. He started to mix up his words, backtrack the entire conversation.

"We don't have to talk about this," he said, sounding panicky and childlike, the lost little boy returning to his demeanor. "Let's not talk anymore, okay? We don't have to talk anymore . . ."

And so we didn't.

Minutes later we arrived at the terminal.

"Goodbye," I said, grabbing my luggage and shutting the car door behind me.

20

IN FEBRUARY 1998, NINE months after my first meeting with Albert, I received a letter from the College of Physicians and Surgeons.

The preliminary review committee had requested further investigation of the issues raised by my complaint. The outcome of that investigation would be reviewed at a meeting in April. Over the coming weeks, I exchanged several letters with the College's legal counsel. In one, I said I was distressed that the College had granted Alfonzo so much time to respond to my complaint. That the doctor would take nine months and, according to Albert, 500 pages to either deny or justify the behaviors described in my complaint was baffling. I suspected he was attempting to discredit me, instead of facing his peers and taking responsibility for his actions.

Near the end of March, the College received preliminary information from Alfonzo. The plan was to examine Alfonzo's response in the context of all the other information gathered throughout the eleven-month investigation, including a copy of my 1,500-page medical chart.

The College also had sought the assistance of an "independent psychiatric expert," who would conduct a review of the various concerns raised and provide assistance to the committee in reviewing my complaint. Another month later, I learned that Alfonzo would provide his full response by the end of May, and only then would the committee be in a position to reach a final decision.

The College's attorney recognized that this matter had taken longer than usual to resolve, but she reminded me that the issues raised by my complaint were numerous and complex.

||||||||||

In the summer of 1998, I called Alice in her home in Ontario. We hadn't spoken in more than five years. She had been thinking of me, too, she said, hoping, praying that I'd packed my bags and left the Styx, and Alfonzo. I filled her in on the outcome of my therapy and the College complaint, and asked if she wouldn't mind writing a statement—just in case.

"I'll do more than that," she said. "I'll hand deliver it right to your door. I'm going to be on the West Coast in a few weeks—could we see each other?"

A few weeks later we met for tea at an ocean-side café.

"I have a gift for you," she said, handing me her statement. "Do with it as you see fit."

"Thank you."

"I have to tell you . . . when I saw your picture, the one you sent me, I could see that the light had returned to your eyes. Tell me: are you seeing anyone?"

"Seeing anyone?"

"Don't play coy. Are you in love?"

"No."

"Tell me you're at least dating."

"A bit. Not much. Not really."

"Why not?"

"Well, I tried, but the men always ask me about my life."

"Yes, I imagine they would."

"I never know what to say. Talking about the therapy never really works; not talking about it leaves a black hole in the conversation, like I'm on a job interview and the employer can't help but notice a six-year gap on my resume. I just mention the word 'cult' and I sound like one of the Mansons."

"You use the word 'cult'?"

"I mention that I was in a therapeutic cult, yes."

"Well, just an idea, but you might want to skip that part. For starters. Leave it for later, you know, date number three, maybe?"

"Sometimes I wish my life were a bit less complicated. You know:

'I grew up wanting to be a teacher so when I was eighteen I went to university and then I graduated and I got a job and a mortgage and a house and maybe a dog and I fell in and out of love a few dozen times until I found the right one and now here I am.' Wouldn't that be nice?"

"Sounds boring. But it's nice to see you laugh. I don't think I ever saw you laugh when you were in the Styx."

"Probably because I didn't. Laughing wasn't in the charter."

"I have to tell you—reading your letter was disturbing. It disturbed me."

"Which part?"

"All of it. The outcome of your therapy. Alfonzo. You know I still feel affection for him; you know that, right?"

"I thought so."

"He taught me everything I know about attachment theory and childhood trauma. He was an outstanding mentor: compassionate, courageous, brilliant. Arrogant. He wanted to control everyone and everything around him, and I know he hurt a lot of people in the process—people I loved, including you. You know we worked together, that I was his surrogate mother?"

"We talked about it at the Styx," I replied, "and the fact that he was 'nearing the big one.' No one really knew what it meant, but we knew he was working with you. Did he inject himself with ketamine, too?"

"Never in front of me, but after a while, yeah, I figured he was taking some kind of drug. It was obvious."

"How so?"

"I could hear him in the next office with Yvette, the two of them whispering, and then he'd come stumbling in. It didn't take me long to figure it out. I was one of the ones who wasn't supposed to know. There were secrets from me about everything."

"Why would he keep secrets from you?"

"Because. I wasn't one of the 'chosen.' I told Yvette, you know, before I left, I told her that I thought the only kind of person who could work as one of his mothers was someone who wanted to become part of 'the family.' It was just too weird otherwise. By the time I figured out he was injecting all my patients with ketamine—secretly—he tried to explain that I hadn't been told because he wanted to do a study comparing those who received the drug to those who didn't. I was supposed to be part of that study."

"How did that make you feel?"

"Outraged. Betrayed. Confused. I talked to my husband about it. I told him that the ethical approach would've been to invite me to be part of the study, to tell me that some of my clients would be injected prior to our sessions. But . . . by then I'd already resigned, so I didn't say a word. I regret that now. Maybe I always will."

"It's weird to hear you talk about your husband. You have a life, don't you? You're a real live person."

She laughed. While I'd always known she was married, that she had her own child, a daughter, we'd never discussed it while I was in therapy. Even at the Styx, we didn't like to think about the fact that our "Mommy" wasn't our real mother.

"How much of my treatment were you aware of?"

"I knew that you were trying to change your sexuality, that he was prescribing all that medication, trying to kill your sex drive, make you straight. I remember you lying in my arms once, exhausted. It was probably after one of your primals. You told me that you were carrying around that vial, the little film container. I was speechless."

"Did you say anything to me? When I was in your arms . . ."

"I told you that if it turned out you really were gay, well . . . I'd love you just the same. It didn't matter to me. I didn't know what else to say."

"What did I say?"

"You were threatened. Part of me wanted to steal you away: from him, from the Styx. But . . . I learned early on never to challenge him. Alfonzo was not the sort of person who invited a collaborative approach."

"Did he ever yell at you?"

"Alfonzo yelled at everyone. A lot of the time he'd yell at a patient, march out of the room and slam the door, and leave me to pick up the pieces. It happened all the time. I got used to it. Funny what we get used to, numb ourselves to. Or else change. Pick up the pieces and move on. It's no excuse, but there it is. Everyone could see what was happening to you."

"To me?"

"To all of you. Other patients talked, you know, how it seemed like you were all members of a cult. The fact that you were all denied a past life, family and friends were excluded from your lives. You could go to work, but you couldn't take a holiday. Even a course had to be approved. The way you were discouraged from talking to anyone outside of therapy, the house, even to me. I stopped by for a visit once, do you remember? You told me I wasn't allowed to just drop by 'unannounced.'"

"I did?"

"Actually, I think it was Clay. But you were there. You all had this blind loyalty toward Alfonzo—'the cause,' that's what the others called it. I asked one of you once, Clay, I think—I asked him if the doctor was paying you to cook his meals and deliver them to his house. He just stared at me. 'We're doing it for Papa,' he said. You were making progress in your therapy, I mean, I could see that, but at what price? Therapy isn't supposed to take the place of living."

Talking to Alice was validating, but I'd had enough.

"I wonder if he ever imagined that we would still be friends, years later," I said.

"I doubt it."

"We must have some sort of karma going on, you and I. Don't you think?"

She took my hand. "I do," she said.

"I hope I don't still look like your ex."

We laughed.

||||||||||

In July 1998, fourteen months after submitting my complaint, I was at my government job, typing up minutes from a meeting, when the couriered package arrived from the College. I slipped the documents beneath a pile of work-related papers and began reading through the 40-page summary of Alfonzo's 500-page response.

As Albert mentioned, Alfonzo had categorically denied all my allegations, including inappropriate conduct, comments, billing, involvement of patients in his personal life, breach of confidentiality, double prescribing, establishing a cult atmosphere, not obtaining appropriate consent, and providing medical care and advice to "a homosexual patient for his homosexuality."

With regards to my sexuality, specifically, Alfonzo's position was that my therapy had not related to my homosexuality and that he therefore did not try to change my sexual orientation from homosexual to heterosexual. He referred to me as being "ambivalent" toward my sexual orientation and sexual practices, and that his "considerable empathy and concerns" related to the effect of those practices on my lifestyle and psychiatric status.

Alfonzo went on to quote several of my primal sessions in which I screamed about wanting to "kill my parents," about how much I "hated gay sex," that I knew I was "not a homosexual," and that he, Dr. Alfonzo, was "the only person alive who could help me reclaim my true identity." I was now blaming him for my own feelings of homophobia, he wrote, when in truth it was actually he who had supported me emotionally in trying to find a healthy relationship with another man. Strangely, several pages later, he referred to his current hope that I was now "living with a nice lady."

Halfway through his report, he responded to my claim that he had told me his father had died in the Spanish Civil War—that his father had been a writer of a small Spanish newspaper, a dissident who opposed Francisco Franco's totalitarian regime, and that in the middle of one night from his childhood, a night that had haunted him for the rest of his life, his father had been taken from their home, lined up outside along with all the other dissidents, and shot. Now, in his report, Alfonzo said that none of this was true: His father had never been a writer; had not died in war; that he had, in fact, lived a long and unremarkable life, dying only recently, an old man, in a small Spanish fishing village.

I met the attorney, Ms. Pearson, for the College of Physicians and Surgeons in September 1998. The office building, situated on a side street in a well-to-do neighborhood, was a two-story relic from the late-1960s covered in bottle-dash stucco. Within minutes of arriving a stylishly dressed woman, like a blond prima ballerina, approached from a long corridor behind the front reception. Our eyes locked.

"Mr. Gajdics," she said, somehow knowing to pronounce my name correctly, "Guy-ditch." Smiling, she extended her hand to shake mine. "Thank you for coming in today . . ."

She led me back down the corridor and into a large boardroom, where she introduced me to her colleague, Mr. O'Donnell. The three of us took a seat at one end of a mahogany table around which must have been more than thirty high-back leather chairs.

"Before proceeding with the expert's evaluation," she began, "we would be interested to hear your general thoughts about Dr. Alfonzo's response."

"My general thoughts? His report was like reading a fictionalized account of the last six years of my life. Not only did he deny all my allegations, he also created a persona of a doctor that treated me as he *should* have. The things he said about encouraging my independence, supporting me in my desire to have a long-term relationship with another man—his interpretation was skewed and revisionist."

"Is that all?"

"For now."

"Thank you. As you know, in light of the doctor's denial of the alleged conduct, we were required to consult the assistance of an independent expert in the field of psychiatry."

"I understand."

"I should tell you first that the expert was not in a position to determine what had happened between the doctor and yourself."

"Okay."

"However," she continued, glancing down at her opened file, "he did say that, assuming your allegations are true, 'Dr. Alfonzo's behavior has been considered acceptable within the framework of his therapeutic model.'"

She looked up. I was expecting her to say something more, to read something else, but she didn't.

"I don't understand."

"Assuming your allegations are true," Ms. Pearson repeated, "the doctor's behavior has been considered acceptable within—"

"I'm sorry," I interrupted, "I heard what you said. I just don't understand. How is cooking his meals and delivering them to his home considered 'acceptable within the framework of his therapeutic model'? Or cleaning his house, or trying to 'convert' my sexuality by making me sniff—" I stopped myself, mid-sentence. "Screaming at me, double prescribing medication . . . injecting us with ketamine . . . how can *any* of that be considered 'acceptable'?"

She did not answer my question, but continued to tell me, by reading from, what the so-called expert told them. "'There are many types of psychiatric therapies that would involve potential confrontation with a patient, limiting a patient's activities, and challenging a patient's sexual orientation.'"

"Okay."

"That should not be interpreted as a psychiatrist stating that your alleged allegations are acceptable. All it means is that there are various psychiatric theories that could be raised at a disciplinary hearing, and depending upon the evidence accepted by a disciplinary committee, any one of them could be justified."

"What about his attack on my character? He's taken isolated incidents from my life, he's even quoted my primal sessions, all in order to make me out to seem delusional."

"Mr. Gajdics, I can assure you that in reviewing complaints, the committee is concerned with the conduct of its members and *not* with the allegations regarding the character of complainants. The committee's focus will be on the concerns expressed in your initial letter of complaint. They will complete their review at their next meeting of November eighteenth, after which they will report back to you on the outcome of their decision."

Our meeting was short. When she asked me if I had any other questions, and I didn't, the three of us left the boardroom together. Mr. O'Donnell walked down the hall ahead of us as I turned to face Ms. Pearson in the doorway.

"I wanted to say," I began. She looked at me. "I mean, I wanted to ask you . . . I know we've been writing and talking on the phone for over a year, but I was just wondering . . . I was wondering . . . if you believe me, if you believe my story."

"Mr. Gajdics," she responded, taken aback by my candor, glancing down the hallway toward her colleague as he disappeared around the corner.

"I know you probably aren't allowed to say . . ."

"I think . . . I think that in the months we've written and spoken on the phone . . . you have always presented yourself as a mature, reliable witness—articulate and professional."

She paused. I smiled and extended my hand for a final shake.

"And I believe you, Peter," she said, clasping my hand with both of hers. "I believe your story. I believe you."

‖‖‖‖‖‖‖

In late September, I interviewed several gay men as part of a sex-research project being conducted through the AIDS organization where I was still employed part-time. Most of the men met me after hours at my downtown office. First names were all I ever knew. I asked them a series of questions about their lives, sexuality, and their coming-out processes, then I let them talk. Some went on for hours. An opportunity to tell someone their story, to be heard, seen, was all that many of the men needed. I listened to them as I'd always wanted, when I was a teenager, someone to listen to me.

One mid-fifties man named Emery, an agoraphobic, asked that I interview him in his home. He lived on the main floor of a wooden three-story walk-up near the outskirts of the city. The long, dimly lit corridor inside his building stunk of cigarettes and fried food. I knocked on Emery's door, and when he opened it, the first thing I noticed were his eyes, their youthful glint that contrasted against his lined face, like cracks in the earth of his age-toned skin.

He smiled and invited me into his sparsely furnished room, the room of his life, with a single bed pushed up against one wall and a mini-fridge and hot plate on a blue laminate counter against the other. Next to his bed were a stack of yellow milk crates upon which were several paperbacks, a framed, black-and-white photograph, and a nightlight. We took a seat at a small folding table in front of the window, a window that looked out over a parking lot, and began our conversation.

In 1960, when Emery was twenty-five years old, the Canadian Public Service "purged" him from his job for being a "practicing homosexual." Soon after, his parents sent him to Montreal's Allan Memorial Institute, the Psychiatric Department of the Royal Victoria Hospital, which had been at the forefront in Canadian psychiatric education and research. Emery spoke openly about his involvement with the Institute, and about its director, Dr. Ewen Cameron, a former head of the World Psychiatric Association, who had been awarded funds from a CIA front organization to conduct brainwashing experiments on innocent civilians, both Canadian and American.

"Can I ask you a question?" Emery said.

"Of course."

"You're gay, right?"

"Yes."

"And you're okay with that? With who you are?"

"Now I am."

"You're lucky."

"How so?"

"Growing up in a different time and place the way you have. Back then we were all considered mentally ill. Cameron thought he knew how the human mind was wired and what he needed to do to fix it. He hooked us up to electrodes, gave us drugs like LSD or sleeping pills. Massive electroconvulsive shock treatments, sensory isolation, insulin-induced comas that lasted months on end."

"Why? What was he trying to do?"

"Wipe our brains clean of all identity, including what he thought was our neurosis. Break us down so that he could build us back up again, his own way. Imprint a new, healthy identity on top of our blank minds. 'Depatterning'—that's what he called it. Most of what happened to me personally I only discovered years later, when I finally read my hospital file. I have no real memory of any of it. I don't know if you can imagine what it's like to have gaps in your life, years, stolen from you."

I wanted to tell him that I knew exactly what it was like, but I listened as he continued.

"For months we were in these 'sleep rooms,' not just homosexuals but married women, straight men, we were all wearing headphones and listening to taped messages that just went on for hours, sometimes sixteen hours a day, seven days a week. Everyone's tape was different, depending on your problem. I thought I was a homosexual: that was my illness. Cameron wanted to erase my brain of all association with homosexuality and replace it with my innate heterosexuality. Or so his theory went. Instead we turned into children. Grown men and women: incontinent, with no past life. By the time I got out in sixty-two, I was a shadow of my former self. I couldn't work. Couldn't think. Couldn't process information, make decisions. My entire memory of the fifties and early sixties . . . of my whole life . . . it was wiped clean, like off a chalkboard. I had to reconstruct everything, my entire personal history, from pictures, from stories people told me, letters that I wrote or received from family and friends. Everything about my former self was erased. Except for my homosexuality. That much never changed. I was still attracted to men."

Thirty years separated Emery's experiences from mine, but the similarities between what he went through with Cameron and what I had with Alfonzo shocked me.

Emery walked to his egg-carton bookshelf and picked up the picture—of a young man with jet-black hair, sea-blue eyes, and a dimpled smile.

"His name was Jim," he said, displaying the framed photograph with pride. "Such a handsome man, don't you think? His parents sent him to the Institute to help 'cure' him. By the time he left, he was a vegetable, physically and mentally impaired. They killed him. Two years later, he killed himself." Emery dusted the frame with his shirtsleeve and replaced it back on the milk crates. "There's more than one way to murder a fag. Cameron was an architect for genocide."

I wanted to ask Emery about his road to recovery, whether he'd ever found love, or forgiveness, reconciled himself with his past. When those who've wronged us do not take responsibility for the harm they've caused, I wanted to know, how is it possible to release them, the hope for their contrition, from our lives? I wanted him to tell me what I could not figure out for myself. But before I knew it, our interview was over, and Emery, visibly shaken, was ushering me out his front door.

I was scheduled to hand out condoms in the park that night—the "public sex environment outreach" part of my job. It was also the part of my job I liked the least, that seemed the least productive. At least it would have been for me had someone handed me a condom through all the years I'd had sex in parks, and cars, public toilets, bathhouses, parkades. Condoms, back then, would not have saved me from myself, my use of sex to fill a void. But part of our funding at the AIDS organization depended on the number of condoms distributed, and so I distributed as many condoms in "safer sex packets," as possible. At least the men liked the flavored lube.

The park seemed busier than usual. Nighttime brought with it the need for sex, and everywhere I looked shadows of men, like scavengers, roamed back and forth between trees. My routine had always been the same; I'd wait until a man approached me along the trail, then tell him that I was not there to "play," but as an outreach worker—and would he like to talk instead?

That night, however, all I thought about was Emery, the years he'd lost to ignorance and hatred, years that he would never get back. His words, *There's more than one way to murder a fag* echoed through me as I heard the sounds of ravaged, ravenous souls, breeding in the dark. The memory of Alfonzo was with me, too, as was the realization that the longer I stayed in his therapy, believing that I could "change" while compartmentalizing my feelings for men, dissonantly, the more likely I was to act on an unconscious sexual compulsion, have unprotected sex with a stranger, and potentially "get AIDS and die."

I left the forest before distributing my quota of condoms. Back home, stripped and in bed, Emery's phrase *an architect for genocide* haunted me to sleep. And before I opened my eyes the next morning, not yet awake but not still asleep, somewhere in between, for a moment I thought I heard someone next to me in bed crying, sobbing.

I awoke to realize it was me.

21

SEVERAL WEEKS LATER I received another letter from Ms. Pearson.

Following their final review of my complaint, the preliminary review committee had now directed Alfonzo to attend a meeting of the ethical standards and conduct review committee. Comprised of four senior physicians and two public representatives appointed by the Ministry of Health, the conduct review committee's task, she wrote, was to be educational, remedial, and to provide advice, guidance, or criticism, as appropriate, on the physician's conduct in order to avoid the recurrence of similar complaints.

I was invited to attend and was allowed to bring with me a "support person" of my choice. Reviews rarely lasted longer than thirty minutes, and I would not be expected to address the committee, although I would be permitted a few words at the end, if I so desired.

In closing, Ms. Pearson stated that she hoped I felt my complaint had been thoroughly reviewed and that my "concerns had been satisfactorily addressed."

I was outraged. Nothing about my "concerns" had been "satisfactorily addressed."

I called my friend Natie.

"You should sue him," she said on the phone.

"What?"

"Forget the College."

"But—"

"The College isn't going to protect you. The College protects the doctors, no matter what they say publicly. A conduct review means a slap on his wrist. It's a joke. You're a joke to them. Find a lawyer and sue him. Make him pay."

"Well, in the meantime," I said, "will you come with me to the slap on his wrist?"

||||||||||

My parents invited me back to their house the following Sunday, and I accepted. Shortly before brunch, my father walked into the kitchen, where my mother and I were talking.

"The search for truth is God's will for all," he said.

I was scrambling eggs at the stove, but his statement stopped me. From glancing back into the living room I could see that he'd been watching his favorite television station, the Catholic channel. No doubt the priest had included the statement on his regular Sunday sermon.

Our conversation throughout brunch, by contrast, was shallow, and that familiar feeling of alienation was setting in. For a change I brought up the subject of the approaching conduct review. I had always been a master of omission, and even though my complaint dealt almost entirely with the issue of homosexuality, I found a way to talk about it without ever once mentioning the word. My mother, as always, knew exactly what we were discussing.

"What is this meeting for again?" my father cut in after a minute.

"My complaint. I told you."

"What complaint? I thought we were talking about your job."

"You know, the doctor," my mother said in a hushed tone. "The one he filed that complaint against?"

I recognized the disturbed glare, registering in my father's eyes. "Just what's the basis for this complaint?" he asked, as my mother walked to the counter and began fiddling with the toaster.

"What's the basis? Didn't you read my letter to the College?"

"Oh, that," he said, "that has *nothing* to do with us."

"Well, I *did* start therapy with that doctor because of what I'd been through at home."

"What happened at home?"

"During my childhood?"

"What about your childhood?"

"The fights . . . spending all that time alone, downtown. Kriska running away . . ."

"What does Kriska have to do with anything? Lots of children run away from home."

"You don't think our family was just a little bit dysfunctional?"

"No."

"You don't."

"Well maybe *you* were dysfunctional, but your mother and I were *never* dysfunctional."

"But—"

"I've told you how I feel, and I expect you to respect our wishes." And, with that, he stood and left the room.

"Why are you doing this?" my mother asked when he was out of earshot.

"Doing what?"

"This complaint. Why can't you let it go?"

"How can you say that after what you survived?" I resented her comment—that I should "let it go." For me that would have been tantamount to crawling back into bed, as I did so often in my teens and early twenties, sedating myself with sleep because it hurt too much to stay awake. I didn't want to do that anymore. I couldn't do that anymore.

"I'm trying to prevent this doctor from doing to anyone else what he did to me," I continued. "I'm standing up for myself. Considering your own traumatic history, I thought that you more than anyone would understand."

"Traumatic?" she repeated, as if mulling over the word. "Today everyone is a trauma survivor. I've never had time for trauma."

I glanced outside. My father was standing in the late autumn chill, alone.

"Maybe," I said. "Trauma might have found you, though."

||||||||||

While talking to Albert on the phone about the upcoming conduct review, he told me that Alfonzo believed my actions over the previous two years were "completely out of character" and that I would never have betrayed him by filing the complaint had it not been for my friendship with Natie and her vindictive meddling.

For this reason alone, I decided instead to invite my childhood friend, Tommy. I hadn't talked to Tommy in nine years, but I called him on the phone. When he answered, for a moment, I said nothing. He said my name.

"How did you know it was me?" I said.

"I heard you breathing.

"You recognized me from my breathing?"

"Peter, I would recognize you blindfolded."

I filled him in on the outcome to my therapy, the College's two-year investigation, and asked if he could come with me to the conduct review.

"Sounds like fun," he said, dryly.

‖‖‖‖‖‖‖

In October 1998, a national media frenzy exploded over the savage beating and death of Matthew Shepard, a twenty-two-year-old Wyoming student, a "homosexual."

"By the time Shepard died in a Colorado hospital," *Newsweek* reported, "his suffering had been transformed into a passion play of sexual politics, touching off a vicious new debate: on one side, civil-rights crusaders who say that federal law can help protect gays from hateful violence; on the other, Evangelical Christians who believe that Jesus Christ can save gays from themselves."

Christ, according to right-wing fundamentalists, now wanted the unhappy homosexual, just as Uncle Sam once had the naive civilian.

As Shepard became the poster child for hate crime, and I waited five more months for the conduct review, I couldn't help but think about all those men and women who were battling another kind of hatred: the one inside themselves that made them want to "change." Theirs was the worst kind of hate crime. I knew, because I'd done it to myself.

‖‖‖‖‖‖‖

On March 24, 1999, nearly two years after filing my complaint, Tommy and I arrived at the office of the College of Physicians and Surgeons for the conduct review. Albert shuffled us directly from reception to a small, private waiting room with two green vinyl chairs and a half-melted plastic plant. The air inside was stale, and the flickering fluorescent bulbs secured behind a chipped paneled ceiling burned my eyes. After a minute, Tommy broke our silence.

"Your mother called me," he said. "Years ago, when you were in that house . . ."

"The Styx?"

"I guess you'd called her one night, sometime in the early nineties. I don't know exactly what you said, but she was really upset."

"She called you?"

"She was crying."

"My mother was crying?"

"She must have called me as soon as you hung up. She said something about you being in a cult, that you were brainwashed. She wanted me to help her. She sounded desperate."

"What did you say?"

"I didn't know what to say. Your mother had never called me before, the whole time we were friends as kids. I also thought you were in a cult. For a while I actually thought about kidnapping you out of that house."

"By the way, what's that cologne you're wearing?" I asked.

"Dalí. I prefer the musky scents, lots of sandalwood and patchouli. Mark Birley had a wonderful top note of oranges mixed with wood and leather. I couldn't decide which one to wear today. Why, do you like it?"

I said nothing, thinking how his pungent cologne smelled just like Alfonzo.

"Dalí used to spread shit all over himself, you know."

"Pardon?"

"And other things, but mainly shit, just before he met Gala, and apparently the result was intoxicating. Gala, of course, being the love of his life."

"Okay."

"He felt the smell of excrement was incredibly sensuous and erotic. When he was young he mixed his own cologne and the main ingredient was shit. Of course there were other ingredients, like olives. But now that I'm thinking about it, if this Alfonzo person had done his research, he would've been aware that the smell of shit has its own sensuous aphrodisiac properties . . ."

I was glad when Albert reappeared from around the corner.

"I'm afraid I have some potentially disruptive news," Albert said, holding a letter.

"What?"

"Dr. Alfonzo just presented a letter to the committee that lays out the reasons why he believes you should not be allowed to attend the review."

"Are you serious? Can you read it to me?"

"I am not in a position to read you the letter. However, I can tell you that he's cited your . . . 'fragile state of mind,' and that he's warned the committee that by listening to them talk about your 'mental instability' it could be 'hazardous and detrimental' to your emotional well-being. He says that it could set you back years in your therapeutic process. He's concerned for you."

"Is he."

Albert smiled and nodded his head.

"Does this mean I can't attend the review?"

"No, no, of course not. But you needed to be aware of the letter. It's up to you whether you attend."

"Dr. Alfonzo will say just about anything to pathologize me. Of course I want to attend."

Albert didn't seem surprised. I think I even caught him smiling as he led us down a hallway and into a boardroom.

The walls inside the room were dark and oppressive. Around a large rectangular table sat three men and three women. All eyes turned toward me as I entered the room. Peter Gajdics, the complainant they'd read about for nearly two years, was now a real live person. Tommy and I took a seat at one end of the table. No one spoke for five minutes; then an older man in a pinstriped suit entered the room, followed closely by Alfonzo, carrying a large box that he dropped next to a seat adjacent to us. There was a frantic manner to his arrival: he appeared confused, disorganized, like a man on the edge, and I imagined that he'd just been led out of a car, chauffeured by one of his "family," because he did not have the mental stability to drive it himself.

Mrs. Humphries, the committee's chair, a mid-fifties British woman with a beehive hairstyle sitting at the head of the table, called the meeting by outlining the reasons for our attendance. Then she walked us through my five-page letter of complaint, which had set the process in motion twenty-three months earlier.

"Dr. Alfonzo, could you please tell us a bit about your attitude toward homosexuality?"

"Attitude?" he said with a raised brow. "I have no particular attitude. Twenty percent of my clients are homosexual. I do find homosexual women more amenable to treatment. But no one knows the cause of homosexuality. Freud pioneered theories based on an emotionally weak father in combination with a smothering mother, that this may cause the male to identify with the mother and therefore choose a love object of the same sex. Efforts to convert homosexuals into heterosexuals have never been successful. But there's a lot of debate about the nature of homosexuality, whether it's an illness or a part of a person's nature. The whole nature-versus-nurture theory. But I know that homosexuality hasn't been an illness since nineteen seventy-three when it was removed from the DSM, so how could I treat someone for an illness that hasn't existed since then?"

"Dr. Alfonzo," Mrs. Humphries responded, already with an edge to her voice, "there is no debate about the nature of homosexuality. None. The Canadian Psychiatric Association has *never* considered homosexuality a mental illness. And the Canadian Medical Association has long considered homosexuality equal to heterosexuality as a sexual orientation. Research into homosexuality is irrefutable, and it is considered neither mental illness nor moral depravity. Moreover, homosexual orientation has been found to be in place early in the life cycle, possibly even before birth. Efforts to repair homosexuals have been shown to be nothing more than social prejudice and could result in severe psychological damage inflicted onto the individual."

Like an animal in a zoo, I had become The Homosexual At The Far End Of The Table.

"Dr. Alfonzo," she continued, "this committee is aware that you practice a highly unorthodox form of therapy which could involve an intensification of the power difference between therapist and patient. Could you tell us a bit about the 'slave and daddy' roles used in your therapy?"

"I'm not sure what you're referring to."

"Your treatment involves a form of primal therapy, does it not?"

"I wouldn't call it primal therapy."

"Your patients undergo regression, do they not?"

"Yes."

"They are therefore extremely vulnerable to suggestion, correct?"

"Vulnerable?" He repeated the word as if he'd never heard it before.

"Could Mr. Gajdics have said things in his therapy that you wanted to hear? Perhaps just to please you as a father figure?"

"Oh no, no no no no no. I don't think so."

"You don't think so?"

"No."

"*Why* don't you think so?"

"I believe that patients can control what they say during their primals. There's never been any evidence to suggest that a therapist can extract from someone something that they did not want to say."

"Are you saying patients *can* control what they say or that they can*not* control what they say?"

"Can*not*. Sorry. Can*not*."

"Have you ever used abusive language on your patients?"

"Abusive language?"

"Screamed at them, called them names or threatened them in any way. Undermined their hopes, exploited their fears, coerced them into behaving or doing certain things. Your chores, for instance. Cooking your meals and delivering them to your home."

Alfonzo laughed. "I'm a Latino. Latinos are temperamentally different than Anglo-Saxons. Sometimes these cultural differences confuse my patients, but I would never scream at them. I know such behavior would never be acceptable. And my meals? Sorry to laugh, but I have a very restrictive diet. My wife cooks all my meals."

Alfonzo's "restrictive diet" was hardly something I could forget, considering all the lists of spices and foods we were to use and avoid that he provided us with, and assumed his "wife," Yvette, was cooking for him now only that we were gone.

"Do you keep your beliefs to yourself? Facts about your life?"

"Naturally," he said, still smiling. "Why would I tell my patients about my life? My patients are all mentally ill. Most are delusional." He glanced over at me. "No offence to them, or to Mr. Gajdics here, but if I wanted to talk to someone I wouldn't talk to a patient. I'd talk to my wife."

I wanted to laugh, too. Or maybe just raise my hand and remind the good doctors and publicly appointed civil servants sitting around the shiny, lacquered boardroom table that Alfonzo had met his wife, Yvette, more than fifteen years ago when she, a "mentally ill patient," was referred to him for treatment, and that she'd continued as his patient, in addition to becoming his common-law wife.

"Dr. Alfonzo, have any of your current or past patients ever witnessed your own therapy, with or without the aid of ketamine?"

"I haven't done active therapy work since the nineteen eighties."

"You haven't."

"No."

"Why then would Mr. Gajdics have said this occurred, that he had witnessed your own therapy, if it had not?"

"Sadly, Mr. Gajdics's ability to blend fact and fiction is characteristic of his kind of personality disorder. For a patient to witness his therapist's own treatment would not be therapeutic. It would break all the rules. It would be traumatic for the patient, not to mention unethical and a violation of trust. I would never do that. I'm shocked that he would say such a thing. Shocked."

Alfonzo's comments were puzzling. If, as he said, it truly was "traumatic," "unethical," and a "violation of trust" for patients to witness their therapist's own treatment, did Alfonzo himself understand that his behavior was, indeed, unethical and a violation and now was lying just to save his profession? Or was he only telling the committee what he knew they wanted to hear even though he did not, in truth, believe it himself?

Either way, listening to the entire conversation was like watching skilled professionals in a game of chess: The committee asked Alfonzo what they knew they needed to ask, and Alfonzo told them what he knew they needed to hear. Truth was the last thing this conduct review was about.

"Dr. Alfonzo, when was the last time you consulted another psychiatrist or the psychiatric community?"

"The psychiatric community?"

"Yes."

"Um . . . I'm not sure what you mean."

"When was the last time you had a conversation with another psychiatrist?"

"I used to attend some meetings."

"When was that?"

"Ten . . . eleven years ago. In Quebec."

"You have not discussed your theories with another psychiatrist in ten or eleven years? Are you conducting research on your patients on the use of ketamine and nurturing in psychotherapy?"

"Yes."

"Well who gives you feedback on your research?"

"Feedback?"

"Who do you talk to about your patients?"

"My patients."

"Excuse me?"

"My patients complete questionnaires, and we discuss their progress together."

"Dr. Alfonzo, are you telling this committee that you discuss your research on your patients *with* your patients?"

"Yes."

"You have no peer review."

"I've found that the patient is the best person to discuss their progress with. Besides, research in psychiatry is not the same as in other branches of medical science."

"Dr. Alfonzo, this committee is not in agreement with the opinion that a psychiatrist's treatment model should be tailored to the requirements of what the patients *think* they need. Especially when those patients are undergoing regression, are under the influence of extremely powerful psychotropics, and would naturally want to do or say anything to please their therapist."

I was struck by Alfonzo's comment, about turning to his patients for feedback, not only because it had been true for us but because it was similar to what I'd read in cult-expert Margaret Thaler Singer's book *Crazy Therapies*, in which she referred to the many "crazy" therapists, many of whom practiced a type of "feeling" therapy similar to Alfonzo's, whose support came mainly from patient feedback, which was analyzed and evaluated by the therapists themselves.

"Dr. Alfonzo, could you explain to this committee your use of ketamine hydrochloride and the general use of anesthesia in your psychotherapy?"

"I use only very small doses of ketamine to avoid the hallucinogenic effects. No more than a quarter to a half cc. I've found that by using the drug, I am able to eliminate the patient's observing ego, thereby allowing direct contact with the patient's child self during the nurturing sessions with the surrogate parent."

He reached below the table and started shuffling through his boxes, heaved one up onto the table and began flipping through the six-inch-thick tabbed binders. "I've brought a research paper that was written thirty or so years ago, in Russia, where ketamine was used to enhance psychotherapeutic processes. If you'll just . . . just give me a minute . . . one . . . second . . ."

I knew the paper he was referencing. Since leaving the house I'd done my own research. The paper was about ketamine-assisted psychotherapy for detoxified heroin addicts—not exactly correlative to my own history.

One of his boxes tumbled back onto the floor and some of its content scattered beneath the table. Before Mrs. Humphries had had a chance to stop him, he was down on his knees, like a schoolboy, crawling under the table, gathering the loose papers and clipping them back into their respective binders.

"If you'll just give me a minute," he said, popping his head up from beneath the table. "I'm sure it's here, somewhere . . . I'm sure I can find it . . ."

Some of the committee members hid their faces in their hands. Alfonzo's pasty-faced lawyer ducked beneath the table and whispered for him to sit back up in his chair.

"Dr. Alfonzo . . . *Dr. Alfonzo*," Mrs. Humphries called out from across the room, "*please stand up*. This committee is not interested in Russian research papers written thirty years ago."

Alfonzo finished clipping his papers back in the binders and returned to his seat, looking more frazzled than when he entered the room.

"Dr. Alfonzo, can you please tell this committee why you would not have used benzodiazepines, rather than the ketamine?"

"I don't want to sedate my patients. I want to stay away from dampening their feeling. It's important that my patients retain the ability to communicate their progress with me."

Considering that I had been taking Rivotril, a benzodiazepine, for most of our years together, and that I had been beyond "sedated" and close to catatonic due to the elevated levels of all the medications combined, Alfonzo's comment left me dumbstruck.

Mrs. Humphries flipped through another voluminous file.

"Dr. Alfonzo, we understand that at one point Mr. Gajdics had been prescribed up to . . . five hundred fifty milligrams of Elavil every day, on top of the other medications."

"That sounds about right."

But taking 600, I wanted to say.

"Five hundred fifty milligrams," Mrs. Humphries repeated, flatly.

"Yes."

"Dr. Alfonzo. Are you aware that five hundred fifty milligrams of Elavil would normally be restricted to the most severely ill patients in hospitals or institutions?"

"Normally, yes."

"You *are* aware of that."

"Yes."

"And that the medication's side effects alone would have caused Mr. Gajdics extreme suffering, not to mention a complete inability to communicate any progress he may or may not have been making in his treatment."

We all waited for Alfonzo's response. He had none. Elavil, especially at the doses he prescribed, had a long and worrisome list of possible side effects, almost all of which I'd experienced, including anxiety, blurred vision, diarrhea, disorientation, dizziness, drowsiness, fatigue, hallucinations, insomnia, decreased sex drive, excessive perspiration, irregular heartbeat, lack of coordination, loss of appetite, nightmares, numbness, rashes, swelling of the testicles, and weight gain. Tricyclic antidepressant overdose, as I had also read, was a significant cause of fatal drug poisoning.

"Can you please explain to this committee your rationale for prescribing such high doses to Mr. Gajdics?"

"I admit, few outpatients require such high dosages. They were needed for Mr. Gajdics because he was quite mentally ill."

There was a suspended moment when I looked around the table at each committee member, and each of them looked back at me. I had worn my best suit, was freshly shaven, and my eyes, I knew, had the clarity and sparkle of a sane human being.

"Dr. Alfonzo," Mrs. Humphries responded, her inflection rising dramatically, "are you trying to tell us that this young man sitting before us here today, that this man is a very, very, very, *very* damaged human being who required five hundred fifty milligrams of medication every day *just to function*? Is this what you are trying to tell us?"

Every person in the room—Alfonzo, his lawyer, Mrs. Humphries, the committee members, even Tommy—had turned and looked at me, and I looked, one by one, at each of them. Several moments, it seemed, were happening in slow motion: Mrs. Humphries's question, everyone's glances at me, all of us waiting for Alfonzo's response. Then Alfonzo turned to me as I did to him, and we all turned back to Mrs. Humphries as he responded to her.

"Yes," he replied.

Some of the members shook their heads in what appeared to be bewilderment. I caught the eye of one committee member. She winked at me.

"He looks great *today*," Alfonzo added like a hiccup. "Obviously my therapy worked."

"Dr. Alfonzo, do you deny all of the allegations laid our in Mr. Gajdics's complaint letter?"

"Yes," he said.

I looked around the room. The members' heads were all faced down at their yellow legal-sized pads of paper.

"Dr. Alfonzo, tell me, please, what could possibly motivate a person, any person, to invent and then spend years of their life pursuing a complaint of such magnitude, unless at least some part of it were true?"

"I now have sixty-five patients. None of *them* are complaining. Besides, most of my referrals are self-referrals that have come to me from other patients."

"Dr. Alfonzo, complainants come to the College without thought of gain but out of concern for the physician's behavior. Even one complaint is cause for concern." Mrs. Humphries inhaled deeply before continuing. "Dr. Alfonzo, your treatment plan is a highly unorthodox form of therapy. The committee is aware that it has never been properly investigated and that it leaves much to be desired at the scientific level. The fact that an experimental program of this type of therapy was run almost thirty years ago is not sufficient. Scientific knowledge *must* be continuously evaluated and reevaluated in order for advances to be made. Moreover, the committee is concerned that you are isolated from the psychiatric community. We are concerned about your future group work with patients, your individual therapy, and your use of ketamine."

One committee member, a man, spoke up for the first time. "Dr. Alfonzo, I have to say that I am not at all comfortable with your style of practice. Personally, I find it extremely distressing. Tell me: When do you plan to retire?"

"Oh, not for a while. Ten years or so."

For several minutes no one said a word. Mrs. Humphries wrote notes and exchanged a hushed conversation with a colleague. Others looked at me and smiled, blinked in acknowledgment. I did not look at Alfonzo, but I could hear him whispering with his lawyer. Tommy had not said a word to me the whole time we'd been seated.

"Dr. Alfonzo," Mrs. Humphries said, turning back toward the

room, "the College will arrange to have your practice reviewed. We will be in touch. Mr. Gajdics, would you like to say anything before we adjourn for the day?"

"Nothing, thank you. I think my complaint letter said it all. But thanks to everyone for their time. I appreciate it."

"Then we're finished. Thank you to all for your time and energy."

I looked at my watch. Despite being told that reviews rarely lasted longer than thirty minutes, mine had lasted more than two hours.

Out on the street, Tommy and I walked to his car in the pouring rain.

"Don't you want to get under?" he motioned, opening his umbrella.

I nodded, turned my face up toward the sky. Rain was what I needed.

"They believed *you*, Peter, not him," he said as we climbed in his car. "He looked like the mad professor, down on his knees, picking up binders, mumbling something about ketamine being used in Russia. I think their only hope now is that he retires one day soon."

"Maybe. Maybe not. I don't know."

This had been the first time that I'd seen Alfonzo in nearly three years. The last time I'd seen him, he had been like a father to me, a demigod; now he was more like a phantom from someone else's nightmare. I didn't know which disturbed me more: his current behavior or the fact that I'd submitted to him for as long as I had, fearing that if I didn't, somehow I'd be punished.

"Where do you want to go to eat?" I said to Tommy, my face still dripping from the rain. "I need a drink."

22

IN AUGUST 1999, FIVE months after the conduct review, I received an envelope in the mail with no return address; inside was a poorly photocopied, four-page document that took me several minutes to decipher. It was a copy of the review of Alfonzo's practice, as conducted by "two independent psychiatrists," both hired by the College of Physicians and Surgeons.

The review had taken place in Alfonzo's office, the document read, on a single day over a period of four hours. The two psychiatrists commended Alfonzo for his availability and cooperation in pulling charts from recent patients. They asked him questions about how he conducted his practice; Alfonzo, in turn, told them of his therapeutic houses, which he stated no longer existed. He explained that his therapy consisted of "about fifty percent cognitive behavioral and about fifty percent feeling therapy," and that its purpose was to "allow retrogression and to link the past with the present." The "about fifty percent cognitive behavioral" comment left me perplexed. If Alfonzo had changed his practice since my days in the Styx, this was news to me. Maybe we had been his guinea pigs.

The doctors discussed Alfonzo's nurturing sessions. Alfonzo affirmed that the powerful emotions that emerged during these sessions connected past events to the present. The doctors discussed the potential problems with regression, their concern about a patient's ability to return to normal functioning. Alfonzo said that his patients emerged fully able to live in the present.

The document concluded with the following summary:

Strengths:
1. *Dr. Alfonzo is trying his best with a difficult patient mix.*
2. *He is well-intentioned and approaches his work with diligence.*
3. *The notion of support and nurturing as a treatment process for personality disorders is not without foundation.*

Weaknesses:
1. *Occasional involvement in nurturing sessions himself. We are clear that this is not a sexual violation but is most likely a boundary violation.*
2. *Giving gifts to patients would be considered a boundary violation.*
3. *Use of Ketamine, which is an anesthetic drug that produces disinhibiting and hallucinatory experiences. This is not a standard, accepted psychiatric practice.*
4. *Potential problems with regression (retrogression) and return to normal function in a short period of time with individuals who are vulnerable in this experience.*

ıııııııı

Natie and I had not seen each other in almost ten months when she visited me in my apartment. Since undergoing a colostomy for stage 3 cancer, she told me, her life had revolved around her now "nonexistent asshole," and the fact that she would have to "shit out of a bag" for the remainder of her life.

For the time being, she was unable to sit for long periods of time, and even when she did, had to use a doughnut-shaped pillow to soften the feeling of sitting on a pinecone. She also went through a six-month course of chemotherapy, which caused the usual symptoms of nausea, vomiting, diarrhea, fatigue, hair loss, skin rash, and mouth sores.

Her recent three-month follow-up test, she explained, came back negative, although her doctor was quick to remind her that these types of tests were not at all sensitive; he could neither confirm nor deny that she had cancer. At times, her feelings of grief, exhaustion, and sadness were almost too much to bear. But she was aware that soon she would have to put this demon in the cage she had built for it in her mind and carry on with life, knowing full well that the demon that was cancer could emerge and consume her once again, this time for good.

Natie and I had always shared a brutal honesty. After lying regressed on a mattress for years, confessing the shame of our childhood sexual abuse and the ways in which we'd sought the love of our parents through hundreds if not thousands of sexual partners, there was little else to hide. Little else embarrassed. Physical nakedness paled in comparison. So I asked about her cancer, about whether she thought there was a correlation between the fact that her childhood abuser had anally raped her and that her body developed colon cancer some thirty-five years later.

"Of course I've made the connection," she said. "I don't have an asshole anymore. The hole my abuser entered me through has been sewn shut. I'd be a fool not to think of that. On one hand, I know that I've survived this crippling disease we call cancer. But the experience of having cancer has meant so much more to me; it's gone far beyond a bunch of microorganisms in my body. It's illness as metaphor. The cancer was a message. It forced me to stop and reexamine how I was living my life, how I should live my life, how I want to live my life. Like you and the therapy. I think in a lot of ways it's easier to have cancer than to go through what you did with the therapy."

"Why would you say that?"

"There's an intrinsic support system built into our culture for making meaning out of cancer, whereas there is no cultural permission at all, at all, for you to make meaning out of what you've experienced. It's hardly even recognized by society as being anything that even happens to people. Psychotherapeutic cults? Conversion therapy? Who goes through that? And if they do, who wants to talk about it, or believe it? The horror of it all provokes disbelief. Acknowledging what you've survived would be far easier if you had some type of public validation for having gone through it in the first place—recognition from your family, or your culture, that what you went through was challenging. Life threatening, even. Cancer, on the other hand, is universally recognized as being a serious, public, catastrophic situation."

"So what do you do with it? When you're alone and there's no one else."

"'Do with it'?"

"The fact that you survived."

"One of the ways I was able to make meaning out of what I went through was by using the experience itself."

"'Using the experience'?"

"The process of encountering this challenge, the cancer itself: it was like a wall against which I was forced to hurl myself. Over and over. It teaches you how strong you are. Trauma gives you feedback about your own inner strength that you just can't get anywhere else. It tests your mettle. No one can take that away from you: who you are because of what you've survived."

"Remember what you said about suing him?"

"What about it?"

"Well . . . I've been thinking about it. It's all I can think about, actually."

"And?"

"Maybe if he'd admitted to what'd happened I'd feel different, maybe then I could walk away, but . . . to deny everything . . . as if none of it was real . . . You really think I could sue him?"

"What do you want to do, Peter?"

"Some days, still . . . I just want to die. Meanwhile, I don't know what else to do but sue him. I'm not interested in revenge, but right now, it's like none of it is real, like none of it even happened. I have to make it real, somehow."

Readjusting her doughnut-shaped pillow, Natie sat up an inch taller in her seat. "I think you should do it. Absolutely. He was unethical with so many of us. Part of my own healing from the sexual abuse was reporting it to the police. Saying publicly that what happened to me was not okay. That one act of vindication helped me to let go of much of my anger toward my abuser. This isn't about revenge, Peter. This is about your sanity. You have to set things right. Unless you stand up for yourself, it will always haunt you. This isn't just about what he did to you. This goes way beyond you. This is political."

||||||||||

After calling fifteen lawyers, I was able to summarize the last ten years of my life in less than thirty seconds, a fact I didn't find particularly heartwarming. I knew I wanted a lawyer in Vancouver, because I'd also been thinking for some time about moving back to my hometown as soon as the lawsuit was filed. Finally, a high-profile lesbian lawyer specializing in human-rights cases, whom I found in an LGBT legal directory, referred me to an attorney she knew.

"He's your man," she told me as I walked out her door. "He's gay, and he's a pit bull."

||||||||||

The attorney, Mackenzie, who was short and round, with a perennial frown across his brow, indeed reminded me of a dog, a gay bulldog, when I met him for the first time in his office in Vancouver's trendy Gastown district one hot August afternoon.

He accepted my case on contingency at the end of our meeting, after I explained who I was and what had happened. At our next meeting, where I filled him in with even more detail, I gave him a six-inch-thick binder of material from the College investigation.

"I also have journals," I said.

"What kind of journals?"

"That I wrote during the therapy. All my primal session reports are in the journals, as well as long passages I wrote after raging at the bat for hours. Many of the pages are ripped because I was still so angry as I wrote. I'm afraid my rants may come across as pretty unbalanced, though, out of context."

"I'll want those from you. We may not want to release them as evidence, but I need to read them."

"Has anyone ever sued their former therapist for trying to make them straight?"

"Not that I'm aware of. This won't be easy. Malpractice suits never are. And they almost never settle out of court."

"I don't want to settle. I want to go to trial."

"This is a long, drawn-out process, Peter," he said, explaining that he would first need to draft a Statement of Claim and then serve it to the defense, who would then review it and respond with a Statement of Defense.

Examinations for discovery would follow, he said, wherein both Alfonzo and I would give sworn testimony under oath to be used during the lawsuit. For tactical reasons, Mackenzie said he preferred that my examination take place prior to the doctor's.

During one of my many subsequent visits to meet with Mackenzie, I rented an apartment on the ninth floor of a high-rise, overlooking English Bay Beach, in the city's West End district. I handed in my resignation with the AIDS organization back in Victoria, and arranged with my government job to be transferred to one of the Crown Counsel offices within British Columbia's Ministry of Attorney General, in Vancouver's downtown core. On September 1, 1999, exactly ten years to the day that I had fled the city, I moved back.

||||||||||

I tracked down my old friend, Pearl, and discovered that she'd moved to Berlin years earlier. I wrote her the first of what became several letters, describing my years in the Styx and my plans to sue Alfonzo.

In her response, which I received a month later, she wrote that my withdrawal from her life, and our friendship, devastated her. She talked with friends, some of whom had been my friends, and together they wondered whether she should dive in and rescue me. "Cult," she wrote, was the word that she and others used to describe what seemed to be happening to me.

Mostly she talked about our final, brief meeting in the ferry café, in 1990.

"You scared the shit out of me," she wrote. "Your eyes looked vacant, like you'd been brainwashed: glazed, absent, not registering a thing I said. Most distressing was that I could find no sense of myself or our past in your eyes or in anything you said. Our parting seemed to cause you no grief, as if nothing of substance had ever been between us. This complete absence of even a memory of me in you made me feel psychotic and sent me reeling. You seemed to be erasing, or perhaps rewriting, our shared history. There was nothing

I could find in you to hold on to in myself. It was a nightmare. I returned home that day and vomited, as if to empty myself of our poisonous exchange.

"I must confess that it is retroactively validating for me to learn about the kind of duress you were under and the amount of medication you were taking. But I am glad that you are now on the 'outside looking in,' and that you're taking action—because Alfonzo behaved criminally, and because you need vindication."

|||||||||

In my Statement of Claim, which Mackenzie filed later that same month, I sued Alfonzo for the following:

- *failure to act in accordance with general and approved practices in the field of psychiatry;*
- *prescribing psychiatric medication (Ketamine) no longer in use in medical practice;*
- *prescribing medication in inappropriate dosages;*
- *double-prescribing medication for his own personal use;*
- *failure to explain or warn me of the side effects of prescribed medication;*
- *treating homosexuality as an illness or disease;*
- *allowing me to witness his own therapy;*
- *directing me to care for his pets, provide editorial services for his book, domestic services for himself and his other patients, and landscaping services and household renovations to his personal property, all without remuneration;*
- *intentionally inflicting mental suffering upon me contrary to his duty not to harm me and for no medically accepted purpose; and*
- *committing battery by injecting me with the drug Ketamine without my knowledge or informed consent.*

In his defense statement, which Mackenzie received on my behalf two months later, Alfonzo denied every allegation contained in my claim. Defense submitted that the action should be dismissed with costs.

In February 2000, defense filed thirty-eight authorizations for release of information on my personal history, directed to twenty-three medical practitioners and fifteen past employers. Then Mackenzie received defense's list of more than 100 interrogatories—questions that I needed to answer about every doctor I'd visited over the previous twenty years: appointments with general practitioners, medical exams, X-rays, dental checkups, and therapists I'd consulted post-Alfonzo.

In March, Mackenzie wrote to confirm that we'd agreed with defense's recommendation for an eight-day trial.

Civil lawsuits such as mine, for more than $25,000, were heard by a judge only within the Supreme Court of British Columbia, one of two superior courts in the province, the other being the Court of Appeal. With the court's ongoing backlog, it was not uncommon for trials to be scheduled up to two years in advance. Lengths of trials also could be altered as the date approached.

I waited four more months for further information. Finally, Mackenzie's secretary called to tell me that the Supreme Court Trial Division had rejected a proposed trial date of December 2001. I didn't hear from her again until October 2000, when my eight-day trial was officially rescheduled for to March 18, 2002, seventeen months away. Unfortunately, we would not know if a judge had been freed up for trial until two days prior to its commencement. If one hadn't, we would have to postpone the trial to some indeterminate date in the future.

I didn't hear from Mackenzie again for another six months, until April 2001, when he called to confirm that my examination for discovery was set to begin December 17, 2001. "By the way, I looked at your journals," he said on the phone.

"Okay. And?"

"We won't be releasing them as evidence. You were right—you do come across as pretty unbalanced in those pages. They wouldn't help us win your case."

꞉꞉꞉꞉꞉꞉꞉꞉꞉꞉

Pisti, my next eldest brother, was still single, self-employed as a gardener, and living on his own when I visited him in his two-bedroom apartment over a weekend. If I was not quite ready to step fully back into the family circle, Pisti had at least remained a point of contact. He also had gained more than forty pounds in the years since I'd last seen him. Beneath the extra weight, however, like a body suit that protected him from his pain, I could see the same frightened boy that Dad chased through the house with a *fakanál*.

My face was buried in a newspaper when he snuck up behind me in his living room with a copy of *Playboy* draped open to its centerfold. "Look at those tits," he said, turning Ms. May in all her glory to face me. "I'd do her."

"What movie would you like to see?" I said, deflecting his comment, and the magazine.

Pisti sprawled the opened magazine on the sofa next to me and looked over my shoulder at the movie listings. "How 'bout that one?" he said, pointing to the latest action flick staring one of Hollywood's hottest hunks.

"He's gay," I said.

"Who?"

"The actor."

"How would you know?"

"Everyone knows."

"But he's married."

I glanced back to see his expression, wondering whether he was feigning ignorance or if he still believed that all men who married women didn't sometimes still have sex with other men.

"Have you talked to Mom or Dad lately?" he asked.

"Not lately."

"You should visit them more often."

"Why?"

"Don't you miss them?"

I dropped the newspaper over Ms. November and looked at him. "How often do *you* see them?"

"Every week. We still go to Mass together every Sunday."

I picked the paper back up. "So you're still the good Catholic son they'd always hoped and prayed for."

"Why don't you talk to them?"

"We don't get along."

"Why do you have to advertise it? I don't tell them what I know they don't want to hear."

"I can't do what you do. Besides, my not talking to them isn't just about my sexuality . . ."

"What's it about then?"

"Don't you remember Dad beating me?"

"You didn't get it half as bad as I did. Or Kriska. I still remember the day Dad told me to break a branch off the tree in the backyard and leave it in the basement so he could beat her with it."

"He beat her with a tree branch?"

"You have to train a child. You have to discipline them."

"You do not 'train' a child. Not by beating them. We should never have been hit."

"You don't think I know they made a few mistakes? You get to a certain point in your life where you either accept what's happened to you or you don't. And if you don't, you're never at peace."

"You've accepted what's happened to you?" I glanced down at his immense midsection. "You're at peace?"

He rubbed his belly, as if inside him lived a baby. "So I like food, so what? It keeps me company. At least I don't go around blaming someone else my whole life."

"I'm not blaming them, I'm holding them responsible. There is a difference. Actions do have consequences."

"Do you still blame me for what I did when we were kids?"

"Which part?"

"Father Raphael."

"Honestly?"

"I thought I was doing the right thing at the time."

"Threatening to tell Mom and Dad that I was having sex with men unless I confess my 'sin' to a priest was definitely not the right thing to do at the time. What did you think he was going to do, perform a miracle?"

"You don't think it's a little twisted that you were having sex with men twice your age, in parking lots, when you were sixteen years old?"

"You were having sex with girls when you were sixteen. And I never had sex in parking lots. We were always at the bottom of the stairwell, below the parking lot."

"You think it's funny?"

"It was just sex."

"'Just sex'? You don't feel the least bit ashamed of yourself?"

"Of course not. Do you? Of the sex you have?"

"Sometimes. Most of the time. Always."

"You feel shame about having sex?"

"I've never not felt shame after having sex."

I looked at my brother, as if through the bars of his cell, a prison of the worst kind: one in which he'd normalized and so no longer even noticed.

"Homosexuality is unnatural," he said.

"Maybe to you, because you're not attracted to men. My homosexuality is the most natural thing in the world to me."

"Cancers are also natural. Lots of things that are bad for us are 'natural.' The Bible explicitly states that no man shall lie with another man . . ."

"Oh, I am so tired of you people using—"

"Us people?"

"Using the words of ignorant men to support your own ignorance. Who wrote the Bible?"

"The Bible is the inspired word of God."

"Written two thousand years ago. By men filled with prejudice and ignorance and absolutely no scientific data."

"You really think that genetics is the wisest position to take?"

"What do you—?"

"If homosexuality has a genetic cause, don't you think it's inevitable that science, or society, would take steps to root it out? Haven't you heard of eugenics?"

"You don't know what you're saying."

"Homosexuals spit in the face of traditional family values."

"That's ironic, considering the home life we came from."

"Your lifestyle will never be accepted by society. *Never*. Men and women are anatomically constructed to procreate. There's no debating that. We fit together."

"Do you ever have anal sex with women?"

"That's none of your business."

"Sorry, I forgot: heterosexuals never have anal sex."

"Didn't that doctor help you at all?"

"With what?"

"Kick the habit."

I'd had enough. I stood and moved back down his hallway, preparing to leave.

"Oh come on," he said, trying to pull me back into his world.

"If it weren't for you, I wouldn't have ended up that doctor."

"What?"

"If it weren't for you and this family of mine, I would've spent my twenties learning how to *love* instead of how to hate myself."

"What is going on with you?"

I turned to face him at the door. "Teen gays commit suicide because of people like you."

"Oh come on."

"People die of AIDS because of people like you."

"I've never killed anyone."

"It's people like you that are killing me."

"*What?*"

"What do you even think of when you say the word 'homosexual'?" He looked at me like a stunned animal. "Because I'll tell you one thing, whatever it is, it's not what a homosexual is. Most of the men I've had sex with watch football, drink beer, and hang out with guys that look just like you." I glanced down at his protruding stomach. "Well, maybe not like you. You wouldn't believe the number of fathers who've picked me up with their little toddler carriages in the backseats of their station wagons."

"Do you have to talk about that?"

"How would you like me to say the truth so it doesn't offend you? You have some kind of weird idea about what it means to be a homosexual, and that's crazy." I turned to leave, turning back to him like I was caught in a turnstile. "No, you know what's crazy? What's fucking crazy? The fact that after all these years, after everything I've been through, that at the age of thirty-three I am still standing here, defending myself to you: my brother. That's what's crazy."

His glazed eyes told me all I needed to know.

"Forget it," I said, opening the door to leave.

"Aren't we going to the movie?"

"Not tonight," I said. "I'm tired."

|||||||||||

In May 2001, I attended my parents' forty-fifth wedding anniversary dinner at a high-end French restaurant. At the table was Pisti, who I'd not spoken to since our last visit, my middle sister, Barbara, and her husband, and my eldest brother, Frank, and his wife, Lisa. Kriska, despite being invited, was, as always for such events, a no-show.

After more than a few glasses of expensive red wine, I didn't even mind so much that I had nothing whatsoever in common with anyone at the table. When I noticed everyone lost in their own private conversations, I leaned over to Lisa, sitting next to me.

"Have you ever considered the possibility that one of your boys might turn out gay?" I whispered, discreetly. I knew that I was taking a risk by asking the question, but considering Lisa had always prided herself on being "open minded," I figured it was a risk worth taking.

"Oh yes," she replied without hesitation, "of course I've thought about it. I've thought about that just like I've thought about them becoming alcoholics or drug addicts. But I know they aren't because they've never been sexually abused."

I expected her to crack a smile.

"Every gay person I've ever met has been sexually abused as a child."

Lisa had never made a secret of the fact that she herself had been sexually abused by her father, before her parents' divorce when she was eight, but her own history did not seem to factor into her current argument about me.

"What about all the straight people who were sexually abused?" I asked. "What about all the gay people who weren't abused?"

"Well were *you* abused?" she asked, turning to face me square on.

Lisa knew that I'd been abused because I'd told her, years earlier, before I'd moved away. My eyes scanned the table. My father was staring at me from across the table. "I don't think that made me gay."

"You don't?" She sounded genuinely surprised.

The dinner was winding down, so our conversation came to an abrupt end. I left the restaurant angry, reminded of the frequency throughout my life with which the same belief system—ideologically insular, pointing to nothing in the real world that validated its flawed argument—had caused me years of depression and confusion, self-hatred, not to mention had walked me straight into the office of one Dr. Alfonzo.

Instead of walking home, I marched directly to the nearest gay dance club. Like a joint that needed popping back into its socket, I needed to be around my own kind, if only to undo the effects of my family.

I arrived close to midnight, bought a drink, and watched as the dry ice seemed to lift the shirtless, sweaty men off the dance floor like a cloud. Then I spotted him, recognized him instantly, standing across the floor, alone. Memories of another time and place assaulted me as they flooded back without warning. A couple of minutes later I walked over. He saw me standing next to him, glancing at him. His cocky expression told me that he thought I was cruising him. He didn't remember me; then again, why would he? More than twenty years had elapsed since we'd last met.

"Your name's Jonathan, isn't it?" I asked, leaning into him.

"Yes," he said, looking pleased, if a bit leery.

"My name's Peter Gajdics," I said, pronouncing my name like I did as a child—*Gay-dicks*. "Do you remember me?"

He turned and looked at me, closer, up and down, but did not respond.

"We went to high school together."

For a moment I thought he'd acknowledge me. Then he turned his attention back to the half-clad men on the dance floor. Perhaps because he did remember me, he did not wish to acknowledge me. "Sorry," he said, distantly.

"You used to call me 'goots.'"

He didn't look at me. Just saying that word, *goots*, reminded me of the way I was taunted daily, starting in elementary school: threatened and assaulted when Jonathan and his friends ran up from behind, pecking me like vultures, punching me in the ribs, slapping me across my face, the singe from their handprints like red hot irons to my flesh. Once, when we were in tenth-grade gym class, he and his friends pretended to like me and called me over to join their group. When I did, he threw an open bottle of liquid paper in my mouth; then he spat in my face and ran off with his friends, chanting, *Faggot . . . faggot . . . faggot.*

The disco beat of Donna Summer called me back to my surroundings.

"You don't remember me?" I asked again.

"No," he repeated, still not looking in my direction.

He was lying. I repeated my name again. "*Gay-dicks.*"

He would not look at me, but mumbled, "Sorry, I don't remember."

"Well I do," I said, stepping around to face him so he'd be forced to look me in the eyes—two boxers squaring off in a ring. "I remember you well. You called me names like 'fag' and 'queer' throughout high school. You were an asshole to me."

I waited for him to look at me, for his eyes to focus in on mine. When they did, I continued. "I saw you standing here, and I wanted to come over and tell you that I lived in fear for years because of you. I thought you should know how much pain you caused me."

I held his gaze until he looked away. Then I turned and walked away, through a cloud of dry ice on the dance floor.

23

THE MOMENT DR. REIMER opened the door to his downtown hotel room, I thought of Sam the Snowman from *Rudolph the Red-Nosed Reindeer*—stout, with snow-white hair, a full but nicely cropped beard and gleaming blue eyes that twinkled as he said, "Come in, come in."

Our conversation began almost as soon as I took a seat next to him at a round table next to a small kitchenette. Then he clarified what I knew already. Dr. Reimer had been hired by Mackenzie to provide an expert medical opinion in my lawsuit against Alfonzo. Without a moment's delay, with pen and paper in hand, he asked me to tell him about my life from the time I was a child to when I left therapy. I did, and without interruption, he listened. Without judgment, he asked for clarification. So supportive was he of my experiences that all three of our four-hour conversations, beginning September 21, 2001 and extending well into October, were the antithesis of all my years with Alfonzo.

When I reached the part about my collapse in the Styx, I asked Reimer what he thought had been its cause. The only explanation Alfonzo had ever provided was that I'd "expiated" my "parental introjects" to the point that my "mental image" of my "self had become dislodged"—one of Alfonzo's many obfuscations roughly translated as: primal had hollowed me out. The medication, he'd always said, had never played any part.

"You most certainly suffered a breakdown of some sort brought on by medication toxicity," Reimer said without hesitation.

"So, in your opinion . . . it was the medication, not necessarily the therapy, that caused my collapse."

"I'm sure the therapy didn't help. But you were taking well in excess of the recommended doses of extremely powerful psychotropics. Simply put, you overdosed. You're a lucky man. It could have been far worse."

"Worse, as in . . ."

"As in not surviving."

||||||||||

Several weeks after Reimer's interviews concluded, I met with the defense's psychiatrist, Dr. Bennington. The day of our first meeting, I sat alone and waited for him in his tiny office chock-full of gray metal filing cabinets, a brown laminate bookshelf, a coat stand, scattered papers, hardcover books, and a large oak desk that split the room in two—a dividing line separating doctor from patient. On his wall were several large framed certificates of medical studies. His business cards, displayed facing out on the desk, read: "General and Forensic Psychiatry." I slipped one into my coat pocket as the doctor—a large, brooding man of sixty-plus years—entered the office, twenty minutes late.

Speaking in a refined English accent, he introduced himself as Dr. Bennington, and then repeated that I should also call him Dr. Bennington. I declined his offer of a Sprite or Coke before he settled in his reclining leather chair, facing me behind his desk. He breathed in a deep sigh, as if he were about to undertake the first step in what he knew would be a thousand-mile journey.

"Now," he said, "before we get started, why don't we set some ground rules. I am a psychiatrist, retained by defense to act as their expert medical opinion in your suit against—" He flipped through his opened file. "Against . . . Dr. Alfonzo. My job is to talk to you, to get to know you, to ask you a few questions about yourself. Do you understand me?"

I wanted to tell the good doctor that English was my first language—of course I understood him—and that while we were at it, I also did not have a mental illness, such as borderline personality disorder, which I was sure would be his eventual diagnoses.

"Yes, I understand," I said instead.

"So. How are you feeling?"

"Well, it's six years since I left the therapy. Things are better now than they were."

Bennington began writing furiously, waving his freehand like a traffic controller, motioning for me to proceed.

"I suppose I'm dealing with the same issues that most people deal with: family, friends, relationships. Except that it's like I'm waking up at the age of thirty-six and I've lost the last ten years of my life."

"You mentioned relationships. Are you in a relationship?"

"No."

"Dating?"

"I tried, I mean I have, but . . ."

"Yes?"

"I'm not seeing anyone right now. I'm single."

For one hour, Bennington asked me about my "coming-out" process, my family's attitudes toward my homosexuality, my reasons for moving away. When we finally returned to the therapy, I repeated Alfonzo's comments that because I did not possess "any of the characteristics of a homosexual," he thought I could be the first to make "the switch over."

"Sometimes I feel guilty about suing Dr. Alfonzo," I said, interrupting the flow of our conversation.

My comment seemed to have been the first interesting thing I'd said to Bennington. He stopped writing, removed his bifocals, and leaned forward in his chair, staring down at me like Gulliver to a Lilliputian. "Please, continue."

"Dr. Alfonzo was like a father. I felt a great deal of loyalty toward him."

"When did that change?"

"About a year after the therapy ended, in 1996. I hadn't talked to my family or friends in years. I was living on my own. I'd go out and—I mean just four or five times—I'd buy a bottle of wine, go home, and drink it down in ten minutes and pass out on my bed. That's how I dealt with the pain. I'd never drunk like that before."

"What sort of pain?" He repositioned his glasses and resumed taking notes.

"Pardon?"

"You said you were in pain."

"Well, I'd just spent six years of my life crying and screaming, drugged out of my mind, isolated from the world and twisting myself in knots to become something that I wasn't. I didn't know what to do with all of that. I was numb. Empty."

"And you left the therapy in what year again? Nineteen ninety-six?"

I repeated that it was 1995, but wondered why he was asking me something that was surely in his file, and that I'd told him only moments earlier.

"Sorry, I should have asked you before: Is there a history of mental illness in your family?"

"What? No. Not that I'm aware of."

"Alcoholism? Drug dependency?"

"Not that I'm aware of."

For a moment he continued writing, then looked up from his notes. "How about you?"

"How about me what?"

"Do you have a history of mental illness? Alcoholism?"

"No. To both."

"Well that's not true, now, is it?" His voice had taken a sudden, accusatory tone, like my seventh-grade teacher was suddenly reprimanding me. "Just a minute ago you told me how you used to buy bottles of wine and drink them down and then pass out on your bed."

"What I *said* was that after I left the therapy I didn't know how to express what I was feeling, so I bought some wine four or five times and drank till I passed out at home. I didn't know how else to deal with the last six years of my life. That's what I said. They were isolated incidents. I never drank like that before, and I haven't since."

He looked back to his file, appearing bored by my response. "It says here you cut yourself." When he looked back up, I saw nothing in his eyes.

"I never cut myself."

"You pierced your nipples with a safety pin. It's all right here."

This time it was an accusation. I blushed. Details from therapy, like confessions to a priest or, for that matter, admissions to a lawyer, were fair game.

"Do you still pierce your nipples?"

There was no "right" answer to the question: either I said "no" and he would write in his neatly summarized treaty that Alfonzo's therapy had helped "cure" me of my pathology, or I said "yes" and my borderline personality disorder would be verified.

"No," I said.

"Tell me about the sexual abuse. You were abused? A stranger, was it?"

I told him about the incident when I was six years old. He continued taking notes for a moment after I finished. "That's it?" he said, looking up with a start.

"Pardon?"

"That's the sexual abuse? That's all that happened? Tell me," he said, leaning forward in his chair, eyes narrowing, as if looking into a microscope, "do you remember if you were attracted to men *prior* to that incident, or if the attraction began only *after* it happened?"

"I was six years old."

"Yes, but can you recall being attracted to men before it happened?"

"I was six years old. I don't think I was attracted to anyone, man or woman, at six years old."

"Did you ever tell Dr. Alfonzo that you wished to be heterosexual? That you wished to be straight?"

"I recall saying that I felt like a crippled heterosexual, yes."

"Well," he replied, tossing his pen on the desk, "if you walked in here and told me that you felt like a crippled heterosexual, I'd think that we'd just need to get rid of everything that's in your way and then you *would* be heterosexual."

"Or," I flipped back, "you could think that I was homophobic and that we'd just need to get rid of my fear and hatred of homosexuals and then I'd be able to admit to myself that I really was gay."

Another faint smile crossed his lips as he picked up his pen. He asked me to explain how Alfonzo attempted to treat my homosexuality as an illness and to make me heterosexual. When I mentioned "the shit thing"—my way of deflecting what I really would have rather never talked about again with anyone—he seemed genuinely surprised and asked for clarification, which I provided. For some reason, I expected a look of horror. Something. He did not acknowledge what I'd said, but once again changed the subject. "So," he said, leaning back in his chair, expressionless, "I imagine it'll be difficult to get the people you knew to testify against the doctor."

"I don't know. I guess if they're subpoenaed they'll have to."

"They know about the case?"

"I called some of them a while back. Most were still in his therapy. I do have one witness, a woman I met in the therapy. She's—" I stopped myself mid-sentence. "I don't know that I should be talking to you about this."

"That's okay, I'm not taking notes. But let's stop here. Do you need a break? Coffee?"

"No."

"Mind if I get one?"

"No, no, of course not."

"Why don't we take ten minutes and then we'll continue."

"Fine."

And, with that, he left the room.

I sat, alone, and waited. Street noises surfaced, honking cars, muffled conversations from down below his third-floor window. Outside his office door, I heard nothing. My own words from the first part of our interview flashed through my mind.

I feel guilty about suing Dr. Alfonzo . . .

Dr. Alfonzo was like a father . . .

I'd go out and buy a bottle of wine, go home and drink it down in ten minutes . . .

I felt like a crippled heterosexual . . .

A streak of panic washed over me. My face flushed. I had wanted to tell him the truth, to be as truthful as I could about everything, but maybe I'd been naive. Unwise. Foolish. I felt stupid, totally unprepared for what I'd stepped into.

"Sorry to keep you waiting," he said as he entered the room again, smiling.

I prepared myself for more questions, for something, an onslaught.

"Well . . . let's see. Where were we . . .?" He sat down and glanced at his files. Flipped through a few pages. Then he closed the files and he looked back up at me. "I think I have what I need. Thank you for coming down."

"That's it?"

"That's it."

||||||||||

Toward the end of November, Mackenzie called me down to his office. Defense had sent him taped recordings of my primals between 1993 and 1995, considered a "normal" part of disclosure of evidence between parties in all civil cases brought before the Court. He wanted to play me portions from several so that we could discuss them face-to-face.

Not until the door was shut and we were seated across from each other did Mackenzie turn on the mini-cassette recorder. When he did, I heard what sounded like a panting animal. Seconds later a voice, my own, pierced through us both.

"PETERRRR, I'MMMM GOING TO KILLLL YOOOUUU . . ."

I glanced back at Mackenzie's door, half expecting his secretary to come rushing in to see who or what was screaming. Mackenzie pushed the small recorder an inch closer in my direction, as if to distance himself from the voice, like an exorcism in full swing. I heard a thumping in the background and knew that I'd moved to the batting station. The pounding added a heartbeat to the session, a rhythmical stabbing that echoed my screams.

"I don't feel safe in this house," my voice continued, breathless. "I don't feel safe with you . . . "

"Be *specific*, Peter," I heard Yvette interject. "Why are you so scared? Answer in your father's voice again. Tell Peter what you're going to do to him."

I took her advice and replied as my father.

"You don't feel safe around me? I'm not going to do anything to you, Peter, I'm not going to do anything to you—*except maybe rip your fucking throat out!*" The sound of me banging the punching bag with the baseball bat continued again over my screams. "FUCKING PETER, O-PEN THE DOOOORRRR. I'M YOUR FATHER, I CAN DO WHATEVER I WANT TO YOUR BODY BECAUSE YOUR BODY BELONGS TO ME! AS LONG AS YOU LIVE IN MY HOUSE YOUR BODY BELONGS TO ME, YOUR BODY IS MINE, SO GIVE ME MY BODY! GIVE IT TO ME!"

"Switch back!" Yvette called out. "Tell him how you feel!"

"This *isn't* your body," I replied, the cadence to my voice having shifted back to "me" again. "This is *my* body. It's on *me*, isn't it? How can it be *your* body when it's on *me*? If this was *your* body it would be on *you*, but it's on *me* . . ."

Mackenzie hit the "off" button mid-voice, popped the tape out of its holder, and replaced it with another.

On this one my voice was fiendish and raspy, howling profanities as if through a throat full of vomit, sounded more like a demon than a man. I winced when I heard me say that I wanted to murder my mother for making me stick my hand up her "cunt." I wanted Mackenzie to turn the tape off. I didn't want to be reminded of what I said or felt "back then."

"You think I can't kill you? You think I can't STAB STAB STAB this knife into your bloody rotten corpse when you're not looking? When you're asleep at night?"

Never before had Mackenzie expressed emotion in front of me, but when he finally turned the tape off and leaned back in his chair, he appeared shaken. He asked me to explain my sessions, the process of primal. We'd talked about that many times before, beginning when I first met him in 1999, but I explained it all again.

"Tell me something," he asked. "After you finished a session like this . . . would Alfonzo calm you down . . . make some effort to bring you back to reality? What happened once you finished screaming?"

I explained, as I had many times before, that the intensity of these sessions was the norm in primal, not the exception. Typically, once a patient, any patient, finished their turn, they'd just sit up on the mattress in the middle of the room, take a moment to wipe the sweat from their face or to dry their tears. Then they'd crawl back to their spot around the circle, and we'd wait until the next person voluntarily ripped open their guts and bled like a wounded animal. We were like a crowd gathered 'round a car wreck: intermittently fascinated, yet terrified.

"But what did Alfonzo say to you after you finished your turn?"

"Not much. Sometimes he'd go off on long, philosophical rants about how his therapy was the best therapy in the world. For the most part he never said a word."

That Alfonzo never reframed my "memories," brought me back to the here-and-now after regressing on the mat, was clearly upsetting to Mackenzie.

"I want you to listen to something," he said, replacing the previous tape with yet another. On this one my breathing was labored, as if I'd just ran a marathon. I could only imagine that I'd just finished a session at the batting station.

"There is no such thing as homosexuality," my voice, rhythmic and assured as a metronome, declared. Mackenzie started fidgeting with his pack of cigarettes. "Homosexuals, what society calls homosexuals, they're all just sacrificial children. Only Dr. Alfonzo understands this. Only Dr. Alfonzo can help me reclaim my true identity—my innate heterosexuality. Without Dr. Alfonzo's help, I'm as good as dead. My life is over. I might as well stop living because that's what it would feel like to have sex again with another man. The thought of it makes me sick to my stomach. Like I want to puke, like I want to shit every last man who ever fucked me out of—"

Mackenzie's hand jerked up, almost involuntarily, and slammed the tape machine off. He took a deep breath, like he was readying himself to blow up a balloon, and released it in one long, nervous giggle. "I listened to your tapes last night," he said.

"What did you think?"

"I think defense is going to want to know why you said what you said, that's what I think. Frankly, I wondered the same thing."

Mackenzie waited for my response. I didn't know where to start.

"Understanding those sessions has taken me a long time—why I said what I said."

"And . . .?"

Explaining the process of primal, like directions on a road map, to someone was one thing; trying to explain any man's heart of darkness was another matter entirely.

"At the time of these sessions, I was taking more than five different psychiatric medications . . . lying on a mattress in the middle of a dark room, regressed . . . convinced that sexual abuse had created my homosexuality . . ."

"What about your mother? You said she made you stick your hand up her—"

"I don't remember that ever happening."

"But you said it."

"Yes."

"Why?"

"I said lots of things that weren't true. Or that were true but not necessarily in the way I said them."

Mackenzie looked unconvinced.

"People say lots of things when they're regressed. It doesn't mean they're *factually* true. The stories I could tell you about some of the things I've heard people say while in primal: parents wanting to kill their children, children wanting to kill their parents. Unfortunately, all the things I said about gays, that they were all just hurt children, they were taken at face value. Probably because it validated Alfonzo's beliefs. My self-hatred fed off his prejudice. We fed off each other. Besides, *everyone* in therapy is a hurt child. If they weren't, they wouldn't be in therapy."

"Do you still believe what you said about sex? About hating gay sex?"

"For a long time, in my life . . . sex with men reminded me of the man who abused me as a child. I couldn't separate the pleasure from the pain."

"But that's not what you said."

"There was this woman in one of my groups, she had been sexually abused as a child. The night before a primal, she'd have sex with two or three guys, then come to the office and lie on the mattress, and the hatred toward those men that came out of her—it was palpable. Alfonzo never told her that the sexual abuse had caused her attraction for men."

"What about when you said you wanted to be straight?"

"Who in their right mind in this culture *wouldn't* want to be straight? Or at least grow up thinking they *should* be straight? But Alfonzo was supposed to *know* better. He was supposed to help me *accept* myself. He was supposed to lead me *out* of my self-hatred, not reinforce it. That was his *job*."

Mackenzie took another steady, deep breath. "Alfonzo is a wacko," he said on his exhale, shaking his head. "I'm not trying to make light of the situation. But I find this whole case so extremely . . . distressing."

"So do I," I echoed. "So do I . . ."

|||||||||

After our meeting, I stopped at Doll & Penny's café near my apartment to read Dr. Bennington and Dr. Reimer's psychiatric evaluations, both of which Mackenzie had handed me on my way out of his office. The café had been Tommy's and my favorite late-night "hot spot" in the early- to mid-1980s. Now near closure, the restaurant was rundown and nearly empty. I took a seat at the back, behind a life-sized mannequin of Liza Minnelli from *Cabaret* and began to read.

In both their reports, Bennington and Reimer agreed about my mental faculties: I was, in their words, "clear-minded, logical, and goal-directed," according to Reiner, and "generally candid and open in [my] demeanor," according to Bennington.

Retrospectively diagnosing me was another matter entirely. Reimer stated that he could see no sufficient current or historical evidence to support a diagnosis of any major mental illness, such as a personality disorder, and attributed my anxiety, unhappiness, and depressive symptoms to the difficulty I'd experienced adjusting to my sexual orientation, as well as to the unhealthy interactions I'd had with my family throughout my coming-out process.

As might be expected, Bennington qualified me as a "wounded human being"—a redundancy in qualifiers, it seemed to me—while quoting extensively from the *Diagnostic and Statistical Manual of Mental Disorders, Fourth Edition* (DSM-IV). All of my panic, despair, and chronic feelings of emptiness were pathological in nature, he wrote, and any anger toward both the therapy and the therapist—my "fall from grace"—was clearly symptomatic of my borderline personality disorder in which, as he wrote, "disillusionment with caregivers could be a feature." That I had also expressed "intense anger" and "negative views" about both my parents—that I had experienced a great deal of distress at their lack of acceptance of my homosexuality—seemed to further support Bennington's diagnosis of a personality disorder.

Alfonzo had never treated my *homosexuality*, Bennington continued, but my "unwanted homosexual urges," all of which, he wrote, was consistent within "conventional" psychiatry's then-position that homosexuality was still considered "a problem to be addressed when it caused distress to an individual."

His inverted logic took me days to decipher.

In sum, it was true that the DSM-IV, as well as the World Health Organizations' own diagnostic manual, the *International Classification of Diseases,* Tenth Revision (ICD-10), no longer viewed homosexuality as a "mental illness"; however, in the DSM, a "persistent and marked distress about sexual orientation" was now cause for treatment; and in the ICD, the anxiety and depression that individuals might suffer as a result of uncertainty about their sexual orientation, or even the wish and efforts to try to change their sexual orientation, was reason for psychiatric intervention.

In other words, as long as "the homosexual," who the psychiatric community had for decades said was "perverted," "mentally ill," and "pathological," and whose cure could come only from reclaiming his innate heterosexuality, was not disturbed by and/or did not wish to change his homosexuality, he was no longer considered to have a mental illness, although treating him for a mental illness that comprised his uncertainty about, or his wish and efforts to try to change, his sexual orientation, was now wholly justifiable.

No sooner had I immersed myself in the reports than a young, effeminate waiter wearing purple eyeliner and a feather in his platinum hair interrupted to take my order.

"Just a chamomile," I said, imagining the box of "Gender Identity Disorder" that the young man would have surely been trapped inside had he fallen into the hands of Bennington or Alfonzo.

Glancing around, I noticed a bearded couple sitting across from me near the back of the café. One of the men ran his fingers along the underside of the other's hairy arm, toward the inside of his lover's open hand. Their fingers clasped, the joining of parts, palm against palm. Then he whispered something in his partner's ear, and together they smiled, as couples in love so often do.

Both doctors agreed on what medications Alfonzo had prescribed, as well as their dosages. Bennington wrote that Alfonzo's use of ketamine—"to enhance the positive emotional experiences of the bonding (reattachment) process"—was safe and justifiable.

Reimer, on the other hand, wrote that its use was completely outside accepted standards of psychiatric practice at the time in Canada, and was therefore unconventional and inappropriate in the extreme. He noted that ketamine, though normally used as an anesthetic agent (most commonly for horses), was also a drug of abuse that could have serious side effects, including dissociation, hallucinations, respiratory depression, and addiction. It was sometimes used as a club drug, he wrote, and had been reported to have effects similar to the street drugs LSD and PCP. He further noted that Alfonzo's so-called "consent for utilization of medication" documents were virtually devoid of clinical content.

Reimer found the dosages of the other medications used by Alfonzo to be extreme. Elavil, he explained, was most typically prescribed in the dosage range of 75 to 150 milligrams daily, and dosages above 150 milligrams were uncommon. Only in unusual cases would one approach the conventional maximum dosage of 300 milligrams daily, and only the most extreme and inconceivable circumstance would provoke dosages anywhere near 500 milligrams. The medications' side effects would have been extremely uncomfortable, he wrote, causing unnecessary suffering. Comprehending and incorporating insights or other learning experiences while in a state of such medication toxicity would have been impossible, causing memory and cognitive impairments and ultimately undermining the psychotherapy's effectiveness.

Unsurprisingly, Bennington never once drew any correlation between my history of sexual abuse and the sexual acting out by clarifying that such abuse often results in periods of promiscuity, dissociation, and compartmentalization, regardless of one's sexual orientation. Rather, my "increasingly promiscuous manner," as exhibited throughout my teens, seemed to him to be synonymous with homosexuality. Any unhappiness I may have experienced around my homosexuality, therefore, regardless of the reasons for that unhappiness, had apparently given Alfonzo carte blanche to help "correct" me.

While Bennington reaffirmed Alfonzo's contention that my homosexuality had never been treated as a disease, he also stated that Anafranil, one of the many medications Alfonzo had used to "deaden" my libido, had been an appropriate form of treatment in my "obsessive ruminations about sexuality"; similarly, my "sexual deviance" had warranted a treatment of aversive stimuli, such as Alfonzo's prescription of having me carry around and sniff from a bottle of feces. Bennington stated:

> "Whilst this treatment, at first glance, seems unusual, there is a form of treatment for sexual deviance that involves the use of aversive stimuli. The use of electric shock is perhaps the best known, but aversive smells have been used, and it would be seen here as appropriate."

At no point whatsoever did Bennington clarify what my "sexual deviance" was.

Conversely, Dr. Reimer viewed the "feces in a bottle" as "almost too bizarre to be worthy of comment," but stated, for the record, that it was not an effective therapeutic technique and that it would have amounted to "a degrading, demeaning, and counter-therapeutic strategy."

"Smelling one's feces," he wrote, would "more likely create confusion and distress in a patient than achieve a therapeutic goal."

Any therapy aimed at altering my sexual orientation would have only deepened and intensified the homophobic psychopathology that I'd already exhibited upon entering Alfonzo's therapy, Reimer clarified, rather than helping me to overcome it. The effects of such "unethical, unconscionable, and severely harmful" therapy would have included prolonged and unnecessary distress, instead of leading to a healthy self-acceptance and sexual lifestyle. Alfonzo's therapeutic techniques could not be justified, Reimer concluded, and involved a problematic mixture of positive and negative effects, not to mention diverting enormous time and energy, which could have been directed to accomplishments in other areas of my life, such as building friendships, love relationships, career advancements, or self-acceptance.

In their conclusions, Bennington had little to add about the reasons why I might have stayed in the therapy, except to say that my current self-acceptance pointed unquestionably to the success in Alfonzo's treatment. Reimer, on the other hand, stated that a "complex interaction" between my psychological vulnerabilities and symptoms and the approach taken by Alfonzo were only some of the reasons why I might have remained in such a therapy "voluntarily." I could only translate this to mean that Alfonzo had been a perfect manifestation not only of my own self-hatred, but also of my father: controlling, unpredictably explosive, and homophobic. I stayed because Alfonzo was not unfamiliar.

When I looked up from my reading, the waiter told me they were closing for the day. I was alone inside the café; the couple had left. I collected my papers, stuffed them back inside my shoulder pack, then walked through the crowds of late-night partygoers, home.

24

ON DECEMBER 16, 2001, the day before my discovery examination, Mackenzie asked that I meet him in his office.

"We need to talk," he said as I entered his office.

"Okay."

"Defense could potentially ask you anything about yourself tomorrow. They want to find out what makes you vulnerable. They want to know what makes you defensive."

"Okay."

"I don't want to be surprised. I need to know the worst possible thing that they could ask you. I want to be prepared."

This was not a difficult question. I told him about the boy I used to babysit, when I was twelve years old. The one I almost molested.

"So you didn't actually go through with it."

"No. I guess not. But I almost did. I tried—"

"But you didn't," McKenzie interrupted. "You didn't do it."

"No. I didn't . . ."

That night I dreamt the grown-up me was back inside the house, the house of the six-year-old boy. Someone was rattling around in the basement, evil rising from below. Terrified, I ran outside. Standing on an empty street in the middle of the night inside my dream, I could hear the child, crying, trapped and alone, still inside. *I might not escape a second time*, I thought as I stood, motionless, listening to the crying, unsure of what to do: remain outside and safe, or run back in and save the boy.

|||||||||

Early the next morning I arrived at the court transcriber's office. Inside a stark, white room I met the court reporter—a mid-fifties balding man. I took a seat next to him at one end of the rectangular table, a wall of windows to my right, and listened as he explained the process of discovering facts: defense counsel would ask me questions, and I was obliged to answer each into the microphone before me. He asked whether I preferred to swear on a Bible or affirm the truthfulness of all my answers. I choose to affirm.

Outside, the snow had just begun to dust the city white; inside, the two of us waited in icy silence. By the time Mackenzie arrived, ten minutes late, I had eaten five of the brightly wrapped candies on the table. Seconds later Alfonzo entered, trailed by not one but two lawyers—the pasty-faced man from the College's conduct review, whose name I now understood was Stanley Morris, and another, devilishly handsome young lawyer with slick, black hair. Mackenzie sat to my left; Morris sat directly across from me; and Alfonzo, I saw out of the corner of my eye, was seated to his lawyer's right, with his second, younger lawyer at the far end of the table, next to him. I would not look at Alfonzo directly.

"Would you pronounce your last name for me?" defense began.

"Gajdics."

"Gajdics," he said, mangling my name's pronunciation, "your name is Peter 'Gad-jax'?"

"That's correct. Except it's pronounced 'Guy-ditch.'"

"And you are the defendant in this action?"

"He's the plaintiff," Mackenzie responded, already sounding annoyed.

"Of course," defense corrected himself, "the plaintiff in this action. Excuse me. You have been sworn to tell the truth on this examination?"

"Yes."

For more than two hours, defense asked about my work and educational history, the childhood sexual abuse, my sexual history, and my deteriorating relationship with my family.

"How did your parents' attitude towards your sexuality affect you emotionally and psychologically?" Morris asked.

"I felt rejected and confused, isolated. I loved my family and I wanted their acceptance. And yet I also felt like they didn't love me. That I really was on my own."

"Would you describe their attitude toward you 'coming out' as homophobic?"

"Extremely."

"How about your siblings? Was there homophobia among your siblings?"

"Yes."

"Just so we understand each other, what do you mean when you refer to someone as being 'homophobic'?"

"That they have a disdain for homosexuals; a fear or hatred toward them; a belief that gay people are intrinsically disordered, perverted."

Morris led me through a series of questions about my "promiscuous" youth. At one point, he asked about my visiting bars "frequented by male homosexuals," and it struck me that no one would ever be asked if they visited bars "frequented by female heterosexuals."

For several minutes, Morris buried his face in a large file; then, without looking up, asked, "Was there ever an element of prostitution in your homosexual activity?"

The question was unexpected. I was taken back to when I was twenty-three, standing on the downtown street corner, waiting for a car to pull over.

"Once I prostituted myself. Only once."

Defense asked that I describe my symptoms upon first visiting Alfonzo. He asked if I entered the therapy voluntarily, how the therapy worked, details on the medications, including ketamine, how I felt about the reparenting sessions, and about details on my breakdown. He asked that I elaborate on my claim that Alfonzo treated my homosexuality as a disease, that he tried to make me heterosexual, about the effects of the therapy as compared with my presenting complaints. He asked question after question, never smiling, sometimes repeating questions two or three times, rephrased.

"I felt better only after the therapy ended," I said, "after the medications were decreased and I spent time away from the house, read gay literature, thought my own thoughts, separated myself from the Styx. My emotional and mental health improved only after I left the therapy."

"Are you saying, then, that contrary to what you wrote in your sessional reports, the therapy given to you by Dr. Alfonzo did not improve your mental and emotional state?"

"What I'm saying and what I've said before is that some of the techniques, like the screaming and the nurturing, those things helped, especially at the start. They calmed my mind. They released my anxiety and my anger. But as my regressions deepened and the medications were increased, as my mental health deteriorated . . . he kept telling me that I had to 'go through the tunnel' before 'coming out the other end' and feeling better."

"And my question was: Did you get better?"

"I think I answered your question: I got better after leaving the house and the care of Dr. Alfonzo."

Following three-and-a-half hours of questions, the attorneys agreed to break for lunch. Before I'd even stood, Morris had pulled from his briefcase a book on the use of ketamine hydrochloride in psychotherapy. He placed it gently on the table, pushed it slowly an inch in my direction, and started talking to Mackenzie about the drug. Half of what he said went right over my head. What I understood, however, was that ketamine was evidently being used in medical practices in almost every country in the world, mainly as a short-term anesthetic agent, with a secondary use as an analgesic agent. The drug was occasionally used for other purposes, including as an aid to psychotherapy, and there was considerable literature about its effects on the mind, brain, and body.

"I should remind you," Morris said to Mackenzie, "that ketamine is an approved drug for human use under the Food and Drug Administration," which I knew was American, although Canada sometimes followed suit with their rules and regulations. "Oh, yes, I also need to tell you that we're going to have to extend the trial duration."

"Why is that?" Mackenzie asked, characteristically deadpan.

"We will have to increase it to five weeks, or twenty-five days, given that we'll have Mr. Gajdics on the witness stand for at least one full week. We will also be flying in eight to ten expert medical witnesses from around the world. Eight days is simply not long enough."

The whole time the defense attorney was talking, he was looking at Mackenzie, though he occasionally glanced at me, but I knew the information was as much for my benefit as it was for Mackenzie's. This was all a scare tactic.

||||||||||

Throughout lunch, which I ate by myself in the back corner of a nearby Japanese restaurant, I fought back tears while thinking about Alfonzo's treatment of my sexuality and that everything he did to me I did to myself. If Alfonzo was a monster, then there had to have been monstrous demons inside of me just waiting to escape.

||||||||||

Morris started the afternoon by asking if I'd ever signed or scrutinized documents about the therapy and my willingness to participate in it. I told him I had not. Smiling, he reached into his briefcase and produced more than twenty consent forms and therapy evaluation reports. The next two hours were spent reviewing the forms' signatures, most all mine, though I had little or no memory of any of them.

"I was taking a lot of medication back then. Most days I could hardly remember what I ate for lunch, let alone the details of a contract. I also trusted Dr. Alfonzo like a father: I would have signed anything he put in front of me."

Defense produced a contract for entering the therapeutic house, signed by me and dated December 14, 1989, the time of our first meeting. I noticed that it was a photocopy, as were all the other documents. There were no originals.

"I don't know how I could've signed this in December nineteen eighty-nine when I hadn't even been told about the house until the following spring. This document also references our house charter, which we didn't even write until we were living in the house in nineteen ninety."

My comment seemed to have little of no effect on defense, who showed me yet another contract, between Alice and me, and asked if I could identify my signature on its final page. I looked at the document; someone had signed it, but it wasn't me.

"Isn't that your signature on the document?"

"No. I can't even read what it says. But it's not my signature."

"So that is not your signature on this document, even though you are stated to be a party to the document?"

"That's correct."

"Well have you read this document before?"

"I don't remember reading it either, no."

"Were you in the habit in nineteen ninety-one of signing documents without reading them?"

His question confused me: I couldn't tell if he was trying to trick me, if I hadn't been clear in my answer, or if he was asking me an entirely new question.

For two hours defense produced consent after consent, each time pointing to my signatures at the bottom of the forms and asking if they were mine. When I told him that I had no clear memory of signing the forms, he asked if I had an "unclear memory."

"I have no memory whatsoever of signing these forms," I told him.

At one point, I accidentally glanced over at Alfonzo. I had not looked at him since he entered the room, six hours earlier. He was looking directly at me, as if through me, arms folded, smirking.

Defense continued producing multiple, self-rated progress reports, saying something about how he wasn't going to review all of them now, although he would at trial. "Were you truthful in the many comments you made about your therapy?"

I glanced at the reports. "I was dishonest about issues around being gay: wanting or thinking that my attraction toward men was decreasing and my attraction toward women was increasing."

"Was that the only area in which you weren't honest?"

"No. I also wasn't honest about how scared I was of Dr. Alfonzo. I never wrote about the way he screamed at me, how humiliated I felt when he told me I was crazy for saying that I was gay, that I was insane for wanting a relationship with a man."

"Well, if Dr. Alfonzo's 'unethical behavior' was so upsetting to you, why wouldn't you write about it?"

"I told him how I felt when I started therapy. We were always arguing. He'd just tell me to 'shut up and do as you're told,' to not contradict him or else he was going to throw me out of therapy. At that point in my life, I had nowhere else to go. I learned to stop arguing. By the time I started writing those reports, I knew not to tell him anything that might anger him: I was scared of him."

Defense quoted extensively from my progress reports, reading that I said the therapy was "a positive experience," that I was "feeling better," that I was "making progress," that the therapy had "saved my life," that I was "highly satisfied with the results of my therapy," that I had "benefited a great deal from the therapy up to that point," that I would "require a lot further therapy to deal with my problems," and that I would "strongly recommend Dr. Alfonzo's psychotherapy" to close friends with emotional problems.

He asked if I'd been truthful in what I wrote, and, if not, why.

"I was as truthful as I could have been at the time."

"You have to explain that one to me again."

"Because I was lying to myself about who I was, I didn't have the ability to be truthful."

"You mean you were lying to yourself about your true sexual orientation, that you were not admitting to yourself that you were homosexual? Is that what you're meaning?"

"Yes."

"How do you know that Alfonzo's therapy didn't help you?" he asked.

"If it had been Dr. Alfonzo's intention to insult me about my sexuality . . . to shame me and to overdose me with medication so that he could help me feel better about myself and my sexuality, then . . . I suppose you could say his therapy worked."

Defense looked at me with eyes like empty graves and asked in a lifeless voice what harm or ill effects had been caused by my therapy with Dr. Alfonzo. I didn't know what to say. It was as if all the other questions had led to this one crucial question, and I had now been asked to articulate how being raped had caused me "ill effects." I managed to say something about the emotional harm caused by his therapy, but after so many years and all that has happened, my words felt stilted, inadequate, pointless.

The eight-hour interview concluded when I told them I was tired and having trouble concentrating. We agreed to adjourn for the day.

|||||||||||

Outside in the corridor, Alfonzo was standing with his lawyers as Mackenzie and I left the office. I motioned to Mackenzie, to tell him not to get in the elevator, but before I could open my mouth, the mirrored metal doors had slid open and all five of us walked in together. Morris and Alfonzo continued their conversation. I saw their mouths moving, but their words were muffled, as if pillows were held over my ears. It wasn't till the elevator doors slid open twenty floors later that I realized I'd been holding my breath the entire way down.

Streams of office workers weaved in and around Mackenzie and me as we stood in the lobby.

"So, how did I do?" I asked.

"Some people totally mess up during discoveries, and their case is as good as over. You did . . . okay."

"'Okay' as in I hurt our case or 'okay' as in I helped our case?

"Okay as in we have a long way to go."

"So, what time tomorrow do we continue?"

"Tomorrow's not going to work for me," he said, shuffling through his briefcase. "We have to reschedule."

"Oh."

"And we're going to have to wait till we finish your discovery before booking the doctor's."

"I see . . ."

"We're also going to have to rebook court time."

"Why?"

"We can't just extend our trial date to five weeks," he said, sounding annoyed that I wouldn't have figured this out on my own. "We won't get a date before . . . two thousand four."

"Two thousand four?"

"If we're lucky. Maybe as late as two thousand five."

I was disappointed when he told me he was running late and that he had to leave, and then he was gone, through the glass turnstile and out the door onto the street. Dejected, I sat on the cold marble bench in the office tower lobby and stared at my reflection, tripled and warped, in the mirrored wall across from me.

||||||||||

As I waited to hear back from Mackenzie, I thought about Europe. At thirty-eight years old, all I wanted was to take the kind of trip through Europe that I knew many twenty-something-year-olds often did after college, sometimes at the same age when I'd first met Alfonzo. Mostly, though, I thought that maybe after the lawsuit ended I could reclaim my European heritage, maybe even find some way to apply for European citizenship.

When I heard that Hungary was poised to join the European Union in 2004, I gathered all the citizenship application materials from the Hungarian Embassy. Unfortunately, I soon discovered that all of that material was available only in Hungarian and would need to be completed in Hungarian, a language my father had never taught me or any of my siblings when we were children. I had heard the story for years: my father, a Magyar, could not speak German, my mother's native tongue, and so the two decided they must speak to us only in English, the language of their adoptive country, Canada.

I visited my parents at their home to ask my father if he would help me translate the application into English. My hope, as I explained, was to apply on his behalf to reclaim his own citizenship—a citizenship he had essentially forfeited when he escaped communist Hungary in the late 1940s—in order that I could apply for my own based on paternal heritage. Hungary's ascension to the Union would enable me to work anywhere in Europe, find a job, maybe even live in Budapest, I told him.

None of that seemed to matter. My father said he would not hand over his Canadian passport, nor would he give me whatever documentation he had left of his Hungarian nationalization.

"I can't help you," he said.

"You mean you *won't* help me."

My mother, as always, was five steps back, through the doorway in the kitchen.

"I mean I *can't*." He turned and left the room, disappearing into their bedroom.

"What is he afraid of?" I asked my mother.

She said nothing. A moment later he reappeared.

"You're on your own, baby."

"I've always been on my own," I said. My words hurt him. They were meant to hurt. "What are you afraid of?" I asked.

But of course I knew, could see the scared little boy that he had carried around inside himself even when I was a little boy, and now a man. Ghosts haunted me, too, but his, it seemed, possessed him entirely.

"You have no idea what I went through in the war."

"Then tell me. *Tell* me, I want to know . . ."

"You have no idea what it's like to live under communism . . ."

"Me applying for this citizenship has nothing to do with you and your past. It's about me and my future."

It was no use. In the coming months, I hired a translator to translate the citizenship application into English, completed as much of the form as I could in English—leaving blank essential questions like "Name of Paternal Grandfather"—and then had the entire form translated back into Hungarian.

The day before I mailed the application to the Hungarian Embassy, my mother called me up to her "office"—my old bedroom on the top floor of their house—where she proceeded to pull from out of her "confidential" files in a two-drawer metal filing cabinet some kind of document, written in German, yellowing with age. I asked if she could translate it.

The date stamped was February 2, 1951, notarized in München, Germany, and drafted from the Displaced Persons' (DP) Camp in Hersbruck, Germany, where my father had lived for a short time after fleeing Hungary for Czechoslovakia. The document confirmed his birthplace as Budapest, his citizenship as Hungarian—"*Ungarisch*."

"Where did this come from?" I asked my mother.

"From the filing cabinet," she said, motioning vaguely to the drawer.

"Yes, but *before* the filing cabinet. Did you know you had this?"

"I knew, but I guess I forgot. Anyway, it's yours now. You can use it."

"Dad knows about this document?"

"Of course."

Downstairs, I thanked my father.

"It won't make a difference," he said, his voice still gripped by fear. "Nothing will help you. You won't get this citizenship. You think the communists are just going to hand over citizenship to you? To *me*?"

"Dad, Hungary isn't communist anymore."

"Oh, you are so naive."

Along with my father's application, which I also completed on his behalf, I submitted my own to the Hungarian Embassy. In essence, I proceeded in the absence of verification of my paternal grandfather's identity, one of the key elements to the entire application. My father, born out of wedlock, had never known his father. Which was to say he'd never met his father. I, however, had grown up with my father, but still I didn't know him.

25

MACKENZIE SUMMONED ME TO his office in late July 2002. I had barely taken a seat when he broke the news.

"This firm has no incentive to take your case to trial. We will have to settle out of court. Sorry."

His words were like an unexpected amputation.

"What if I don't want to settle?"

"Peter . . ."

"What if I say I don't agree to settle? It is my decision, is it not?"

"*Peter*, this firm has already spent more than 15,000 dollars on disbursements alone. We could spend another fifteen before we even walk into court. I would be in a tough position if you insisted on going to trial, if we could settle, since I would then have to go to my partners and explain the details of what this suit is costing them. This is a business decision, Peter. This is about money."

"This has never been about money. Not to me . . ."

"Besides, defense has shifted its focus away from our claims of impropriety on the part of Alfonzo and to the effectiveness and validity of his therapy. Like the shit in the bottle: that *could* be seen as a justifiable form of treatment. Considering you allowed the doctor to make you sniff it."

"*Allowed him?*"

"Within the confines of Alfonzo's paradigm, this form of treatment did have its own internal logic."

"Alfonzo's 'internal logic' was barbaric and homophobic, and I had been under the impression that you agreed with that."

Defense would be flying in experts from around the world, Mackenzie explained. Even if I were awarded a substantial settlement, which he said was "unlikely," with what his firm could spend in expert witnesses alone, "you could still go bankrupt." I would be in my late forties or fifties before the matter was even concluded, he said. "Do you really want to spend the next ten or fifteen years of your life fighting this? At the end of the day, I still have to tell my partners why I think we should take this case to trial, and there just doesn't seem to be a reason why we should."

"What about all the reasons why I filed the suit in the first place? To stop people like Alfonzo from inflicting this type of harm on anyone else in the future. To create legal precedent. Bring public awareness to this kind of abuse of trust. People have been subjected to this type of abuse for decades. Isn't that enough of a reason? This doesn't bother you? You could just walk away from this?"

"Trial has never brought closure to *anyone*," he replied, ignoring my previous remark. "Rarely, if ever, do plaintiffs walk away from the experience of litigation with a feeling of restitution. More often than not, they leave more damaged than before. Settling is in everyone's best interest."

Regarding the possibility of my case creating legal precedent, Mackenzie explained that the Canadian Medical Protective Association—the mutual defense organization responsible for providing indemnification to all licensed doctors in the country—sent out details of all malpractice suits to all their members, including causes of action and information about settlements, excluding amounts.

"Their bulletins would dissuade physicians from practicing similar types of therapy in the future," Mackenzie assured me.

He'd explained the different types of damages before, but once again, he told me that the Canadian courts had put a ceiling on the amount that could be awarded in these types of cases.

"I suggest we make an offer of 150,000 dollars, all-inclusive, with a deadline of today at noon, at which point our offer would be irrevocably withdrawn."

"And you can assure me that this organization—"

"The Canadian Medical Protective Association."

"That they'll report on my case, that it'll be written up and sent to all practicing psychiatrists, explaining the essence of my case?"

"Bulletins are mailed out automatically."

"Okay. Fine. Make the offer."

We waited a month to hear back from the defense; when we did, they rejected our offer and countered with an offer of $40,000, which we countered with $75,000, all-inclusive. For three months we heard nothing. Mackenzie agreed to call and ask for their response. A week later, he called to tell me that defense had rejected our counter. Three months worth of faxes and phone calls followed. Defense made inquiries about how much we'd spent so far on disbursements. Mackenzie set deadlines, which the defense promptly missed.

In late November 2002, I met with Mackenzie to discuss defense's latest offer of $45,000. We decided to counter one last time; either way I had resigned myself to settling, if only because I could not stand one more day of uncertainty.

By early December, I instructed Mackenzie to accept defense's latest offer of $60,000, all-inclusive, on condition that we receive the money within the week.

I was at my office job on December 13, 2002, my thirty-eighth birthday, when Mackenzie called to ask if I could be in his office within an hour. The money had arrived.

The two of us were sitting in his boardroom, one hour later.

"You probably realize that we've never drawn up a contingency agreement," Mackenzie began—a statement, delivered in his typical monotone voice, that seemed to signal more alarm bells. He went on to say that the rules and regulations of the Law Society of British Columbia—the regulatory body of all licensed lawyers in the province—prohibited him from charging a contingency if we had not signed such an agreement. In these kinds of circumstances, he said, charging me billable hours "would be appropriate," even though those hours "totaled more than 30,000 dollars." He paused, as if waiting for my comment. I said nothing. "However," he continued, "in the spirit of what we had agreed to at the start of this suit, we have deducted from that amount enough billable hours in order to bring the total owing to us down to what you would have been charged had we drawn up a contingency agreement at thirty percent."

"I have a question. By accepting this money, I'm not agreeing to not write about my experiences, right?"

"There is no such agreement," Mackenzie said. "But if you're asking me, I would recommend that you not write about Alfonzo or anything to do with the therapy."

"Why is that?"

"I can't tell you what to do, but my suggestion is to take the money and move on with your life. If you wrote about the doctor, you'd be setting yourself up for a lawsuit."

"Even if I changed everyone's name?"

"You'd have to change most of the details in order for all the people involved not to be identified. Even so, my advice is to put this whole experience behind you and to just move on."

"What about him writing about *me*? He still has more than a hundred taped hours of me saying hateful things about gays."

"There's nothing we can do about that. He's free to use it, if he changes your name."

"So he can write anything he wants about me, but I can't write about him."

"My advice to you is that you don't. I can't tell you what to do."

"In terms of the Medical Protective—"

"The Canadian Medical Protective Association."

"They'll definitely document my case."

"You'll need to contact the association yourself. What they choose to do is outside my—"

"Choose? I thought you said they document all malpractice suits in their bulletins."

"I have no knowledge about which cases they choose to document. There is nothing I can do about that."

"So how do I find out if—"

"You'll have to just call them yourself."

I half expected him to say something more. He didn't.

I signed the final letter of agreement sitting on the table between us, and Mackenzie handed me a check. After costs and disbursements totaling $15,000, Mackenzie's fee of $13,500 and various taxes, my amount was for $30,793.08.

I stood, shook Mackenzie's hand one last time, thanked him, smiled, and left, without fanfare or catharsis. As if I'd been pushed back into invisibility.

In the ensuing months, after numerous phone calls, I discovered that the only way for me to view the bulletins from the Canadian Medical Protective Association was through a library in Montreal. Because of copyright laws, the 2003 "Information Letters" could not be faxed to me; however, the librarian was kind enough to read through the only three bulletins published since the beginning of 2003.

No details of my suit were documented at all.

For four years I had also been reading through the College of Physicians and Surgeons' quarterly bulletins, distributed to every registered medical practitioner in the province, which contained decisions of complaints brought before the ethical standards and conduct review committee, the same committee that reviewed my complaint in 1999.

The details of my complaint to the College of Physicians and Surgeons also were never included in the quarterly bulletins.

||||||||||

When it was announced at my job in 2003 that all government employees in British Columbia would be offered early retirements—or, in my case, three-week cash payouts for every year of employment—I accepted the offer, calculated at roughly $9,000, and started to plan my trip to Europe, with or without my Hungarian citizenship.

I emailed Ingrid, a maternal cousin twelve years my senior, in Linz, Austria. Ingrid and I had met only once before, during her visit to Canada in 1978, and though we'd had little in common at the time, for some reason I'd always felt a connection with her. In my email I told her I was planning a trip to Europe and wanted to spend time with her. She was thrilled. So was I. To connect with my relatives in Europe, the life my parents had escaped, had always been a dream, one of the many mocked by Alfonzo.

||||||||||

In preparation for Christmas 2003, I was standing at my mother's side rolling out dough for ten poppy seed strudels when she started talking about the camps. Many of her stories, by this time, were familiar, but each time she told one they always seemed new.

"Before the war we were segregated, ostracized, Germans living in a non-German country, foreigners in our own home, today's Serbia. After the war, we were sent to camps. State-sanctioned ethnic cleansing. Those of us who survived, or escaped, were declared 'stateless.' Persona non grata. When I finally made it into Austria, after my own escape, I had to have a friend swear before a judge that I really existed. In the eyes of the government I did not even exist."

"Did you tell people you were German?"

"Not when I arrived in England. I was Austrian."

"So you hid your identity."

"Not hid, survived. I did what I needed to do in order to survive. People assumed I was Yugoslavian because I was born in Yugoslavia. I just didn't tell them I was German. Even today, seventy years later, you tell someone you're German and they think of one thing and one thing only."

"Can you help, please?" I said, mildly panicked, motioning with my floured hands at the holey dough, which had not been my desired outcome. "You're better at this . . ."

"Patience . . . patience. When you've lived as long as I have, you develop patience for things like this, that's all . . ."

"Whatever it is, your hands are more tempered than mine . . ."

She put her apron back on and began kneading the dough. "Where was I with my story?"

"You had left Yugoslavia . . . "

"I escaped into Romania, then I went to Austria, and on to England."

"Where did you live in Romania?"

"I worked for a Jewish family. They knew I'd escaped a concentration camp so they gave me food and a bed. Every day potato soup and a slice of bread, but it kept me alive."

"How long were you there? What did you do?"

"Three months. Nothing. I lived incognito. No one saw me during the day. I was scared of being caught and deported back to the camp."

"How many of our relatives were in camps?"

"My brother escaped from a children's camp. My grandmother died in a death camp when she was ninety. My cousin, Ingrid's mother, she was taken to Dnipropetrovsk in the Ukraine, and worked for two years in a cement factory. My great aunt was moved from one camp to another. She watched her grandmother die, and then her mother. Finally she decided that she was not going to be next. She escaped when she was sixty-five."

My mother had told me the story of her own escape many times before, including in the story she'd written for me when I was nineteen.

By early 1947, she had been jailed in the barren pantry of the OZNA headquarters for several months. The approaching weekend meant that soon her tormentor, the camp commandant, would return for his weekly interrogation. Still, she managed to fall into a deep and restful sleep. In the middle of the night she awoke, not frightened or startled, but peacefully, sweetly.

And as she woke, she heard her mother, who had died years earlier, saying, *You must go now*.

Mice scampered across her feet as she sat up; and then the church bells began to chime—four chimes for the full hour, and then two. With no thought of capture, she stood, unfastened the panel in the door, and stepped through the opening and into the hallway, by the espalier trellis. She didn't question the possibility of escape or whether she might succeed. Her mother had told her it was time to go, and so she did.

She lay on her belly and crawled soldier-like across the smooth tile floor. Only after she'd passed the kitchen, where she heard the guards breathing not five feet away, did she stand. Baskets of chrysanthemums hung from the wrought-iron bars of the trellis: she used them to steady herself, climbed the height of the building, one rung at a time, grabbed hold of the drainpipes, and heaved herself up onto the gravel roof. Down below, a courier left the building's front door, and then the windows were thrown open wide. Lying on her stomach, with the brightness of the harvest moon reflected off her white blouse, she was in full view for all to see.

But her mother's voice was still with her, encouraging her fainting spirit: *You must go now.*

When the commotion below subsided, she slithered up the crest of the roof, where the east and north joined at an angle. A couple of times she disturbed dried leaves and bits of granite, but no one seemed to notice as it scattered to the ground. Soon she reached the top of the roof, where she could see the guard at the south end of the house.

She just watched him for several minutes. He had a pattern of walking from the door of the house to the corner of the street, his gun slung over his shoulder, and shouting across the street to a second guard, who was standing watch at another store. They exchanged a few words in Serbian, then the second guard would go south as the first walked west. When he reached the door again, he would turn and then take at least three to four minutes before returning to the headquarters. This was the time she had to use—when one guard was down the side street and the other guard's back was turned.

The moment one guard was down the street and the other's back was turned, she lowered herself down the water pipe, then landed on the metal-lined awning with a thump. For a moment she thought that someone would come looking to see what had caused the noise. Instead, the guards made their usual joke as they reached their corners. She knew she had to move; time was slipping away. She threw her shoes down onto the boulevard, preparing to jump, but just as she did, a crowd approached from a nearby hotel. They were singing in Hungarian, seemingly drunk, and walked under the awning and over the sandals. They didn't look up.

After they had passed and the guards had had their little chat, she jumped. Pain seared through her ankle and shot up her leg, but she grabbed her sandals and began to walk.

A block later, she approached the small hotel as its front doors swung open. Before anyone left, she had turned and walked in another direction.

She passed the house of the local police. The lights inside the office were on, and two policemen were lying in the open windows, looking out onto the street. It was a warm night. They were smoking.

Her shoes were still hidden in her blouse, since she'd had no time to put them on, and her ankle was swelling fast, but she walked straight, with conviction and confidence, as though she knew precisely where she was going.

Two blocks later, an old man she had known rode toward her on a bicycle. He had been a policeman during the German occupation, but had spied on the Germans. They were only a little more than a block away from the police headquarters. One shout from him and she would have been caught and returned to jail. He rode his bike right past her, never once looking back.

From across a broad dirt road, she could see the entrance to the cemetery, a desolate stretch of overgrown meadow with the fourteen Stations of the Cross lining one side, and in the distance, rows of wooden crosses and one black marble mausoleum. She knew this was her last chance to visit her mother's grave. She knew that. But time was slipping away, so she couldn't stop. Soon she reached the sluice gate and waded through a slow part of the river Tisa, its icy water like balm to her bluing ankle. By the time she emerged at the other side, the water had revived her fading spirit. She was more determined than ever to cross the border and enter Romania, the neighboring country. Freedom was within her reach.

"He had some type of special interest in me," my mother said, scrubbing the counter of dough as I brushed the ten finished strudels with egg wash. "I've never understood why, exactly."

"Who?"

"The camp commandant. My tormentor. The man I called my tormentor."

"He hated you?"

"It was never as simple as hatred. That was their way of torture, the communists. Interrogating you as if you were a great and terrible criminal, forcing you to 'confess.'"

"Confess what?"

"You never knew. At one point, when I was in solitary confinement, they gave me a typewriter and told me to type my confession or else they'd kill me."

"What did you write?"

"I didn't know what to write, so I wrote about my life. My childhood. They tell you to confess, and when you had nothing to confess, your life became your confession. You second-guessed yourself. 'Maybe there really is something wrong with me.' After I escaped, when I was still in hiding, I actually wrote a postcard to him back in Serbia, telling him that I'd survived."

"You did—what?" I looked up from the strudels.

"I don't think I told this to anyone; in fact I think I just remembered it, right now, as I was talking to you."

"What did you do?"

"He'd always said that if I tried to escape he'd hunt me down and kill me, but I always knew that I'd be free. Always, I knew it in my bones. That was me at twenty-two: sticking it to him, telling him he hadn't won."

"You knew his address?"

"I sent the card to the camp, back in Serbia, where I'd escaped."

"Do you still remember his name?"

"I remember his hands. He beat me, repeatedly. I'll never forget his hands."

By this time, we were sitting at the kitchen table. My mother was staring out the window at an aspen tree with its heart-shaped leaves arched overhead.

"For a time when I was already living in England I couldn't stand up. I had lumbago."

"What's that?"

"My lower back—I'm sure it was from the concentration camp, when they put me in the ice cold water. Anyway, I'd walk to my factory job in England, hunched over. Finally, by the time I got to work several blocks later, I could stand up again. Sometimes I couldn't get out of bed. I was paralyzed. I had a recurrence of it for years, the paralysis. The last time I had it was when I was pregnant with Kriska."

"You never told me about this paralysis, the lumbago."

"I remember, when I was living underground in Romania, there was a church, in the town center. I'd heard stories about it, how beautiful it was. More than anything, I wanted to see that church, but I couldn't risk being caught. Well, early one morning, before sunrise, I took the streetcar to the town center. The church was built all in stone, like all the great churches in Europe. I'll never forget the moment I walked through that arched entrance. The first rays of sunlight were beginning to stream through the stained-glass windows, and the walls, everywhere you looked the walls were carved out of black marble. There were hundreds of candles, all lining the aisles. Something happened to me when I entered the church that day. I had an experienced that's stayed with me my whole life. No voices, nothing anyone can ever know for sure. Such peace entered my very soul, my mind. A perfect certainty that I would make it safely to wherever it was I had to go. I was not alone. Well, of course, as it turned out, I was caught in Hungary, and then again in Austria, twice. But there was always someone along the way who helped me escape, again and again. To help me go further, and further, until I made it all the way to England. Sometimes I still wonder whether my mother's spirit was at work, guiding me to freedom. You probably think I'm making this all up."

"Of course not."

"The facts of that part of my journey would seem fantastic to some people, even miraculous. Especially in today's secular world. Unless you believe that when we ask for help . . . it is always forthcoming, somehow. Providing we ask in the true spirit and for the right reasons."

"You really believe that?"

"I do. I must."

"I wish I had your faith."

My mother took my hand in hers. I noticed the blue veins glowing through her aged skin, like translucent tissue paper, and her fingers, crippled like brittle twigs, curled around my own.

"Thirty-four months of labor and death camps. When a person no longer believes in man, nothing is left but despair or God."

"Have you ever asked yourself why you survived? How it is that one person survives something like that, and the next person doesn't?"

"I've thought about that over the years, and I really do believe that I survived because my captors never touched the core of who I was. They might have killed my body—God knows they tried—but they never touched my spirit."

||||||||||

Later that night, I was back in the car with my father. Neither of us said a word the entire ride home. He parked the car outside my apartment. I was hesitant to leave, and I knew he wanted me to stay and talk.

"I know that your difficulty with my sexuality has nothing to do with not loving me."

My father looked at me, surprised, but he didn't shut me down. He listened.

"You're from a different world . . . a different culture. I understand that. I also know you've always wanted to have a relationship with me."

"Of course I do. I'm your father."

Even after all these years, he still pronounced the "th" in "father" as "t."

"Yes, well, I guess what I've always found difficult . . ." I had to stop and remember to breathe, stop myself from crying. "What I've always found difficult is that I remember how you brought me up talking about God and Christ, but all I ever wanted was for you to tell me about you, my father."

"But I do tell you who I am. More than you know. When I tell you about my faith, I reveal myself to you." He was silent. Then, as if reading my mind, he continued, "You mean about my childhood. You want me to tell you about my life before. I wouldn't know what to tell you. I wouldn't know what was real from what was imagined. I spent so many years trying not to remember, and now . . . I know I cried from birth to when I escaped Hungary. You know about my mother, that she died in the war, that I was raised by various foster parents in the country. You know I never had a father. You know that I was a bastard."

My father had never said that word aloud: "bastard." The fact that he could now, in old age, weakened my heart.

"Your mother and I were orphans of the war."

"Do you still think about your mother?"

"Of course. I pray for her soul every night . . . Some day the Lord will call me home . . ."

"Please don't talk like that . . ."

"There's nothing wrong with that. But when He does, when I'm gone, I want you to remember me. It means so much to your mother and me that since you moved back you want to come home and be with us. It means so much, so much . . ." He cleared his throat, as if to interrupt his tears. "To be continued," he said.

"What?"

"Our conversation: to be continued. Okay?"

"Okay. I'd like that."

I reached over to hug him goodnight. I wanted to tell him that I loved him, I understood him. I forgave him.

"I love you," my father said for both of us, as I held him in my arms.

|||||||||||

One week before I left for Europe, in April 2004, my father asked if I could find his mother's grave.

"She's buried in Vecsés," he said when I was at the house, maps of Europe spread across their dining room table. "It's a village twenty minutes outside Budapest. I don't know if her body will still be there. But if it is, if you are able to get out to Vecsés, somehow . . . I mean if you have time, that is . . . it would mean a great deal to me."

"When was the last time you saw her grave?"

"In nineteen forty-five, I was—how old?"

"Fifteen," my mother added from the living room.

"Fifteen. There was a wooden bench beside her grave. I stood at the foot of her grave and I cried for hours, until there were no tears left inside of me to cry. Then I fell to sleep on that bench. I was exhausted. In the morning I left before the main gate, an iron-winged gate, was opened again from the outside. Maybe the bench will still be there. If you find her grave . . ."

"Maybe Csilla could help," my mother said.

"Csilla? Who's Csilla?"

"Csilla is related to your father's stepbrother. She would be your cousin of sorts." My mother said the words matter-of-factly, as if I'd heard it all before.

"You have a stepbrother?" I asked my father.

"Stephen, yes; by marriage, not blood. His father married my mother. He lives somewhere in Vancouver, but I haven't talked to him since the early seventies. His wife's niece, Csilla—she used to live outside Budapest. I think she's around your age. She should speak English. I could try and see if we could reach her. Maybe she could help."

After a lifetime of secrecy, all of this last-minute "help" hurt my head.

"If you do find my mother's grave . . . if you're able . . . maybe you could also bring me back some soil from her plot? One day I would like to be buried with that soil."

26

I LEFT MY JOB in April and traveled to London. For three days I walked from South Kensington to Notting Hill and on to Soho, around the Globe Theatre, over the London and Tower Bridges, sat through *Les Misérables* not once but twice in the West End, toured Buckingham Palace, lunched across the street from Harrods department store in Chelsea, and stood staring for hours at the works of Gauguin, Dalí, Picasso, and Rodin at the Tate Museum.

In a brief exchange of letters before Europe, my friend Pearl and I agreed to meet at La Marianna, an Italian restaurant near her home in Schöneberg, Berlin.

We greeted with a hug, like two old friends, which, of course, we were.

"How do you like Berlin?" she asked, once we were seated at our table.

"I stepped off the train from London and a neo-Nazi walked up to me and started screaming in German."

"Well, this is Germany."

"He sounded pissed. He had a Mohawk and his face was covered in tattoos of swastikas. I wasn't expecting this kind of culture shock. London was like something out of *Mary Poppins*, and Berlin, well . . ."

After some small talk, we both fell silent. Too much to say, no easy way to begin.

"Do we need to talk about the last time we saw each other?" I said.

"Do you want to talk about it?"

"You know I'm sorry."

She took a sip of her wine. "I don't think about it anymore. I . . . stay away from the memory."

"Yes, but I hope you know how sorry I am, today. For cutting you out like that—"

"For the longest time, I couldn't even touch the memory of you. I couldn't even think about you. It's like you and everything about our time together was in a block of ice in my heart. I was frozen. You must know I loved you. You have to know that . . ."

She reached across the table to hold my hand. I held hers.

"Yes," I said. "And I loved you."

|||||||||

No sooner had I arrived into Budapest-Keleti Pu, the city's main international train station, than my father started to send me long, dictated emails through my middle sister, Barbara. He said he'd been in touch with his long-lost stepbrother, Stephen, and that during one of their many conversations, they realized that Stephen's daughter, Mary, was a friend of Kriska's back in Vancouver. They'd talked often and even gone hiking together, never knowing that they were, however distantly through marriage, related.

My father also told me that my mother had managed to track down an envelope, dated August 5, 1968, to my father from his niece, Erzsébet. "Yes," he wrote, "I had a sister, or rather a half-sister. Her name was Margit."

He told me his niece's married name ("Máte") and address in Vecsés. Erzsébet was barely three years old when my father left Hungary, he wrote, and would be in her early sixties now, "if she was still alive."

He encouraged me to try to look her up.

"Your sister has attached to this email a photograph of my niece as a child, along with her family." He then identified the family members, including Erzsébet's father, who had been an officer in the communist secret police—Hungary's ÁVO, as it was commonly called.

"Also attached," he wrote, "is a photograph of my mother's grave, which I know you have never seen before. I do not have directions to the gravesite, but this photo may help you recognize the site. I was not present when my mother died. I've been told she was caught in the bombings. I honestly don't know what to believe."

And then, it seemed, the family history I had longed to know for so many years came tumbling out of my father—a series of foreign names and occupations. My whole life I had asked my father to tell me anything—anything at all—about his "previous life" in Europe, and now he was revealing more than I could absorb while alone in a foreign country, six thousand kilometers from home, without the native language or a friend.

There was Imre, his stepfather, an architect who helped design the Budapest airport. There was Stephen, the stepbrother he had mentioned, who had been knighted in Hungary for his role in the revolution and was now considered an enemy of communism. And of course there was Margit—his half-sister, long deceased—and her daughter, my father's niece, Erzsébet.

Then there were his personal feelings—spoken to me like the father I'd always wanted, and had searched for through my relationships with so many other men.

"You have always asked that I share with you some of my life stories. My past has always confused me, and I fear time has not helped make any of it easier to understand. Long ago I buried what seems was my life, but with Stephen reappearing, and you now in Hungary, I can't escape any of it. Events long forgotten are resurfacing. One memory blends into another, and I am overcome with feeling. Day and night, I dream of the past. I know there is much more to all these stories. Part of me would like to know. A larger part of me is scared to ask."

Toward the end of the email, he told me of one of those memories—a national tragedy that became strangely personal.

In 1956, he said, during the height of the Hungarian Revolution, the prime minister, as well as all the members of his cabinet and their extended families, had escaped the bombings on the street and were being kept alive in the Hungarian Parliament Building. One day, the Russians arrived, loaded them all onto a bus "for safekeeping," and drove off. They never returned. It was later revealed that the Russians had taken them to an undisclosed location, shot every one of them, and buried them in a mass unmarked grave.

"After the Berlin Wall fell and the political climate became freer," he wrote, "the new government in Hungary revealed the location of the mass grave. They dug up the bodies. All of Hungary wept . . .

"Now, look again at the photo I sent you of my mother's grave. The mass grave was on the other side of the chain-link fence, head to head with my mother."

I read his email several times to make sure I fully understood the gravity of his message. The sadness of it all—my father's words, what he must have carried around inside himself all these years, even my own reaction—was crushing.

"Say a prayer for all those who died that fateful day many years ago," he wrote. "And please say hello to my beloved mother. I miss her very much. I love you, Peter. Sleep well and be safe."

As promised, my father also called Csilla, in Budapest, who agreed to meet me the following week.

||||||||||

I found an enormous baroque post office on my third day in Budapest, but neither of the two tellers inside, whose gaunt faces never smiled, spoke a word of English. Chained to the wall by one door were over twenty phone books, all, of course, in Hungarian, each bearing no clues as to which I should use. When I opened them all, one after another, I found pages of the name "Máte." After twenty minutes of browsing, I found not one with an address anything close to what my father had provided, so I left.

Before leaving Canada I had read all about the female "gypsies" on Váci utca—a main shopping street in the city and one my parents had said I must visit—who were known for approaching "American-looking" men and speaking to them in English. *Do you have the time? Do you know where so-and-so street is located?* If the men responded in English, the women would ask them out for a drink. Together, they would visit nearby bars, talk, drink, flirt; and when the bill arrived, past midnight, the total amount owing would be inflated by several hundreds of euros, and the mafia would appear from a back room, demanding to be paid "or else." I had done my research and been forewarned.

So when I walked down Váci each night, passing stores like Nike,

Zara, and H&M, and was approached by women in candy-colored wigs, I drew on my toughest inner Magyar and gave them all a firm: "*Nem*"—one of the few Hungarian words I knew, but enough. I was no one's meal ticket.

Everywhere I walked, day after day, my father's voice was with me. Up Andrássy út, back and forth across all the bridges, over to Matthias Church in Buda or throughout Margit Island, even sipping Bull's Blood inside Gundel restaurant by Heroes' Square or eating slices of *zserbó* squares outside Café Gerbeaud—shadows flocked two steps before me. I was anticipated by ghosts. The isolation each day was palpable, and when night arrived like an unwelcomed visitor, I hardly ever slept.

Late one evening I left my rented flat on Wesselényi, around the corner from the Dohány Street Synagogue and a few short blocks from the downtown core, and walked west to the Puskin, an English-speaking art house movie theater.

The film was *Monster*, Charlize Theron's dark and gritty portrayal of a serial killer. After not having heard a word of English for weeks, I thought that familiar sounds and syllables might reassure. But no sooner had the film begun than it seemed only to reinforce much of the atmosphere I was trying to escape in the Westernized but highly oppressive city of Budapest. Sitting in the theater's worn velvet seats, I could not help but wonder where I belonged, if I belonged anywhere. Now all I thought about was how I could have ever believed that Budapest was part of who I was.

The day after the movie, I visited the Central Market Hall at Vámház körút, at the foot of the Liberty Bridge. For hours I walked up and down aisles of wicker baskets overflowing with multicolored peppers, loaves of freshly baked rye bread dusted in flour, counters of Ungarische salamis and hundreds of sausages draped like spiced piping above the butchers' blocks below, racks of spices and jars of jams and picked vegetables, apple strudels, slices of vanilla krémes and Dobos tortes, poppyseed squares.

Upstairs, tourists bustled shoulder to shoulder past tables of elderly women selling embroidered tablecloths with roosters or traditional Magyar folk designs, crystal and textile jewelry. Around the corner, stalls of hot food, a smorgasbord of smells, arrested my senses. Beef goulash, *paprikás csirke*, cabbage rolls and sour cream, bratwurst and sauerkraut, sweet and savory lángos, some smothered in peaches and dollops of cream, others with cranberries, still more encrusted in garlic and herbs. I paid my forints and edged toward an open bar stool overlooking the bottom floor of the market. Stewed plums in cottage cheese dumplings squirted sweet explosions in my mouth. For the longest time, there was nothing but the aftertaste of childhood.

Back at my flat, I stripped off my clothes and roamed naked, room to room. Located on the second floor of a stone tenement building, the flat was accessed through a rounded stairwell, marred by graffiti, and a walkway overlooking an inner courtyard where worn bedsheets and women's braziers hung in the muggy midday air.

After the gothic entrance and winding stairs, the flat itself was almost utilitarian, with furniture from IKEA and a washing machine that took three hours a cycle. Each room inside led to the next, and all in a circle: bedroom, living room, foyer, laundry room, bathroom, bedroom. Naked and making my way from one room to the next, I paused in the bedroom the second time around, turned on the flat-screen, lit a cigarette, and reclined on my bed. I flipped channels, past newscasts I did not understand, dubbed episodes of *Sex and the City*, and to a porno—a man and a woman, but still.

Hours later I opened my laptop on a coffee table in the living room. Determined to start writing a book about the therapy, to not lose sight of it, maybe even make some meaning out of all of it, I stared at the flickering cursor on the blank electronic page.

||||||||||

Standing on the causeway at the edges of the Danube the next day, I thought of my parents. High atop the Gellért Hill across the river-banks, the Liberty Statue—erected first in 1947 in commemoration of the Soviet's defeat over the Nazis, later revitalized after the fall of communism in 1989—gazed down upon all of Budapest.

In 1947, the year my mother escaped the communist concentra-tion camp in Yugoslavia, crossing the border to Romania, my father also fled a rising communist regime in Hungary, seen at the time as a "savior" to fascism, for what was then Czechoslovakia. So many crossings. Both of my parents had been born only a few hundred kilometers away from one another, yet each escaped their homelands in search of freedom and what they'd hoped would be a far better life for themselves and their children thousands of kilometers away in some place otherworldly, called "Canada." History had shown, for all of us, in one way or another, the oppressor was once the savior. We had all sought freedom, escaped, and started again.

||||||||||

I met my cousin Csilla at the Astoria hotel, on Kossuth Lajos utca, late one Monday morning. Csilla seemed rushed from the moment we met. Dressed in oval Gucci glasses and a skintight, patchwork skirt, she looked as glamorous as a young Zsa Zsa Gabor.

"Quickly, sorry, we need to rush, it's my car, I'm parked illegal," she said.

Then we were out on the street and around the corner and inside her red Škoda, parked on the sidewalk with a line of other cars. In another heartbeat, we were on the road, speeding toward Vecsés, twenty miles outside of Budapest. While Csilla drove—or rather, defied gravity by crossing multiple lanes of traffic nearly every other second—I peppered her with questions, most of which she could not answer. All I knew, which she did corroborate, was what my father had explained to me. Csilla and I were not "blood" relatives: her mother's sister was married to my father's stepbrother, Stephen, whose blood father, Imre, had married my father's birth mother, Rozália. Or, as my mother liked to summarize before I left for Europe: "You're related twice around the block."

When we arrived, Vecsés looked like something out of a Norman Rockwell painting: moss-eaten barnyards, overgrown weeds through unused railcar tracks, abandoned storefronts, a stray elderly man walking aimlessly down an otherwise deserted street, one lone pig-tailed girl on a rickety, three-speed bicycle.

Because of a flower stand that spilled out onto a side street, Csilla spotted the cemetery easily, on the left off the main road through

Vecsés. We turned the corner, parked the car, and walked through the winged, iron-gate entrance and into the graveyard. Everywhere I looked there were alleyways of tombs, marble sarcophaguses, statues of angels and weatherworn crosses, death dates from centuries before I was born.

"My father told me about a wooden bench near the grave of his mother, but I have no idea where to look, or even if it's still there," I said.

We returned to the office across the unpaved street where a woman with slug-like eyebrows and jet-black hair greeted us in Hungarian. We told her my grandmother's name (Rozália Gajdics), and, after searching through stacks of large, dusty ledgers, the woman said she'd found the site of the grave in her books. I quickly bought bouquets of flowers and votive candles from the street florist, and then followed as the woman led us back into the massive burial ground.

Rozália's grave was second to last along a dirt path near the rear of the graveyard. The soil was now crusted and weed-heavy, with purple wild flowers sprouting up throughout. There was no wooden bench beside the grave, on which my father said he'd slept that last night. I looked behind the cracked headstone, to the other side of the old chain-link fence, where I knew there would have been the site of the mass burial ground.

Csilla and the woman looked on, five steps back, as I lit the candle, and introduced myself to my grandmother. I told her that my father loved her, had never stopped missing her, that she now had grandchildren of her own, even great-grandchildren. I was glad she could not ask me why I was not married to a nice girl. I wanted to "pray" for all the dead, the mass killings, but all I could find in my heart was silence. So I stood there, in silence, head bowed, until finally I knelt down and dug up a handful of soil, placing it in a little red satchel to take back to my father.

We turned our attention toward Rozália's daughter, my father's half-sister, Margit, whose own daughter, Erzsébet, I had been trying to locate in the stack of phone books back in Budapest. As my father had mentioned, Margit was likely to be buried in the cemetery, as well.

He was right. We found the plot fifty meters away. The grave was well maintained with fresh daisies in an iron jug and a half-burnt votive. I lit another votive and stood for a moment's silence before all three of us returned through the winged-gate entrance to the office.

I asked the office woman—as translated through Csilla—if there was record of who was paying for the graves' upkeep. Again, the woman checked her ledgers, and said that my father's niece and her husband, Tomas, had been paying for both graves. The phone number listed was out of service, but I showed her the address my father had provided, and she told us the location was five minutes away. The fact that I had traveled all the way from "Kanada" in search of family seemed to thrill her.

"*Köszönöm szépen*," I told her as we left. ("Thank you very much.")

We drove to the address, but the house was abandoned. Not to be dissuaded, we stopped in a nearby pub, where Csilla asked the owner if he'd ever heard of Erzsébet and Tomas. He seemed to recall them living about six houses down the street, he told us. One at a time, I knocked on all the doors; each of the owners told us to try three or four doors down.

I rang the door of the last house on the block, a stucco bungalow with four stone steps leading up to a rickety screen door. Moments later a middle-aged man with puffy, sun-bleached cheeks and frizzy white hair opened the creaking screen. Csilla introduced me, mentioning my father's name and "Kanada." Without hesitation a panicked frenzy washed over him.

He extended his hand, pulled me in, called, "Erzsébet! . . . Kanada! Kanada!"

Erzsébet appeared, looking like a middle-aged Cabbage Patch Kid in a blue-and-white polka dot dress. She scrutinized me up and down, listening intently as Csilla hurriedly explained the situation in Hungarian: I was her cousin. I had traveled from Canada to find my grandmother's grave and hopefully some of my relatives, whom my father had not seen or contacted since fleeing Hungary over fifty years earlier.

Erzsébet's initial excitement soon gave way to an edge of stunned trepidation as she spoke back and forth between Csilla and I, fast and excited, with Csilla translating as much as she could, both of them overlapping, everything confused. Languages converged like a mesh of train tracks—Erzsébet speaking in Hungarian to Csilla, Csilla speaking in English to me, and occasionally Csilla speaking the wrong language to both of us.

"I have brain freeze," Csilla told me, in her accented English, at one point.

Still standing, I pulled from my coat pocket a black-and-white photograph of my father as a young man in 1948, dashing in a pin-striped suit, to show to Erzsébet. Tears welled up in her eyes, and she took the photo from my hands. She motioned for us to sit. The shadowed room was filled with lace curtains and doilies, a frayed jacquard sofa, and smelled of mildew and fruit brandy.

The rest of the twenty minutes in her living room was a whirlwind of dialogue, all of which I had no hope to understand. Language, yet again, became my barrier to information.

"Your father's cousin, Emma, she's still alive," Csilla told me after several minutes. "Erzsébet says she lives in Budapest, in the fifth district. She would be the last surviving daughter of one of your grandmother's siblings. Your aunt."

"Does Erzsébet have her address, even a phone number?"

"Yes, yes, *egan*, of course, she'll give it to you."

"Can you ask more about my grandmother, my father's mother? How she died?"

"She says your father can talk to Emma herself. But your grandmother didn't die in any bombings, like you said."

"How did she die?"

No one would answer. Erzsébet and Tomas were already leading us out, but not before I snapped as many photographs of them as seemed reasonable. Then we all hugged and said goodbye.

Csilla and I said next to nothing during the car ride back to Budapest. She was in a hurry to return home to her husband and child in Budakeszi, an hour's drive, so she dropped me next to the Chain Bridge in front of the lions. It was early evening, but the sun was still baking hot. How do you thank someone for helping you find your grandmother's grave—and family you never knew you had—in a country whose language you do not even speak?

"*Köszönöm szépen* . . ." I said, as we hugged on an off-ramp by the bridge.

And then Csilla, so fashionable in Gucci, climbed back in her red Škoda. In another heartbeat, she had merged with a sea of oncoming cars and was gone.

|||||||||

I began to walk, not because I knew where I wanted to go, but because I didn't know where I was. Gypsies littered the Ferenciek tere underground, beneath the busy city streets, that smelled of concrete bones and cold stale urine. One legless man cupped his hands for forints, while a fat busker perched wide-kneed on a two-legged bamboo stool strung Csárdás songs for euros. After twenty minutes I walked on, past one storefront window after another, all of them showcasing various brands of dishwashing liquid, body soap, toothpaste, and toilet paper: the dawning of democracy.

When I looked up, some forty-five minutes later, I was standing across from the Hungarian National Museum on Múzeum körút.

In a pay phone across the street, I called home to my parents.

"Dad, I'm in downtown Budapest . . ."

"Peter? Is that you . . .?"

"I just got back from Vecsés, with Csilla, we found your mother's grave."

Silence.

"Dad? Hello?"

I could hear my father mumbling to my mother; then she came on the phone.

"Peter? Is that you . . .?"

"Mother? I was telling Dad that I just got back from Vecsés. I found his mother's gravesite, I found it . . ."

As they'd done for years, my father picked up the second line and then all three of us were on the call together.

"You saw my mother's grave?" my father said. His voice, even on the phone across continents, sounded childlike, forlorn. "Did you see the bench?"

"Csilla and I found the grave just like you said, off the main road in Vecsés," I said. "The woman in the office found your mother's site in a ledger and your sister's as well. She took us across the street and we found the plot. The bench was gone, I'm sorry. But I left flowers and I lit a candle and I said a prayer, Dad, and then I asked her who was paying for the graves, and it was her daughter, Erzsébet, who's been paying for the upkeep. So Csilla and I—we drove and we just starting knocking on doors, one at a time, until we found her. I showed her your picture. She remembers you, she cried when she saw you. She gave me Emma's address."

"My cousin, Emma? She's still alive?"

"I have her address. You can write to her."

And then the line disconnected.

|||||||||||

If Hungary had been all about my father's side of the family, I left Budapest, at least temporarily, to visit my cousin Ingrid in Linz, Austria, because of my mother's side of the family. The day after I arrived, Ingrid and I drove the autobahn to visit my mother's eighty-two-year-old cousin, Adam, in Munich, Germany. There were no speed limits on the autobahn, a fact not known by me beforehand, and which left me, as Ingrid sped along, clutching the dashboard in a state of near terror the entire three-hour drive.

We arrived late in the evening. Adam's wife, Maria, and their two daughters did not speak a word of English, so Ingrid was called upon to translate everything. Maria insisted we eat "a typical late-night German supper," which turned out to be a spread of sliced meats, cheeses, dark breads, and red wine. I was not accustomed to eating at 11:00 p.m., and the food was like lead in my stomach. When I thought that no one could eat a morsel more, dessert—a six-layer white chocolate torte with whipped cream topping that Maria had spent the day preparing—arrived with black coffee.

After supper, as his daughters cleared the dishes, Adam and I tried to figure out, as translated through Ingrid, exactly "who we were to each other."

We began talking about how we all were related and, like the dizzying cobblestone streets throughout Europe, the conversation quickly found its way around an array of unexpected genealogical corners.

Adam produced one tattered photo album after another and began pointing to nameless faces, at least nameless to me, although I did recognize my mother as a girl in one. Dressed for a costume ball, she looked like a youthful Habsburg, the royal monarchy that ended with the demise of the Austro-Hungarian Empire, in white wig and pink chiffon ball gown. Naturally, Adam spoke to me in German throughout. I smiled politely and nodded. When he realized, yet again, I did not speak his German, he raised both inflection and pitch, as if speaking louder and more forcefully might cure me of my failure to understand his words.

I awoke early the next morning, on the anniversary of D-day, June 5, 2004, to the news of Ronald Regan's death. Within the hour, Ingrid and I were back on the autobahn, driving toward Dachau. I had wanted to visit a concentration camp since arriving in Europe. Considering my mother's past, I thought this was a part of my history I should witness.

Upon arriving at the parking lot, outside Dachau, I could easily have mistaken the grounds for a university campus. Twenty-something-year-olds sat beneath elm trees, beside beds of flowers, smoking, talking, laughing. Birds chirped.

We parked the car and walked fifty meters to the entrance. Crossing the threshold, all sounds of birds ceased; there were no flowers or trees, only rocks and palpable foreboding. A barbed-wire fence enclosed the grounds' perimeter, and within it, a number of memorials and churches had been raised to honor the dead. On one plaque I read of how the Carmelites had built a church on the grounds in the 1960s, led by a one-time survivor.

We found a crematorium and, in front of it, an altar for the ovens.

Hanging on a wall inside the barracks next door, I saw framed pictures of prisoners who had been shot deadprisoners. Because it was the anniversary of D-day, the camp was stuffed with tourists, many American. Groups snapped photos of photos of bloodied corpses, and moved on—mementos from a war long ago for their albums back home.

The "Map Room" displayed a series of framed maps of Europe with colored stars pinned next to all the—as the sign above the maps read—*Concentration camps set up in Europe during World War II.* Eagerly, I scanned the maps, one after the other—looking for one of the camps where my mother, and many of my relatives, had been incarcerated, or died, in the former Yugoslavia: Kikinda, Petrovgrad (today's Zrenjanin), Molidorf (today's Molin), and Rudolfsgnad (today's Knićanin). When I didn't find them, not one, nor any mention of Yugoslavia at all, I realized that the "Map Room" identified only National Socialist (Nazi) concentration camps set up during the war. All my German (*Volksdeutsche*) relatives, including my mother, had been jailed in communist concentration camps erected after World War II under Josip Broz Tito. This was not a memorial for my mother's people, for any of my relatives. Theirs was a minority still without notice, gone unrecognized—silenced, for the most part, even in the history books.

|||||||||

After Munich, Ingrid and I set off on what turned out to be a two-month whirlwind European tour.

From her home back in Austria, we flew into Rhodes, Greece, where for two weeks we sunned on a pebbled beach and ate all meals in Greek resort-style buffets, including daily shots of ouzo, and traveled by foot-passenger ferry across the Aegean for a shopping spree at a Grand Bazaar in Turkey.

From Greece we flew to Paris where we drank vodka martinis for seventeen euros a piece at the Buddha Bar; strolled the Left Bank and Latin Quarter; shopped for funky designer wear along the Champs-Élysées; stood beneath the Arc de Triumph and traveled up the elevator to the top of Eifel Tower; toured Notre Dame de Paris and Sacré-Coeur de Montmartre; and browsed antique shops in the famous St-Ouen flea market.

Gelato, as I soon discovered in Rome, where we landed in a plane the size of a large bus, was an actual food group to most Italians, and we ate more than our fair share while splashing next to the Trevi Fountain or at an outside café in Piazza Navona. After lunch across from the Coliseum for ninety euros, we decided on only coffee and cake in the ruins of Castel Sant'Angelo. We walked the Roman Forum; sat in reverential awe inside the Pantheon; got lost, along with a cast of thousands, inside St. Stephen's Basilica; toured the Vatican museum; and craned our necks to stare up in the Sistine Chapel at Michelangelo's "The Last Judgment."

|||||||||||

"Do you know about your Hungary citizenship?" Ingrid asked on the Spanish Steps late one night, the two of us engulfed by a sea of Italians, all laughing, singing, drinking.

She'd asked about my citizenship many times before, hoping that if I received it while still in Europe, I would never leave. However, even in Budapest, I'd tried to visit various offices that were responsible for issuing citizenships such as mine. But with the names of streets and buses and underground metro stations in a language I could not hope to understand or remember, let alone spell or pronounce, all my efforts were of no avail.

"No word yet, I'm afraid."

"But what are your plans?" she asked. "Will you stay? You know you can live with me in Austria. I would like it if you stayed. I wish you would . . ."

"That's very kind of you."

Then she lowered her voice to a hushed tone. "I want to tell you something now," she said, "something . . . I have not told anyone before."

I turned to face her.

"I'm . . . like you."

"What do you mean?" I looked at her angular, masculine features, "butch," as I might've branded her back home. Though I'd told her nothing about the doctor or the lawsuit, she knew, of course, that I was gay. A *schwul*.

"Haven't you not wondered why I'm never married at over fifty years old?"

"It occurred to me, yes . . ."

"Austria is not America, you understand. I could never tell anyone here about my inner life . . . and so I live behind a wall."

||||||||||

Back in Linz and exhausted from all our globetrotting, Ingrid suggested we spend a few days in Bad Ischl, one of the many spa towns in the lake district of Austria.

After driving through the Alpine foreland, with a view toward the east central Alps, we checked into our spa hotel, the EurothermenResort. First and most pressing order of business: change into our thick terry bathrobes and head to the outdoor salt-water pool, around which twenty or thirty lawn chairs reclined in the late-day sun. As Ingrid basked outside, I walked into a separate cavernous passageway, steps from the indoor pool, with more than thirty different steam and sauna rooms, where I lounged and sweated with crowds of naked tourists and Austrians for the next hour.

Dinner, that first night, in the recently refurbished hotel restaurant, was a seven-course bonanza. We paced ourselves and started slowly, with dark European breads and crusty rolls, three different kinds of smoked trout, Gorgonzola muffins, warm and cold pickled salads, and a pear mousse. A cup of consommé with sherry and vegetable cubes followed, and then a plate of tender liver of lamb in red wine balsamic with mashed celery. To cleanse our palates, we were served a sour currant sherbet, then moved onto the main course: saddle of veal in herb crust on ramson gravy, steamed asparagus, and potatoes cakes. Finally, the crowning glory: raspberry-lime parfait on rhubarb ragout and puff pastry.

If Bad Ischl during the day was magical, at night it was pure whimsy. After dinner, Ingrid and I walked the winding cobblestone streets past churches, typical Austrian boutiques, the famous Zauner Café, a movie house plucked from a 1950s Frank Capra film, through manicured parks with statues of the Austro-Hungarian composer Franz Lehár, and the Habsburgs, Emperor Franz Joseph and his wife, "Sisi." Everywhere the scent of fresh flowers and dry leaves wafted through the evening air. Our first day ended with peach schnapps in the hotel lobby while live musicians played a bizarre mix of Austria folk songs with accordions, and cover renditions of seventies American rock music, like Don McLean's "American Pie" and Led Zeppelin's "Stairway to Heaven."

There was only so much of a good thing I could stand, however, and after three days in Bad Ischl, I was ready to return to my far-less luxurious flat in Budapest. At the train station in Linz, Ingrid would not look at me. We drove to the door.

"I don't need to come in," she said, the two of us still sitting in her car.

"What are you talking about?"

"You don't understand," she said, facing away.

"What? What don't I understand?"

"I wish you had more German so I could tell you what was in my heart. I do not have the English for my sadness."

"Why are you sad?"

She turned to look at me. "Have you heard about your citizenship?"

"Not yet."

"So you will leave and never come back. I'll never see you again, I know it . . ."

"Ingrid, I'm just going to Budapest. I'll see you later."

"And then you'll be home to Canada."

"Or not. I don't know. You really won't come in and wave goodbye?"

"I'll wave and then you'll be missing, and I'll have to cry to myself all the way back to my flat in my car alone. We can say goodbye here."

I reached over and hugged her.

She hugged me back, and then I stepped out of the car. Seconds later, outside the doors of the train station, I glanced back, but she had driven away.

Since Hungary had joined the European Union only in May, all trains between Vienna's Westbahnhof and Keleti Pu were still from the communist era, an old and dank relic, smelling of grit and stale smoke. The entire trip lasted close to five hours. I didn't mind. I smoked my Camels when I wanted, sat in the restaurant car with white linen tablecloths, and ate goulash and cold cucumber salad.

No one spoke English, and all currency on the menu cards was in forints. I kept a cheat sheet in my wallet (forints = euros = dollars). Calculations occupied me mentally.

As the train rattled along, snaking past towns with strange names like Hegyeshalom and Győr, my thoughts drifted again to my mother: shipped between camps by cattle car; and my father, orphaned, lying flat on his stomach on top of trains in the frigid winter nights through Hungary and Czechoslovakia because he had no money for a ticket. Like my parents before me I was a foreigner. I felt as I always had back home: displaced. Only now there was right reason to explain my isolation: I was not at home. I had no home. I was an outsider, and free. Homeless in the birthplace of my father.

27

THE STORY, AS I heard it recounted months later when I returned to Canada in September 2004, was that my parents were checking out of Safeway, their neighborhood grocery store, when my mother, who was paying the cashier for their big Tuesday shopping, handed my father a "scratch" lottery ticket. My father, not really understanding how the whole business worked, scratched the ticket with the back of his car key.

"Does this mean something good?" he said, handing the ticket back to my mother, who was still signing their Visa bill. She looked at the ticket and saw the picture of three laptop computers.

"We won!" she screamed from the lineup of shoppers, holding up the ticket. "We won!"

"Well . . . I think *I* won, actually," my father said, taking the ticket from her hands.

The new, full loaded laptop arrived at the store for pick up ten days later. Wasting no time at all, my seventy-four-year-old father registered in a community center course to learn "how to use the damn contraption." The course covered all the essentials: how to plug it in, turn it on and off, open and save a Word document, start typing.

He set up shop in his new office, in the basement of the family home, typing every day, two fingers at a time. No one knew what he was writing, and he wouldn't tell a soul, not even my mother, who worked simultaneously at her own desktop, in my old bedroom on the top floor of the house, which was now her own office.

Mid-afternoons they met in the kitchen for lunch.

"Homemade soup and good Hungarian rye bread," they said often, "are life's staples. What else is there?"

When I visited on Sundays, my father would ask that I follow him to his office "to answer all my questions."

"How do I print?" he'd ask, facing his laptop, eager as a schoolboy. "How do I center text . . .?" "Can I type Hungarian letters and accents . . .?" "What if I want to add a red heart at the top of a page, or maybe a picture of a bird or a squirrel; can you show me how to do that?"

For hours I taught him everything he asked, writing down notes on scraps of paper he kept tacked to the wall around his laptop, beneath pictures of the Virgin Mary and a crucifix. A two-volume English-Hungarian/Hungarian-English dictionary that I'd bought for him in Budapest now sat beside him on his desk.

Every few months I'd receive an urgent phone call at my new office job, again with the Ministry of Attorney General in downtown Vancouver.

"SOS!" he once shouted, the moment I picked up the phone at my desk. "SOS! SOS!"

"Dad? What is it? Are you okay? Is Mom okay?"

"Squiggly lines are all over my computer and my cursor's gone missing. I swear it was here a second ago!"

"Squiggly lines?"

"Under the words. Red, squiggly lines. I can't get rid of them."

"That's just the computer telling you that you misspelled a word, or that your grammar's wrong."

"'Telling' me? What do you mean my computer is 'telling' me? How can my computer 'tell' me something? And what about my cursor? It's dropped off the screen."

"Dad . . . you shouldn't just call me and scream out 'SOS' like this—I thought you'd had a heart attack, or worse!"

"When are you coming home again? I have so many questions about my computer that I need you to answer. I need you . . ."

When he and I did, on rare occasion, start to talk about his new secret writing project, he said he was "piecing" his life back together, "one memory at a time."

"Can I read it?" I asked him one Sunday when we were down in his office. "Please?"

"Maybe when I'm dead."

"Oh come on, that's not fair. I've been waiting my whole life to read something like this. Maybe I'll have questions for you. Besides, you're going to live for years . . ."

||||||||||

I started dating Angelo, a Greek man I met at a local gay dance club one Sunday night. Unencumbered by the shame of past years, our sex, after the third date, was high octane. Primal, even.

We met for coffees, never hesitating to kiss hello in public, held hands on our way to movies, dined in tapas restaurants, lay in bed for hours, awake or asleep, dreaming and waking in each other's arms, limbs holding limbs, torsos alive with passion. Angelo was in culinary school to become a chef, and I loved to cook and bake, so we spent hours in the kitchen of his condominium, devising elaborate meals. Nothing about our time together called to mind my childhood fears of men, or, for that matter, sex. Everything about our union felt normal, and natural. Necessary even. I was happy.

||||||||||

One Sunday, I asked my mother if she knew what my father was writing.

"I have always tried to avoid asking your father too many questions about his life before we met. I knew he was suffering, and I didn't want to make it worse. We accepted each other without too many questions in either direction. I think he now feels compelled to write about all of it. And all because of you."

"Me?"

"You ripped the lid off this box. Applying for your Hungarian citizenship started him down this road. Visiting his mother's grave probably sealed it. Now he can't stop."

When my father was out of his office, I opened his Word document, what looked like the beginning of a book called *From My Memory*, and read an early passage:

> *Every day when I was five or six, my nanny, a Swabian lady called Aunty Elizabeth, walked me to kindergarten with the Franciscan*

Sisters, dressed in large white wimples and long brown habits, with big wooden crosses dangling from their waists, and then home again in the afternoon. I carried my schoolbooks tied with a string, buttered buns in a lunch pail, and my most prized possession: the crayons my daddy had given to me on Christmas day.

First we passed through the forest full of white birch, weeping willow, acacia and chestnut, and I saw croaking ravens swooping and hopping branch to branch. Then we walked around a lake filled with waterfowl and ducks, geese and swans, both black and white, with long, crooked necks, all chatting and screeching. Socializing, I thought. Gossiping. Finally we walked over a bridge hanging on two chains, and entered the Sisters' forted convent. My trips to and from school each day were magical.

Sometimes I slept in between my mommy and my daddy in the big bed, and in the morning I ate my favorite breakfast, cream of wheat with brown sugar and a glass of ice-cold milk. In the afternoon I worked in my daddy's barbershop, in the front room of our house, brushing all the fallen hair from clients' suits and then sweeping the floor with my broom. My hard work never went unnoticed, because when I finished my daddy handed me a few loose coins, and then he thanked me with a big "peach," by crossing his index finger with his thumb in a sweeping motion on top of my head. I always gave my earnings to my mommy for safekeeping. "Your future tuition fund," she'd tell me.

On Sundays, mommy took me to the big house of God with stained glass windows and gold ornaments. People sang and knelt praying on the marble floor. Mommy closed her eyes while she was down on her knees and so I did too, because I loved my mommy so much and I wanted to be just like her.

At home I fed the animals in the barn, all the pigs and the sheep. I harvested fresh herbs and vegetables from the garden for mommy's homemade chicken soup, or else sometimes I wandered alone outside for hours, smelling all the fruit trees, apricots, peaches, apples, pears, plums. Every year by harvest time the grapes grew up and overhead the length of our outdoor porch, and they turned blue and filled the air with a sweet buttery fragrance. Birds swooped and sang melodies. Yellow and black thrush and fork-tailed swallows nested and delivered sustenance to their young. I'd seen the storks before by the banks of the Zagyva, and so I knew what they were when I watched them standing one-legged atop our red brick chimney, their white wings spread for flight, long beaks pointed up into the breeze. Every day there was so much to see, and smell, to taste. I was a happy little boy.

Then one day my mommy was gone. In the morning, when I woke up, and after school, when I returned home, she was nowhere. Aunty Elizabeth bathed me like usual, she dressed me in my cotton nightgown, knelt beside me as I said my evening prayers, kissed me on my cheeks and tucked me in for the night. Even the next morning, when I opened my eyes, she was bent over me, smiling. But still no mommy.

After school on the second day I approached the house through the back wooden gate holding tightly to Aunty Elizabeth's hand. I walked through the garden, and the inside laundry room, down a long corridor. Next to the kitchen I smelled an overpowering fragrance. Still holding her hand, we entered the main sitting room, which was full of people, all dressed in black, holding something hanging from their hands. Black drapes covered all the windows. In the center of the room was a tall table. I couldn't see the top because it was so high and I was so little, but I walked toward it.

The crowd of people all parted. I saw my daddy, dressed in a black suit; he was sobbing. Someone brought me a stool. I stepped up. Lying flat on her back was my mommy. Her eyes were closed. She was asleep. Her countenance was so beautiful. All I wanted was to lie down beside her, to kiss her, like I always did in bed. I bent down and I looked into her face. "Mommy is sleeping," I said. From the back of the room someone called out, "She is dead." I bent down again and I looked closer. Someone else giggled. I repeated what I'd said before: "Mommy is sleeping, yes, yes, she is sleeping." More giggles. And then my lower lip began to dance.

Never before had I heard the words death, or cemetery, but as the procession moved out into the street, toward a long black car, all I wanted was to go with my mommy to the cemetery. The car drove away and I stood staring down the long street.

Nights followed where I cried myself to sleep. In the mornings I awoke from strange dreams with wet undergarments. My soul had been submerged into something dark and mysterious. Before, I had always

*slept in the center of the big bed between my mommy and my daddy.
Now only daddy lay beside me. I missed mommy so much. Sometimes
I started crying and I couldn't stop. I hid in the pantry, or out in the
garden. I hid anywhere I could find and I cried myself into a frenzy,
until I started hiccupping, until I saw double. My sister, Manci, she
called me a one-eyed monster, and that made me cry even more. When
my crying stopped, then I only yearned for more tears. Tears now were
my only comfort.*

*For days after they took my mommy away I sat on a stool in front
of our house and I stared down that long street. Next door there lived
a little girl about my height with long ponytails. She sat beside me,
both of us staring with vacant eyes down that long and empty street.*

||||||||||

My father received his first letter from his cousin, Emma, barely three
months after my return from Europe. Emma wrote to my father that
she had received a phone call from Erzsébet almost as soon as I'd left
her house. When Erzsébet said that her uncle's son had just arrived
on her doorstep from Canada, Emma could not believe her ears. For
almost sixty years she had believed my father dead. The communist
police had searched for him, she wrote in an early letter, but he had
vanished. He wrote back, explaining that he had crossed the border
illegally into Czechoslovakia. He knew that he would never return
to his native country; he would need to cut all ties.

My father and Emma began exchanging letters. Sometimes they
talked on the phone, although my father said he preferred letters to
phone calls.

Emma, my father told me, was "the keeper of family secrets." But
"between her fits of tears, and talking a mile a minute in Hungarian, I
can't keep up with her," he said. "After all these years of not knowing
anything about my past, I'm overwhelmed."

He had many questions for Emma, and she tried her best to
answer them all. How many siblings did his mother have? Where were
his uncles and aunts all born, and where did they die? Did everyone
know about him, that he was "a bastard"? Who was his father? And
how did his mother die?

This last inquiry of my father's—about how his "mother died"—flattened me. I could not conceive of what it must have been like for my father to never know, or to think he knew but only because he'd imagined a story to fill in the gaps, how his mother's life had ended. The idea that she had "died in the bombings" had become a safe bet, even though it was all conjecture because he had never even lived with his birth mother, certainly not at the end of her life, and I'd heard this all before, many times. It was one of the only things about my father's past that I had heard. As a child, whenever I'd ask my mother to tell me anything about my father, or his parents, she'd say, "His mother died in the bombings."

He asked Emma if she could please try to locate his birth certificate. "Any evidence that I exist," he told her in one of his many letters. Emma, already past seventy years old, traveled by tram and metro throughout Budapest, visited churches, St. Stephen's Basilica, the hospitals, and religious archives. She asked questions and reported back to my father on what she'd found. I asked him if he could tell me what she found, but he said, "It's personal." In these moments of secrecy, still withholding himself from me, all I saw in him was more fear.

Meanwhile, for nearly three years I had been waiting for news from the Hungarian Embassy about my application for citizenship—an application, the embassy staff had politely, but assuredly, emailed me on numerous occasions, that was "a long shot," considering the lack of original documentation verifying my father's Hungarian birthplace, as well as his own father's identity.

On the same day in late August 2005, as if both roads to our independent quests had intersected, Emma phoned my father with the news that she had located proof of his nationality in the church archives in Budapest, as the embassy staff emailed me with the news that my passport had arrived from Hungary; I had been accepted as a Hungarian citizen. As it turned out, officials in Budapest had been able to verify my father's birth themselves, and, consequently, *his own* citizenship had also been granted back to him. My father was once again a citizen of his home country. He had been repatriated.

Two days later, after receiving both documents in a couriered package, I stood in my father's living room and handed him his proof of citizenship and newly licensed Hungarian birth certificate. No pomp and circumstance. My mother watched nearby.

"I don't understand," he said, now holding the document. "What is this?"

"Your Hungarian citizenship."

"What do you mean?"

"You're a citizen of Hungary again."

He stared down at the document. "That's not possible."

"I told you . . . before I could get my own citizenship, the Hungarian government needed to grant yours back to you first. Mine was based on yours. So there it is. You have your citizenship again."

He stared down at the document, silent.

My mother later told me that he kept it stashed in a drawer by his bedside, next to a rosary, purchased with my mother at Guadalupe, and a picture of the Virgin Mary.

|||||||||

I continued writing my memoir before my office job early each morning and well into every evening. Guided mostly by notes I had taken throughout the therapy, my journals in which I'd transcribed specific conversations from the Styx and with Alfonzo, voluminous documentation left over from the College complaint and lawsuit—including Alfonzo's 500-page rejoinder—as well as recorded primals, I was able to map out the sequence of events from when I met Alfonzo, through the therapy, out the other end, and headstrong into a lawsuit. I wrote to make real what at times still seemed unreal.

I also researched the word "Styx." In all my years at the house, no one had so much as mentioned why they'd chosen to spell it this way. A simple search revealed that the word, "Styx," had originated as *stugein*, meaning, "to hate." In Greek mythology, the Styx, or "the river of hate," separated the world of the living from that of the dead.

Explaining it all to Angelo, whom I'd been dating now for more than six months, was something else entirely. I gave him a copy of an essay that I'd been writing and told him to read it. He did, but then complained that "this is interesting, but it takes so much of your time." Angelo began to experience my writing as direct competition for his attention and affection.

Late one night before bed as the two of us were talking in my apartment, my laptop open, journals and papers spread across my living room floor, he picked up my Walkman, which contained a recording of one of my primal sessions. Horrified, I told him to hand me the Walkman.

"That's a taped recording from a therapy session," I said. "Please give it back."

"I want to listen for myself," he said.

"It's private."

"I'll be the judge of that," he said.

He put on the headphones.

"Don't turn that on," I said, my heart now racing, palms sweating.

He placed his finger on the play button and smiled.

We were sitting across from each other in my living room, and the thought that at any moment he might hear my recorded primals, a whiff of bedlam, ripped me open and left me feeling violated. I lunged for the Walkman, grabbed it out of his hands.

"*Get the fuck out of here,*" I screamed.

"Geez . . . I was only joking," he said.

Nothing about my reaction made sense to him.

Days later he presented me with an ultimatum. "I don't understand why you can't just let go all of all that and move on with your life, instead of constantly reliving your past."

I'd heard these kinds of comments from him before: "Move on with your life," he'd say, or "Let go of the past," or "Get over it"—all comments I'd learned to understand meant something like: "I'm tired of listening to you talk about this subject." Or maybe even: "What you're talking about makes *me* uncomfortable, so will you please just stop?"

"I'm not reliving my past," I said. "I'm trying to make a difference for the future."

"I still think you need to let it go. You spend way too much time writing. You have to choose between me and your writing . . . "

"*Excuse me?*"

"You can't have it both ways."

I broke up with him the next week. I chose.

|||||||||

I didn't mention the subject of my book with my family either, since I'd learned to skirt issues that would only lead to more conflict. Despite whatever reconciliation my parents and I had achieved, topics around my "gay self" were still taboo. Recently, my mother had even handed me a letter she'd written to a local newspaper and asked me to give her my "thoughts." She had been writing letters to newspapers and politicians for years. The first line of her letter had read: *I am writing in firm opposition to the recent legalization of same sex marriage in Canada.*

I had to broach the subject of my book with my mother eventually, though, as I knew that certain details from her life—and, to a lesser degree, my father's—needed to be included in my book's trajectory. My years in the therapy would not carry the full weight of their experience—to me personally, definitely not within the confines of a book—out of the context of my family history. I had changed the name of virtually everyone in my book, except my own, but my mother was my mother.

The entire situation troubled me, ethically and morally. Baring my own soul was difficult enough; what right did I have to divulge any of her own "secrets"? My mother, I knew, would never grant me "permission" to write about the conversation when she told me she'd been raped in the camp, that much I knew. I couldn't even mention that conversation again to her, to anyone. I searched out books about the ethics of real-life writing, but found little that could help me navigate the sticky issue of how to write about one's own life when it intersected—as it almost always does—with another's, particularly when that other person is one's mother who has a history of trauma and sexual abuse.

Two books, however, did help. In *The Secret Life of Families: Truth-Telling, Privacy, and Reconciliation in a Tell-All Society*, author Evan Imber-Black, Ph.D., helped me distinguish secrecy from privacy when she wrote that, "Toxic and dangerous secrets most often make us feel shame, while truly private matters do not. Hiding and concealment are central to secret-keeping, but not to privacy." There was no revenge to my act of writing. I simply wanted to write the truth, maybe even to discover the truth through the act of writing. Finally, I read Judith Herman's *Trauma and Recovery: The Aftermath of Violence—From Domestic Abuse to Political Terror*, in which she stated, "Remembering and telling the truth about terrible events are prerequisites both for the restoration of the social order and for the healing of individual victims." Writing, for me, brought an order of truth to the chaos of lies and deceit.

After months of anguishing, finally I approached my mother when we were alone in the kitchen after one of our Sunday brunches. At the very least, I felt I owed her a request to write about her years in the camps.

"You know I've been writing a book," I said.

My mother looked at me. "About?"

"The therapy. My lawsuit against the doctor."

She looked away, busied herself at the sink, separating plastics from recycling.

"I wanted to ask . . . I mean . . . I was hoping you would give me . . . well, your permission. I wanted to be able to write about some of your own experiences in the camps as well, juxtaposed against my own story."

"Why would you want to do that?" She turned back to face me.

"I'm your son. Your life has affected me. Is that okay?"

Again, she turned away, silent. I waited.

"Yes, that's fine," she said.

No other words, and no mention of specifics. What exactly she was consenting to was unclear, and I couldn't bring myself to ask. Bringing up her rape, specifically, felt out of the question, as I still was not permitted to talk openly about my own sexuality around her. Our fights from years ago were buried deep below the surface, land mines, and I could not risk resurrecting more estrangement.

But I also couldn't stop writing. My essay "Surviving the Cult," an almost academic account of my years in the therapy and the lawsuit, was published in the UK-based magazine *Gay Times* in January 2006.

||||||||||

My parents and I added midweek dinners to our weekly brunches. Not since childhood had I prayed with them—doing so would have felt like submission. But when they made the sign of the cross before each meal, thanking God for all their blessings, the food and their children's health, I bowed my head out of the same sense of gratitude. Their unyielding faith in God, whether shared by me or not, comforted. After years of estrangement, our time together settled my heart. What I believed held less importance than my own unyielding love for them. I wouldn't change, and neither would they.

We toasted each other's health with Jägermeister, ate meals that I spent hours preparing—schnitzel with pickled cabbage, roasted potatoes with bacon and Hungarian cucumber salad with sour cream and dill, tortes for dessert, black coffee and pálinka—all the while veering into any number of hot topics: abortion, which they wholeheartedly opposed even while I defended a woman's right to choose; capital punishment, which all three of us denounced; the sexual-abuse scandal throughout the Catholic church, which they still refused to believe could have occurred; even Hitler, who my mother mentioned often and could not, perhaps because of their shared nationality, bring herself to condemn. In this and any other issue related to my mother's years in the camp, which she spoke of more and more often, my father and I typically fell silent. Nobody could argue with her when it came to any subject related to her three years in a concentration camp.

At the end of every night when I put on my coat to leave and return to my downtown apartment, I said a word or two of Hungarian to my parents. "*Viszontlátásra, Apu és Anyu . . . Szeretlek.*"

To which my father always responded, "*Viszontlátásra, Péter. Szeretlek.*" ("Goodbye Peter, I love you.")

||||||||||

My father continued asking me computer questions—how to make bulleted lists and tables, borders, and colored fonts. He wrote love poetry for my mother using elaborate fonts, affixing pictures of hearts and angels that he'd found through "Clip Art." Google became his new goldmine as he searched for anything he could find about all the towns and villages where he'd lived as a child.

"I want to show you a picture of one of the houses where I lived as a young boy," he said to me one afternoon during a visit after work.

"What do you mean?"

"I found it on Google. I printed it to show you. It's still just as I remember it."

"You found a picture online of a house you lived in as a child?"

"Well, of course."

"What do you mean 'of course'?"

"Everything is in Google," he told me. "Don't you know?"

To his amazement, he learned that he could now email all his letters to Emma through her son—my father's nephew, István. He spent weeks composing each letter in Hungarian, painstakingly using all the features available in Word for accents. Once completed, I helped him copy and paste the letter into an email.

"You're a magician," he'd say each and every time I clicked "send," and the electronic *swoosh* told us his words were whizzing across the hemisphere to Budapest.

"Not really. This is pretty basic stuff."

"Well, from where I'm sitting, you are a kind and gentle sir, a wizard on the keyboard."

Kindness expressed to my father was kindness returned, and my heart swelled.

Emma began including old black-and-white photographs from my father's "missing years in Hungary" in her letters. The single bed in his basement office—his "cave," as he now called it—was soon blanketed in a patchwork of foreign faces, ranging from the 1950s to the 1980s.

"I want to show you something," he said to me in his office one Sunday. He handed me a grainy photograph of an elderly couple standing in the middle of a field, wheat billowing in the air behind them. "These are my grandparents, my mother's parents. They lived in Pocsaj, a small Hungarian village. I lived with them for a short time after the death of my mother."

"You did?"

"István and Sofi. Stephen and Sophie. I smoked a pipe for years because my grandfather smoked a pipe. The smell reminded me of how much I loved him."

"What was he like, your grandfather?"

"Very kind, but quiet. When he talked, I listened. That was the way. He taught me a lot. Here, follow me . . . "

I followed my father up the stairs to the den, next to the kitchen. From behind the upright piano he pulled out a long teacher's stick, and then he pointed it up at a large framed map of "The Kingdom of Hungary," pre–World War I, hanging on the wall.

"This is the Hungary I love," he said. "Before it was chopped up and parceled away. You know that I was born in Budapest." He pointed to the capital near the center of the map. "But I grew up mostly in the surrounding countryside, in Pocsaj"—he pointed to the eastern area of Hungary, close to Debrecen—"where I lived with my grandparents, in Hajdú-Bihar County."

"You know," I said, glancing down at the picture of his grandparents, "if you like, we could scan some of your photos and include them at the end of your book."

"You can do that? But . . . how is that possible?"

"Your printer has a scan feature. It's simple."

Over the coming days I showed him how to scan and paste photographs into his Word document. When he disagreed with the order in which I pasted the photographs, I showed him how to arrange them into whatever order he preferred.

Days later when I returned to the house, all the pictures were deleted.

"What happened?"

"I have to scan them again. The order was all wrong."

"Dad, remember what I showed you, that you can just cut and paste them? You don't need to delete them, you can just move them around."

"I don't remember. Can you show me again, please?"

Month after month, the same situation repeated. He couldn't remember how to cut and paste, so he deleted all the photos, and we started from scratch.

"Technology is such a miraculous invention. In my own life I have seen so much progress, so much change. The evolution of the soul is a miraculous thing. God loves all his children, and we show him our reverence with keen minds and loving hearts."

|||||||||

I had also continued secretly reading from his book when he was away from his office.

One evening soon after the hearse took my mommy away, Aunty Elizabeth dressed me in my nightgown, as usual, knelt beside me as I said my evening prayers, tucked me in, read me a story, and kissed me on both cheeks. I loved my Aunty Elizabeth, almost as much as I had loved my own mommy.

The next morning my sister, Manci, not Aunty Elizabeth, was in the kitchen, cooking my cream of wheat. And then Manci, not Aunty Elizabeth, walked me to school. In my confusion and my eagerness I forgot my school bag with a sandwich, my drawing paper and crayons, my one possession in the whole world. I told Manci that we had to turn back. We could not, she insisted, and on we walked: through the forest, around the lake, over the bridge, into the convent, where the Franciscan Sisters took me by the hand to kindergarten. At noon, when it was time to return home for lunch, no one came for me. Not my sister, or my daddy, no Aunty Elizabeth. Again, I started to cry. The Sisters tried their best to console me, but it was no use.

Later that same day a strange woman appeared at the convent and she took me by train to the orphanage in Budapest, which was nothing more than a junction place for children-in-waiting for adoption, like myself. My mommy had never been my mother, I soon learned, and my daddy had not been my real father. I had no father. Other children like me were in the orphanage and had no mothers or fathers either, only men and women that were paid by the State to house a child who could help clean their homes, tend to their farms, care for their animals.

Over the next several years I was moved from house to house, from family to family. For a bed I always slept under a horse blanket in the barns. Because I could never stop crying, I always became a nuisance to my latest "parents" and so the woman from the State eventually reappeared months or a year later and returned me by train to the orphanage.

Sometimes I thought to myself, How can I dream a bigger dream? I knew I wanted more out of life, but at the same time my life felt like a big bad dream. The anxiety was relentless, I was forever nauseated and my stomach growled with pain. I was sure that something was growing inside of me, that my heart was out of place inside his my own body.

With no family "stories" to share with anyone, I just listened and did not say much of anything as others went on about their own mothers and fathers, their brothers and sisters, aunts and uncles. Simple words like my mother said this, or, my mother did that, or the rest of my family told me so-and-so would have enriched my life, maybe given me some self-confidence. But I had nothing.

Well into my teenage years, if I saw a mother with her child, even a mother pig feeding her piglets, my heart ached for what I knew was missing and I'd burst into tears. I could not speak about my deep inner sadness to anyone. I was emotionally mute, cut off from others, isolated and alone, always in search of the mother I never knew.

I was fifteen years old in 1945 when news of my birth mother's death reached me one day by letter carrier where I was living with my latest parents in Slovakia. I knew what I had to do. Early the next morning I said goodbye to my foster parents, and I travelled by train to the Kőbánya alsó railway station in Budapest. I walked along the west side of the Danube, from the bombed-out Horthy Miklós Bridge. At some point my body could no longer move, so I sat near the murky waters of the river, overpowered by sadness. I had no money or friends, no real family. I yearned for tears. Instead, I saw the river, black and dirty. I regained my composure, stood and spat into the water. Then I walked back to the streetcar and I waited. Finally, the number fifty arrived. With my last precious change I paid my way and I travelled to Vecsés.

It was noontime and windy when I arrived at the cemetery. The big trees were shedding their yellow leaves. I walked to where I'd been told was my mother's grave, second to last at the end of a long dirt path near the rear of the grounds. I read the inscription on the stone headpiece, *touched the soil that blanketed her final resting place. This was the end of the line; my life-long search to know my biological mother was over. All my childhood dreams were lying six feet under. More than anything else I wanted to lie down beside her.*

I knelt down on the left-hand side of the grave and I began to pray, repeating the same words till I was faint with exhaustion. "Oh my heavenly Father . . ." I had not eaten or slept in days. There was a long wooden bench at the foot of the grave. My eyes were already half-closing when I stretched out on it. Dogs barked in the distance. The sounds reassured; they told me I was alive.

When I opened my eyes again it was morning, sunlight and the promise of life. I had slept through the night on the wooden bench at the foot of my mother's grave. Blackbirds were talking on all the poplar trees. I looked around but saw no one. Once again, I knelt by her grave and I began to pray, or at least I tried. Ravens screeched and swooned.

An elderly man with a heavy moustache was opening one wing of the iron-gate for the day as I approached the entrance from inside. Each man, old and young, looked at the other but said nothing. People trickled in as I left. I sat down on the gravel road by a chain-link fence. My throat was dry and parched. All I wanted was to bark or howl, for someone to listen to me, to hear my pain. My eyes fell shut. I began to cry.

||||||||||

The next time I saw my father, all I wanted to do was hug him. He was typing away in his office when I arrived at the house.

"Come in," he said from his seat at his laptop. "Sit down and talk with me . . ."

"What are you working on?" I said, clearing away some of the photographs on the single bed to sit across from him.

"I was rereading different passages that I wrote."

"Such as?"

"An incident with my father."

"You met your father?"

"I think so, once."

"What do you mean, you think so?"

"You have to understand, I did not have a childhood like you had a childhood, a home, two parents that loved you, brothers and sisters, school and friends. Even a country where you were free to think your own thoughts. What I have are stories handed down to me through relatives. For years I did not even know what was real from what was imagined. But there is this one story . . ."

"Can you tell me?"

"You would like to hear?"

"Absolutely."

"Well . . . okay. It was a Sunday. I know it was a Sunday because we ate chicken soup, potatoes, and vegetables for supper, which we ate only on Sundays after church. I was tired after our big meal, so I slept in the bed with my mommy."

I could never interrupt my father and share with him my own stories of "mommy" from the Styx. My father's "mommy," I understood by now, was also not his biological mother. As an orphan, he had never lived with his biological mother, but his adoptive "mommy" had still mothered him as if she were his own. He'd loved her like a mother.

"Anyway, every Sunday afternoon my mommy and I went out for a stroll in the park, and so we did on this day, as well. Just the two of us."

"You remember all of this?"

"Of course."

"It's just, you've never talked about it before."

"So on this Sunday, instead of the park, my mommy took a different route. I said something about wanting to go to our special place in the park, but my mommy put her index finger up to her lips and I knew not to act mischievous. We walked for a long time, and then we arrived at a big garden restaurant with round tables and colorful umbrellas. We sat at one of the tables. My mommy opened her handbag. It was black. She took out a mirror. I remember, she powdered her face. To me it was just so funny, like she was patting her cheeks with—what's it called? The dust from a writing board? On the wall?"

"Chalk?"

"Yes, chalk dust. And I could hear a man's voice inside the

restaurant; he was singing in Hungarian. *Sárbogár, dombbogár, gyógy-izsd meg a lelkem*. I can still hear the music like it was yesterday."

"Can you translate it?"

"No, it would lose its zest."

Then he told me the story of the one and only time he met his biological father.

First another woman appeared from the building. She hugged his "mommy," and sat down at the table. She was dressed all in black—black hat, black net hanging down over her face, black dress, black handbag—with her lips "painted bright red." She talked to his mommy in a strange language that he later realized must have been German. He had no idea who this other woman was, but he knew he liked her. Occasionally, she'd look at him and smile, her face still shrouded by the black net.

A soldier arrived at the table, clicked his heels, tipped his head, and said something to the women in German. He was tall, my father said—"very tall, and he had a black moustache. He was dressed in high black hoots with shiny spurs on each heel, and he had a sword hanging from his left side." The soldier also had more than one gold star on each side under his chin on his uniform, my father explained. Listening to him recount this singular event from what was almost eighty years earlier, I honestly did not know what to think. How could he have "remembered" so much detail—remembered it all and never spoken a word about it? What sort of turmoil must this have caused him?

The soldier signaled to another man with a white cloth hanging from his arms, the waiter, who brought my father a dish of ice cream. "Oh it was so good, chocolate and vanilla, I just munched down on it." Then the soldier gave him "a little 'peach'" on the top of his head. I remembered this expression from his book, so I asked him what he meant.

"A 'peach'—it was a sign of affection."

After that the solider tipped his hat toward the black-dressed woman, clicked his heels again, and left through the same gate from where he'd arrived. The woman stroked his cheek, lovingly. Soon after that, she also left. He was alone again with his mommy.

The whole way home she didn't say a word to him, but he could tell that she was sad. "I never liked it when my mommy was sad," my father said. "Her sadness made me sad too."

Later, much later, in his life, my father said he "came to understand" that the woman in black had been his biological mother and that the soldier had been his father.

"Do you mention the name of your father in your book?" I asked.

"Yes, because of Emma's help. Before my mother died, she asked her sister—Emma's mother—to make sure my whole history was passed on to me one day. From the dying wish of my mother, and then my aunt, now Emma is helping me piece this all back together."

"And?"

"And what?"

"Can you tell me?"

"Tell you what?"

"The name of your father."

"Why are you so interested in my father?"

"Why wouldn't I be interested? Our name could have been his name."

I waited for my father to answer; he said nothing. This quest to learn the identity of my grandfather had been a recurring theme throughout my life, at least since I had learned, as a teenager, that our family name, Gajdics, was not my paternal grandfather's name but my paternal grandmother's maiden name.

In 1992, while still in the Styx, I had contacted a private investigator through the Hungarian Embassy and asked questions about my father's past, to which I received a poorly written letter, months later, stating that there was no record in the Hungarian archives of anyone by my father's name. Even while in Budapest I had hired a retired Hungarian diplomat, specializing in genealogy, to conduct research into my father's past and, hopefully, unveil my grandfather's identity. However, after meeting the elderly diplomat in a local pub, where I handed over a considerable sum of American dollars (his request) in a brown paper bag, he told me that his wife needed surgery—my eyes on his hands now lying flat on the bag of cash—that the money would "help," and then he picked up his cane and hobbled off. For months afterward he sent me cryptic emails, all containing nothing of value about my lineage, and then I never heard from him again.

"Well?" I said to my father, still waiting for his response.

"Why don't you just wait till I'm dead? Then you can read the whole thing for yourself."

28

IF AFTER EUROPE MY heart had opened even more to my parents, my relationship with my sister, Kriska, hemorrhaged. When we spoke on the phone, she was cold and withdrawn.

"I guess you've moved over to the other side now."

"What side?"

"Mom and Dad's side."

"That's ridiculous, I'm not on anyone's side. I just want peace."

"But you go to the house now all the time."

"So?"

"What are you expecting from them? They'll never accept you, never. Only I accept you in this family."

"That's a cruel thing to say. Besides, you don't know what will happen in the future. Do you even try to talk to them?"

"Why would I talk to them? They've never talked to me."

"Do you even know what they went through in Europe?"

"They've never told me."

"That's a child's response. Why don't you ask them?"

"Do what you want. I don't care."

"Yes, you care."

"Whatever."

Each time we argued, month after month, the memory of her eyes, the night she ran away from home, and my sense of abandonment as a child once she was gone from my life, flooded back. That pain was still raw—and so was her anger. Wounds picked open but not, apparently, healed. Or maybe they'd healed, but the scars still remained.

Either way I stopped calling her.

||||||||||

After brunch one Sunday, my mother turned to face me while I was cleaning the dishes. "I'd like to read your writing."

It took me a moment to orient myself to her request, and then to respond. "What?"

"Your book. I'd like to read what you've written."

"Why?"

"Well you said you were including stories about my life. I don't want my life experiences associated with anything to do with your 'gay' lifestyle. Do you understand me?"

"But I asked you. You gave me your permission."

"I did not give you permission to use any of the stories I gave you when you were nineteen."

"But—"

"You just want to write about that time in your bedroom when I told you I was raped, but I was never raped, *I was never raped*. You tricked me into saying that, *you tricked me*."

I was now the accused. She continued staring at me, fear streaked across her face. Stunned, I stood in the doorway, unable to speak. Defend myself against—what? Moments later she turned and left the room.

I turned back to the kitchen, sat down, stood, was numb.

||||||||||

The following week, my father, sitting in his regular spot at one end of the kitchen table, would not look me in the face. "Mother says you're writing a book."

"That's right."

"About what?"

I glanced at my mother.

"I hope you're not dragging your mother's and my good name through the dirt."

"Pardon me?"

"Our good name, your mother's and my good name. I don't want your mother and I associated with your homosexuality." He spit the word out like a sleepwalker, staring back at me through the hatred of his dream.

"Your 'good name,'" I said, "is also my 'good name.' Besides, this book is about me—what I went through with the doctor. You have *nothing* to worry about."

"Just think about what I'm saying."

"I don't know *what* you're saying."

"You must know how I feel about your lifestyle."

I glanced again at my mother, who sat silent in her seat.

"*It's filthy, it's immoral.* I don't agree with it, I've *never* agreed with it, and I never *will* agree with it. I don't want to be blamed for how you turned out."

"I've never blamed you."

I ended the conversation when I told both my parents that I was through, as a *middle-aged* man, defending who I was. I left their house in a storm.

Days later I received an email from my brother Frank. A stock-broker-cum-businessman by trade, my brother and I had little in common. If Kriska had run away physically when I was a child, Frank had left emotionally soon thereafter. I could hardly even recall him from my childhood, let alone a time when we had a single conversation together as adults.

Though Frank didn't wish to read any part of my book, he said he was writing now in order to impress upon me that my "actions could bring about hardship and sadness to others." He urged me to make sure that my book's content "would not cause sadness to anyone, was factual, not proprietary to others," and that if it was, I had the "expressed permission to use it. But the consequence for using unauthorized information was punitive," he wrote. "Everyone knows that slander is a nasty and distasteful word. I do not say these things as a threat, nor do I say them without knowing the meaning of them myself."

The email left me panicked. I was definitely only writing fact, and yet I did not want to "cause sadness to anyone." The two, it seemed to me, were not mutually exclusive.

I called him on the phone, asked him if Mother had put him up to the email, and what could possibly be gained from sending me such a message.

"You are obviously writing something about the family," he said, his rising voice pitched with anger, "and I'm here to tell you to be careful. Do not bring shame to this family. I, for one, do not want my sons growing up with the shame of anything you now feel compelled to tell the world."

Our conversation was brief.

Do not bring shame to this family.

My sister, Kriska, called me the next day.

"What's going on with you?" she said.

"What do you mean?"

"Everyone in this family is really upset with you about your writing."

"Thanks for the vote of confidence."

"You know, Peter, none of us think that anything will ever come of your writing. You should just give it up now."

I said little in response, made some excuse, and hung up.

For weeks and then months afterward I told myself that my family's words, and whatever my mother had said that had prompted them, had nothing to do with me, that my family loved me, that they wanted nothing but the best for me. I told myself that they did not understand, that they were afraid, but that I should not live in fear, should keep writing, keep loving, love my parents, choose love. I told myself what I needed to think in order to keep going and not sink back into the melancholy, or worse: outward spite.

|||||||||

I returned to counseling, this time with a Jungian, where I talked about my shadow, and my parents, about how my brother's email had the same muzzling effects as my fear of Alfonzo after I'd sued him, when I was sure he would stalk me and stop me from talking. But between my need to speak the truth through my writing and my need not to cause harm to my parents, both of whom I knew would say they'd been harmed should they ever read what I wrote, I felt trapped, existentially landlocked.

As I struggled through my brother's threat—through the self-delusion that I'd build up in my mind to protect me from the truth that my own family did not have my best interest at heart, and that fear of the truth-teller can make even, or even especially, the ones we love turn against us—I submerged myself in the writing; spent longer hours at my computer; and wrote another essay about the therapy that was published in the August 2007 issue of Harvard University's *Gay & Lesbian Review Worldwide*.

‖‖‖‖‖‖‖‖

After avoiding my parents for months, my father sent me a letter by regular mail.

"I would like to apologize for my words," he wrote. "I realize now that I shouldn't have said these things to you. Sometimes, in the 'heat of the dispute,' words fly, as was the case here, regrettably." He went on to again make reference to my writing, my "lifestyle, whatever that means," to say that I do "have the right to [my] own life story." The letter concluded: "I hope, Peter, that our short squabble will not sever our relationship. You, Peter, were always close to my heart, and I wouldn't like to find this otherwise. As you were always a loving son to us, I hope that in your heart I too am a loving father. I am sure that Mother would concur with all that I have said. See you at our dinner table—soon."

His entire letter was typed in a special script font—not one I had shown him—and signed "With love, Dad," the "D" in the word three pitches larger than all the other letters.

We never mentioned the incident again.

29

I RETURNED TO UNDERGRADUATE classes at Simon Fraser University, in the Department of Gender Studies—a formal discipline of academia that had only been in its nascent stages when I first met Alfonzo in 1989. More than anything, I wanted to understand my own behavior.

In the midst of all my classes with some 300 other students—most of whom were now half my age—I won a 500-word memoir contest through *Opium*, a literary journal in New York. Within days of publication, an editor from another journal, *New York Tyrant*, asked to publish an excerpt from my book draft. Within a few months I traveled to Seattle to read my short memoir at a "Literary Death Match," like a literary *American Idol*. Writers at a "Literary Death Match" typically read something "funny," and so my short memoir, which was based on the therapy, met with noticeable gasps from the three judges and small audience in a theater at the back of a coffee house, and then silence as I took my seat on the stage after. I didn't win, and before I left for the night, the organizer of the event, a thirties-something man named Todd, approached me by the door.

"You would have had my vote, but I think your stuff was just too dark for the judges. Sorry, man. By the way, did that thing with the shit really happen?"

|||||||||

News that California's state legislature was attempting to pass a bill banning therapies aimed at trying to "change" the sexual orientation of minors, the first potential law of its kind worldwide, prompted me to write another short essay about my own experiences. Published as an on-line Op-Ed by *The Advocate* in October 2012, I closed, stating:

> *In retrospect I could see that I had always objectified my sexuality; for nearly six years I had talked about 'leaving homosexuality' as if 'the gay world' was a thing in itself, some 'thing' that I could leave behind, move beyond. But if my experiences taught me anything it was that a change to the 'map' of my identity from homosexual to heterosexual would never change the 'territory' of my experience from same-sex to opposite-sex desire. A map is not the territory it represents. 'Chasing symbols is like settling for the map instead of the territory,' Deepak Chopra once wrote. 'It creates anxiety; it ends up making you feel hollow and empty, because you exchange your Self for the symbols of your Self.'*

> [. . .]

> *Enacting laws to make it illegal to practice reparative therapy on anyone under the age of 18 is only a start. Reparative therapy may be a lie, but the lie begins not with the idea that we can change from gay to straight, but with the belief that we are who the culture tells us we are, that a change to the map of our identity is a change to the territory of our experience. And no one, no matter what age, is safe from that.*

‖‖‖‖‖‖‖

"I have a favor to ask you," my father said after one of our weekly dinners. "I was hoping you could take a picture of the backside of my head, just head and shoulders."

"Okay . . . but why?"

"In memory of the father I never knew. Could you do that for me?"

"Of course . . ."

I brought my digital camera the following week.

"How do I look?" he said after dinner, combing his hair. "I got a haircut today . . ."

"Very handsome."

He put on a clean white shirt and a blue, double-breasted blazer, even though the picture wouldn't show either, and then a wide-brimmed fedora. I recognized the hat as one he had owned since we were children. He had always worn a hat to Sunday Mass.

"I suppose it's close enough to the one my father might have worn."

He faced the curtain in their living room, and I snapped several pictures of the backside of his head, then I showed him the images right away on my camera.

"I still can't believe you can show me these pictures so soon. Amazing."

"Well, what do you think?"

He looked at all the shots. "The father that was forever faced away from me," he said.

Sometime later that evening we were in the living room.

"I've been thinking," he said, "would you still like to read my book?"

"Would I? Of course . . ."

"Well, then . . . I would really appreciate that. Perhaps you could even help me smoothen out the rough edges. English, you know, was not my first language, or even my second, or third. I'm not sure, but I might have repeated a few memories here and there."

I copied his book to a memory stick that night.

What I found when I read it from start to finish over the coming months was more than mere repetition; my father's memories were largely circuitous. He would chronicle specific emotionally traumatic events, only to approach the exact same events pages later from a slightly different perspective, with additional or even contradictory details. Similar to what I'd done for years in primal therapy, my father was peeling away the skins of his own onion, circling himself, one memory after another, all in search of a core self or clear narrative that might reflect back to him who he was, or at least who he had been.

I spent weeks trying to edit all of his memories into a coherent, linear narrative, to "smoothen out the rough edges," only to realize that the way in which he told his story, his "voice," was as much the truth of his life as the memories themselves. Lifelong secrecy and compartmentalization had left my father with a great deal of confusion, conflicting memories, even "false narratives."

For instance, at one point in his book he said he visited his mother's grave "the year she died, in 1947," after which he immediately left Hungary. Later, he recalled it was 1945. From my own visit to her grave and the carvings on the tombstone, I could easily verify that she had indeed died in 1945, but the two years between his final visit and his exit from Hungary were now a mystery. In yet another part of his book, he said he emigrated from Germany to Nova Scotia on a Swedish ship in August 1952, but over 200 pages later, he wrote that he arrived on May 26, 1951; still later, he said it was May 20.

No matter. Whatever the date of my father's arrival in "the New World," not speaking a word of English, I'm sure he suffered through the same isolation that permeated my first visit to Budapest in 2004. With no common language, a person is forced into introspection. Eyes turn inward even as legs walk forward. Nothing but the past seems familiar.

During these months of editing—since he'd begun writing about his life, in fact—my father began to change. No longer did he shy away from topics around his past. He talked directly and purposefully about the life he had lived, the secrets he had kept, surprising even my mother when he did.

It was because of this openness, because of the book he was writing, and because he was now back in touch with his long-lost and highly knowledgeable cousin, Emma, that—finally—the sad, fascinating, explosive mystery of my father's family finally revealed itself.

My father was born in 1930, the result of an illicit affair between my unmarried grandmother Rozália and her employer. Rozália had been working as a nanny at the time, and her employer—the children's father—was a Hungarian count: Count Dégenföldy-Schonburg. When the count's infidelity came to light, he and his wife sent Rozália back to her parents' farm in Pocsaj. The count would never know his son.

The scandal was heartbreaking for Rozália's mother—my great-grandmother—in particular, because this was not the first time her daughter had given birth to a "bastard child." It was the second. Just three years earlier, Rozália had given birth to my aunt Margit—whose grave I'd visited in Vecsés—the result of an affair by a man no one ever knew.

News of Margit's birth had so upset Rozália's father, in fact, that he tied a noose around his neck and hung himself from the rafters of his barn—cut down and saved, minutes later, by his wife, my great-grandmother. Shame, it seemed, was steeped into the bones of my ancestors.

Although Rozália's father had been able to compose himself after Margit's birth, agreeing to keep the girl and even helping to raise her with his wife while Rozália was away on the nanny job, Rozalia's mother feared his reaction with this second child. Soon after Rozália returned to her parents' farm, her mother, with the help of her other daughters, schemed to send Rozália into hiding in a convent until after the baby, my father, was born—ensuring her husband would never learn of the baby's existence. As a newborn, my father was then swiftly placed in the care of the Hungarian state and was shuffled from orphanage to various foster families and back for years to come.

So it was in this foul climate that my father got his start in life.

Reading about my grandfather's name, *Dégenföldy-Schonburg*, reminded me of my childhood fear around my own name. As ridiculous as it was to me now, back when I was child I had honestly believed that my name, which we'd still pronounced "Gay-dicks," was somehow responsible for "making" me gay. I could not escape my name as a child—my name was "me," who "I" was—and so I'd learned to fear myself. But I was not my name; a name was like a map, and by a stroke of fortune, my own could have been another, and still I would have been myself; still I would have been "me."

If I had come of age before 1869, when the word "homosexual" was first coined, maybe then I might have been called "sodomite" or "uranian," if I would have been called anything at all. Maybe I would have remained nameless, invisible, with not even a shadow to look back at. Without a name that frightened, maybe everything would have turned out differently.

||||||||||

Now I knew about my father's birth, but I still knew nothing about my grandmother's death. There always had been vague mentions of "bombings"—and the timing was certainly right. According to everything I'd been told, she died during World War II.

Sitting in my parents' kitchen one day, I raised the issue of my great-grandfather's attempted suicide.

"There are parts to this story I did not want to write in my book," my father said.

"Such as?"

"Erzsébet, for example. You visited her in Vecsés . . ."

"Of course. She seemed hesitant to keep in contact . . ."

My father explained that years after he'd been sent off to the orphanage, Margit returned to the care of her mother, and the two stayed together as mother and daughter. Rozália eventually married a man named Imre, a wealthy architect, and the three lived as a family—a traditional family—in Budapest.

But their happiness wouldn't last. It soon became clear, my father said, that Imre was not the family man he seemed to be. "Imre was a . . . how shall I say . . . " my father started.

"A predator on the young?" my mother added.

Right around the middle of the war, Margit became pregnant with her stepfather's child. She was fifteen.

"Imre groomed Margit into a secret affair," my father continued. "Their daughter, Erzsébet, my niece, was the product of that affair. When my mother discovered what had happened . . . she went mad. Some reports have it that she attacked Imre with a butcher knife and so he institutionalized her. But that's where she died: in a mental hospital outside Budapest."

"I thought you said she died in the war. In the bombings . . . "

"No," he said. "She died in the mental institution. I have pictures, Emma sent them to me."

"This is unbelievable," I said, realizing, perhaps for the first time, that my father's silence all these years had not been an affront to my worth or value as a person—but a reflection of his own hardened resolve to protect himself.

"Now you understand why I did not want to talk about my past.

It has taken me my life to figure it out, and to come to terms with it. I could never have explained this to you before. I could not even explain it to myself. I hid from it. I was too ashamed."

||||||||||

On December 30, 2013, my father told me he'd been diagnosed with lung cancer.

"What does that mean?" I said, stunned.

"It doesn't mean anything," he said. "I'm not going anywhere."

Tests had been conducted, results had been analyzed, news had been delivered.

In addition to the other medications that he had been taking daily for years—three for high blood pressure, a blood thinner, an antiepileptic for burning "pins and needles" in his feet, an antidepressant, which he said he took for sleep, and up to twelve Tylenol with codeine daily for overall "pain"—he would now be prescribed "another medication."

Life carried on, days with no mention of cancer. No one ever used the word "chemotherapy." I visited my parents as usual, cooked brunches, dinners, and all our favorites desserts: *zserbó* squares, *mákos tészta,* and *aranygaluska.*

"I'm not sure if I ever told you," my mother said during one dinner, "but as a child back home in Modosch, we always ate *aranygaluska* with a clear soup. First our soup, maybe chicken, then our *aranygaluska . . .*"

My father had stopped writing his book and reread passages while alone in his office. His life story, largely passed down from one generation to the next and committed to word now by "memory," reflected back to him the life that he had lived, who he had been, who he was.

Sitting with him in his living room after dinner one night, he asked me a question. "I don't want to make a big deal out of this, but . . . let's assume I don't live."

"*Dad . . .* "

"We have to talk about this. If I don't live, I'd like you to finish my book, edit it as you see fit, make sure everyone gets a copy. Your brothers and sisters. I wrote it for all of you. To tell you who your father was. Where I came from . . ."

I was speechless.

"Will you promise me?"

"Well, of course I would finish it. But you're going to live."

"Peter, we are all going to die. Me ahead of you, in all likelihood, but all of us, eventually, will return to God's Kingdom. I am not afraid. I have my faith. Your mother and I both have our faith. It carries us through life. We have never been afraid of death."

"And it comforts me to know you feel this way . . ."

"Your mother and I hope that you return to Church one day, but . . . we also understand that is your choice. You're a grown man. At the very least, we would hope that you know you are loved. We love you."

"And I love you . . . I look at the two of you, how much love you feel for each other, still after all these years, and your faith in God . . . and it's like a guiding light in my own life. Everyone has to live a life, but not everyone has that kind of guiding light of love. It means a lot to me . . ."

"Now . . . can I ask you to do me another huge favor?"

"Anything."

"Pluck out these damn hairs in my ears. They're driving me nuts they're so itchy."

||||||||||

My father's health was fragile, though stable—or so we all thought—when a mental-health journal agreed to publish another essay I'd written about the therapy and my lawsuit in June 2014. The special issue, the editor had clarified, would be devoted to "psychiatric medication."

In late August, on the eve of the publication, the journal's editor contacted me to say that some members of the journal's governing board had objected to my essay on the grounds that they'd found my story to be "in bad taste," generally "offensive to psychiatry." They didn't want to publish my essay, but agreed to hear any rationale I might be able to provide as to why it should be included in their magazine.

344 / PETER GAJDICS

My editor was outraged, and said as much to the board, and to me. Considering the journal had been created specifically "by" and "for" survivors of mental health to provide a venue in which they could voice personal experiences about a system that sometimes ended up harming the very people it was meant to help, she found the board's hesitation reprehensible, bordering on censorship, as well as undermining her own role as the sole acquisitions editor.

Still, she asked me to comment.

I reiterated to the board that I thought it important, in this "supposed politically advanced day and age," to read true-life stories about psychiatry's treatment of homosexuality. My lawsuit had settled out of court only in the not-too-distant past. Political and personal change had, of course, occurred since the days of my treatment. "Conversion therapies" were now almost universally denounced by all official mental-health organizations, including the World Health Organization. In 2013, California had become the first state and jurisdiction anywhere in the world to pass legislation banning conversion therapy for minors. Other states had since passed, or were about to introduce, similar legislation—events that would have been unheard of during my own therapy.

I was convinced, however, that any official change about the so-called diagnosis and treatment of homosexuality from within the boundaries of psychiatry would not necessarily change what was still in the hearts of some, though not all, of its practitioners, as well as any number of other mental-health providers. Changing laws was not the same as changing hearts. When all was said and done, some members of my own family still could not look me in the eyes and talk about the fact that I was "a homosexual," occasionally even lapsing into debates in front of me about how "certain interest groups want special rights" and are "wholly responsible for the fall of Western values."

To assuage any of the board members' fears about a potential libel suit, I explained that all names in my essay had, of course, been changed. Only my own name was "real."

After days of back and forth, the board concluded that there was an "ethical responsibility to honor the testimony of peers," particularly those concerned with experiences of abuse—abuse made possible in the first place by ignoring or silencing the voices of victims. They acknowledged the courage it took to break out of any abusive relationship: Speaking, writing, and testifying in court all required enormous bravery and had the potential to affect, and improve, the lives of countless others in the future. Testimony in whatever form might reach out, directly or indirectly, to men and women trapped within abusive relationships with professionals who seemed to be under the mistaken impression that the Hippocratic Oath was *first do harm*. One member of the board said she felt "ashamed" that the organization had even stumbled over the issues raised by my story.

The essay appeared in the journal as originally planned; the board's chairperson, who wrote a lead-in essay for each issue, however, withdrew his ordinary introduction because he did not want to be "too closely associated" with it. And though it had been initially planned as the main article, my essay ended up being buried, mid-issue.

In any event, no sooner had the essay appeared in print than my father's health, far from stable, declined.

30

THE FIRST TIME WE watched him hobble across the living-room floor with his walking stick, or even when he complained about razor-sharp pains cascading down both legs, no one, not my mother nor any of her children, connected my father's inability to stand upright and walk with the cancer. Or if we did, no one said it aloud.

"I can't walk," he told us, barely seven months after the initial diagnoses of lung cancer. We all encouraged him to walk even more.

"You need to keep up your strength," we said.

In the early hours one autumn morning, my mother rose from bed to use the bathroom, tripped and tumbled to her side, the kind of fall that might have almost gone unnoticed by any healthy person. But at eighty-nine years old, she didn't have the strength to raise herself back up. My father, staring, horrified and helpless, at his wife now clutching the handle of her bedroom dresser, found he could neither stand nor walk to her aid from the bed, just four feet away.

"Call Pisti," my mother told him.

Somehow—no one knew how—he made it to a phone, called my brother, who flew out of bed and drove the two miles from his house to their home. An ambulance arrived minutes later and then my mother, with my father staring on, grief-stricken, was taken by stretcher to the hospital.

The next day my brother Frank drove my father to the hospital for his first scheduled radiation treatment, then home later that day. He went straight to bed. The next morning, moaning and incoherent, he could not rise from bed.

"Oh my darling," he kept repeating from bed, wavering in and out of tears, "I could not help my darling . . . "

Frank called oncology, who said my brother should bring our father to the palliative unit as soon as possible.

For the next three weeks I, along with my four siblings, visited both parents every night in the same hospital—my father on the eleventh floor in palliative care, my mother in the hip-replacement unit directly five floors below him; they shared almost exactly the same view of Vancouver's downtown skyline. My father's cancer had metastasized to his bones, doctors advised, hence the pain in his legs. Radiation would continue, at least twice more, but he would never return home. If he survived at all, which they said was unlikely, he'd be moved to hospice.

I had to explain the word "hospice" to Pisti. I remembered the word from my days as a home-care worker, from courses I'd taken in palliative care and books I'd read, notably Elisabeth Kübler-Ross's *On Death and Dying*. But we didn't discuss the possibility of our father's death each night we met for dinner at a burger joint and then drove to the hospital. We talked about our favorite albums from the 1970s: Elton John's *Captain Fantastic and the Brown Dirt Cowboy*, Queen's *A Night at the Opera* . . . We talked about people who lived with cancer for years, about how after four months our father could be transferred to a long-term facility, where we would visit him daily.

During one dinner, the conversation turned to our father's book, all the years he'd spent in his office writing.

"He tried to talk to me once about his writing," Pisti said, "you know, about his childhood. We were in his office. He started to tell me a story about his life as an orphan, and his mother. I guess it's one of the stories in his book. The more he talked, the more uncomfortable I felt. He never talked about his life, and now he was opening up about such personal, emotional subjects. I didn't know how to listen to him. I interrupted . . . I asked him some political question about Hungary, totally off point. He got mad. He told me to forget the whole thing, and he stormed out of the room. I'll always regret that. He was trying to open up with me after years of silence, and I shut him down. I know Dad was brutal with us when we were kids, but . . . you know, I don't think he was a bad man."

"Good people sometimes do bad things," I said. "Especially when they're in a lot of pain."

"How do you do it?"

"Do what?"

"Read about all his heartache. I couldn't do it. It makes me too sad."

"I've lived in that world for a long time. Nothing about what he writes is all that foreign to me. What do you think I was doing in that therapy for all those years?"

"I don't ask you about that because I know it's private."

"Or maybe because it makes you uncomfortable."

"Well, I just want to thank you. For the record."

"For what?"

"Helping Dad the way you have. All the work you put into his book. No one else in this family could have done what you did. If you hadn't gone to Europe and found his relatives, *our* relatives, well . . . I don't think he would have even written that book."

⁞⁞⁞⁞⁞⁞⁞⁞⁞

After three weeks, our mother was discharged from the hospital and returned home. Her hip had been dislocated and bruised though not broken as first thought, and snapped firmly back into place.

"I thought this would all last," she told me as we sat again in her living room, now without my father.

"What would?" I said, from my father's chair, across from hers.

"The good times; our lives together. We always knew, of course, it wouldn't. All those wonderful Sunday dinners with you. Do you know how much joy you've given us?"

I glanced down at my father's slippers, still lying next to his chair, a sign that he might yet return home.

Within days of my mother's discharge, my father was transferred to a hospice facility, which looked like a private bungalow, across the street from a botanical garden with cascading waterfalls, at the end of a cul-de-sac. Inside his room—one of only fourteen—plush curtains draped over shuttered windows and big, comfy pillows were spread across a luxurious gray sofa "with a pullout bed," the hospice staff explained, "in case any one of you wants to spend the night."

An ivory crucifix hung on the opposite forest-green wall from where Dad lay in his motorized bed, and below it, a flat-screen TV. He had his own wheelchair-accessible bathroom; and we could visit the kitchen—around the corner and down the hall from the 24-hour nurses' station—for snacks, juice, and coffee whenever we wanted. Even his pain medication, morphine, was regulated by injection, once every four hours, with regular "top-ups" every two hours. The province's government-funded health provider would cover $5,000 of the total $7,000 amount owed each month. When I heard the cost, I asked one of the nurses, outside his room, how long patients typically stayed at hospice.

"Some remain here weeks, maybe a month."

Of the three CDs lying next to the portable CD machine by his bed, Dad chose "Pachelbel's Canon in D by Seascape," which we played on repeat, day and night.

He slipped in and out of consciousness, was delirious one day, ordered us to "sell the damn house," lucid the next day, asked how "this will all work when I go home." No one, not even my mother, had the heart to tell him that he would never go home again.

For the first time in his adult life, he asked for milk. "A big glass of cold milk would be so nice," he said one night.

With a propensity for kidney stones, he had never been able to drink milk as an adult, but I remembered from his book that his favorite drink, as a child, had been ice-cold milk.

During one visit, while Pisti was getting his milk in the kitchen, I held his hands and told him, yet again, that I would finish his book and make sure each of his children received a copy. His fingers were thick and strong, the hands of a man who had worked with machinery—full of life—not the hands of a person who could one day not live.

"Dad . . .? Are you in pain?"

His eyes remained closed. "My pain is not physical," he said, weakly.

I wondered if he kept his eyes closed to avoid seeing me looking at him dying.

"Are you afraid of death?" I asked.

Pisti had told me not to ask the question, but I'd said our father might have *needed* to be asked the question, "by someone."

"I am not afraid of death . . . I am only afraid of leaving your mother alone."

Late one Saturday, three weeks after being taken to hospice, his face was pallid, ghostlike, his pupils smoky, as if behind them he'd already begun to leave his body. Death happens slowly, I remembered thinking later, like leaving a room gradually.

He had also stopped speaking English.

"*Istenem . . . Istenem . . . Istenem . . .*"

I knew this Hungarian term: "My God."

"*Istenem . . . Istenem . . . Istenem . . .*"

His dinner lay uneaten by the side of the bed: roast beef with a scoop of mashed potatoes, baby carrots, and twigs of asparagus. Pisti crushed one of the few medications he took orally into his dessert, an individual chocolate soufflé, and fed it to his mouth. Still delirious, eyes glassy, his lips parted and the soufflé slid in and down, spoon after spoon.

The next morning, Sunday, I awoke early, and as I did I noticed that Pisti had called my cell at six o'clock. In the back of my mind I knew, I must have known, something had happened. I went about dressing, washed my face, made my coffee, toast, and eggs, all the while never not thinking that as long as I didn't return my brother's call, my father was alive.

Finally, I called. Pisti said that, at midnight the previous evening, after returning to his own apartment, he had felt compelled to return to our father's bedside, where he found him fighting for breath.

"He won't live through the night," the night nurse had said before administering a dose of medication to help clear his lungs, help his breathing, stop the pain. All night Pisti sat by my father's bedside, holding his hand, keeping watch for imminent death. Early that morning, Pisti started his round of phone calls.

I jumped in a cab and arrived at the hospice within the hour. My sisters couldn't be reached, but my two brothers and my mother and I stood by the bed.

Unconscious, his breathing was shallow, gurgled. Then it slowed to a murmur. Slowed until the spaces between each breath were longer than the breaths.

A priest arrived to deliver Last Rites.

"In the name of the Father and of the Son and of the Holy Spirit . . ."

A friend of my parents, a nurse from church, arrived seconds or maybe an hour after that. She felt his pulse. "It won't be long now," she said.

We stepped closer. My brothers said something, I'm not sure what.

"I love you, Dad," I said, words I'd said before but now they would be final. "Thank you for the life you gave me, for your love . . . for my love of Hungary, your homeland . . . I'll always think of you when I go to Budapest. I love you, Dad . . ."

My mother, crying, took his hands. "I love you, dearest," she said, leaning over his body, kissing his forehead, stroking his cheek, gently. "I love you . . ."

Seconds later, as if in response to my mother's expression of love, a pronounced intake of air, deep and prolonged, swept through his body, and his face twisted, almost unrecognizably, from side to side, and then everything stopped: his breathing, but also all of us as we watched, unmoving, unthinking, our own breaths hanging on his last exhale.

A minute later he surfaced again, for one final gasp. Then he was gone.

||||||||||

Three days later, my mother asked me to write and deliver his eulogy at the funeral. We were in her living room at the time.

"Me? But . . . I'm the youngest. Don't you think that would offend Frank? Or even Pisti?"

"You're the writer. Dad would want it to be you. It meant a great deal to him that you helped him with his book. He was very proud of you."

In the eulogy, which I delivered after the funeral before a crowd of roughly 200 parishioners, including my mother, sitting ten feet before me, I described my father's childhood as an orphan in war-torn

Budapest, without a mother to hug him or a father to hold his hand. Because he had no "Earthly Mother," early in his young life he had adopted his "Heavenly Mother" as his own on Earth. No matter what his hardship—nights alone, crying; mornings in tears, praying; various foster families; the Russians' invasion into Hungary, Soviet rifles pointed at his head—he knew that "She" would forevermore walk beside him, holding his hand. Through rising tears, I described events from my father's life that even my siblings did not know and that I knew only as a result of working on his book—because of the trust my father had placed in me.

"My father was not an easy man," I said, near-breaking but steady, mid-eulogy. "War brings trauma and leaves scars, some of which the children of the survivors end up needing to heal in themselves."

It was the one part of the eulogy I had worried my mother, to whom I'd given a copy beforehand for her blessing, might have vetoed.

She did not.

I went on to say what I believed. "The mark of any man, however, is the love he brings to the world in spite of his pain. The mark of any person is the love that lives on in the hearts of those who knew him. Love does heal wounds, and there is no doubt to anyone who ever knew my father that he loved deeply; that my father was a deeply sensitive, caring soul. He named the squirrels that visited his backyard and the black crows that drank in the birdbath on his and my mother's porch. He loved his garden; he loved cooking jam with my mother. He loved his birth country, Hungary. Anyone who ever knew or met my parents, at church on Sundays, at the symphony or the grocery store, knew how much they loved each other. He was completely devoted to my mother, and after fifty-eight years of marriage, my father still loved her as much, or more, than on the day they married. That kind of love never dies.

"The philosopher Emmanuel Kant once said, 'Those who live in the memory of the ones who loved them are not dead, only far away. Dead are those who are forgotten.' Though his body may leave us, my father's love will never die, because it will live on in the hearts of his entire family, forever. I love him very much."

|||||||||||

At the internment, hours after the funeral, as the priest said a final prayer, each member of my family sprinkled a handful of the soil I'd brought back from my grandmother's grave in Vecsés onto my father's lowered casket. Another wish fulfilled.

My sister Kriska approached me before I climbed back in the hearse. "That part of your eulogy, when you said war brings trauma, that the children need to heal it in themselves . . . "

"Yes . . . "

"I'm glad you said it. For all of us. Thank you."

|||||||||||

Over the coming weeks, I reread my father's entire book. His words were like a conversation from the grave. He told me stories. I cried. Within the context of my father's life, my own past fit. We had stepped in the way, my siblings and I, of ghosts.

Then I stopped crying, and he told me more stories as I prepared the book for my mother to give to my siblings. I had already spent the past year editing the book—retaining as much of my father's voice while sharpening some of his more disorienting memories with corrected punctuation or grammar, adding a sentence or two to bridge what at times were confusing leaps of logic, subsuming a few of his overly repetitive memories into one streamlined reflection. Then I formatted all the text, numbered pages, reordered pictures at the end according to how I knew he would've wanted them to appear, and even named all of my Hungarian relatives. Working on my father's book also helped me return to my own—I jumped back and forth between the two, from father to son. One would likely not have been completed without the other.

Finally, on the front cover of my father's book, I added one of his black-and-white "movie star" photos from the 1950s, his swarthy complexion and thick, curly hair complemented by a wool suit. And on the back jacket, as an ending to the story of his life, the book he'd written "from memory," I added one of the recent photos of the backside of his head—tufts of gray hair poking out from under a wide-brimmed fedora.

"The father that was forever faced away from me."

On the mattress in the Styx I had mourned the father I never knew and, for all intents and purposes, never had. Both my mother and my father had died for me in primal, and I was orphaned, like my father, estranged even from myself, my nature; at war and imprisoned, solitarily alone, like my mother. Then I returned home and was given the gift of fourteen additional years of conversations and arguments with my parents; dinners and desserts; exchanges of gratitude and forgiveness; expressions of love. The heart beats fast until it doesn't, and the only thing that lasts is what is real, what can't be changed.

Remembering this brings me peace.

Acknowledgments

Heartfelt gratitude to my tribe, past and present: Thomas Lisicar, Cynthia Woodward, Patrick King, Alana Samson, Bryan McIver, Catherine Racine, Eric Marchand, Jule Epp, Pam Howard-Jones, Ingrid Kröblinger, Cathleen With, Didi Mitchell, Nancy Leach, Alice Ages, and Dixie Black.

Thanks to my writers' groups at Lambda Literary Foundation and Banff Centre for the Arts, particularly my teachers, Ellery Washington and Bill Schermbrucker.

For their early editorial feedback, thanks to Claire Robson and Arnold Dolin.

I am indebted to Jeff Moores, wherever he is, for championing the work early on.

Special gratitude to Alan Rinzler, who helped bring it all together near the end.

No book is complete until it is published, and so I want to praise Alban Fischer for his design, Carol Killman Rosenberg for her eagle-eyed final editing, and most especially my publishers at Brown Paper Press, Wendy Thomas Russell and Jennifer Volland, for scrutinizing my every word. Thank you.

PETER GAJDICS is a recipient of a writers grant from Canada Council for the Arts, a fellowship from The Summer Literary Seminars, and an alumni of Lambda Literary Foundation's "Writers Retreat for Emerging LGBT Voices." When not in Budapest, Hungary, his home away from home, Peter lives in Vancouver, Canada. *The Inheritance of Shame: A Memoir* is his first book.

More information can be found at inheritanceofshame.com.

Brown Paper Press engages readers on topics of contemporary culture through quality writing and thoughtful design. Unbound by genre, our press delivers socially relevant works that advise, guide, inspire, and amuse. We champion authors with new perspectives, strong voices, and original ideas that just might change the world.

Please visit us at brownpaperpress.com.